THE GIANT BOOK OF CREATIVITY FOR KIDS

THE GIANT BOOK OF CREATIVITY FOR KIDS

500 Activities to Encourage Creativity in Kids Ages 2 to 12
—Play, Pretend, Draw, Dance, Sing, Write, Build, Tinker

Bobbi Conner

Illustrations by Denise Holmes

ROOST BOOKS
BOSTON AND LONDON
2015

Roost Books
An imprint of Shambhala Publications, Inc.
Horticultural Hall
300 Massachusetts Avenue
Boston, Massachusetts 02115
roostbooks.com

9 8 7 6 5 4 3 2 1

First Edition
Printed in U.S.A.

⊗ This edition is printed on acid-free paper that meets the American National
Standards Institute Z39.48 Standard.
♻ Shambhala Publications makes every effort to print on recycled paper.
For more information please visit www.shambhala.com.

Distributed in the United States by Penguin Random House LLC
and in Canada by Random House of Canada Ltd

Designed by Allison Meierding

Library of Congress Cataloging-in-Publication Data

Conner, Bobbi.
The giant book of creativity for kids: 500 activities to encourage creativity in
kids ages 2 to 12: play, pretend, draw, dance, sing, write, build, tinker / Bobbi
Conner.
Pages   cm
ISBN 978-1-61180-131-6 (paperback)
1. Creative activities and seat work. I. Title.
LB1027.25.C65 2015
372.5—dc23
2014017615

Creativity is contagious. Pass it on.
—ALBERT EINSTEIN

Contents

Acknowledgments

The activities and ideas that found their way into *The Giant Book of Creativity for Kids* have been percolating for years, and many people have helped along the way.

First, a huge, heartfelt thanks goes to the outstanding child development experts, creative professionals, and parents who shared their wisdom about creative, active kids over the twenty-four years that I hosted *The Parent's Journal* nationwide on public radio. Such collective wisdom provided a strong foundation for this book. A special thanks also goes to the individual professionals and parents who offered quotes, creative tips, and childhood memories that are included in this book: Thomas Armstrong, Lindsey Ballenger, T. A. Barron, Suzanne Bloom, Robert Coles, Stephanie Stein Crease, Sandi Dexter, Kate Drag, Marti Erickson, Barbara Esbensen, John Feierabend, Cathy Fink, Kathryn Finney, Sally Gladwell, Daniel Goleman, Stanley Greenspan, Melanie Hall, Edward Hallowell, Jane Healy, Angie Holleman, Carla Lathbury, Susan Linn, Fredelle Maynard, Kristi Sayers Menear, Bonnie Simon, Jill Stamm, and Susan Striker.

I am thankful for the wonderful, generous group of parents and families who graciously offered to evaluate all of the activities considered for inclusion in this book during the early stage of writing. Their critique, suggestions, and creative ideas were invaluable. Thanks to Lindsey Ballenger, Kim Calderon, Ginny Crawford, Meredith Hickerson, Angie Holleman, Victoria Lewis, and their families: Nathan, Olivia, Mallory, Samantha, Matt, Ella, Alex, Libby, Rob, Ford, James Bullitt, Harrison, Michael, Victoria, Vaughn, Lee, Trey, and Zachary.

Thanks to my literary agent, Jim Levine, for finding just the right publisher for this book and for his support and enthusiasm from beginning to end. Thanks to Kerry Sparks at the Levine-Greenberg-Rostan Literary Agency for her excellent brainstorming skills.

The Shambhala Publications/Roost Books team has been a fabulous, positive group to work with at every turn along the way. A big thanks goes to my editor, Jennifer Urban-Brown, who provided keen insight, guidance, and marvelous editing skills. I have thoroughly enjoyed her can-do attitude and wonderful appreciation for childhood creativity.

The illustrator Denise Holmes has captured the fun, high-spirited nature of childhood creativity in the drawings she created for this book. Bravo, Denise!

Thanks to the other members of the Shambhala/Roost team: Sara Bercholz and Julie Saidenberg; assistant editor Julia Gaviria; designers Daniel Urban-Brown, Jim Zaccaria, and Allison Meierding; and publicist Steven Pomije. Thank you, all, for your commitment, dedication, and marvelous attention to detail that resulted in a handsome, playful book to celebrate childhood creativity!

Thanks to Carol Brown, Terry Helwig, and Anita Wallgren—treasured friends who offered tremendous support and encouragement during the writing of this book.

And finally, I wish to thank my family: my husband, Billy; my children, Cass, Livy, Peter; and my mom, Charlotte. I feel blessed each day to have such a loving, supportive, creative, and fun family.

Introduction

W hat if all forms of childhood creativity and originality were outlawed? What if parents were told that reading bedtime stories or singing songs to their young children was a giant waste of time?

What if the assessment experts of the world placed zero value on each child's artwork, poems, stories, jokes, songs, school performances, inventions, creative questions, and imagination?

What if the global chief of learning proclaimed that creativity habits and skills were without merit and should be deleted from the everyday lives of children, effective immediately?

What if it was decreed that every toddler should have a smart phone for amusement rather than a box of crayons and paper?

What if someone in charge in your community said, "No more art, music, dance, plays, puppet shows, story time, writing, tinkering, inventing, or creative thinking in childhood"?

What if children were required to spend 95 percent of their free time consuming high-tech, commercially produced games and electronics and were allowed only 5 percent of their time to do their own original creative projects?

Disbelief. Indignation. Outrage. Rebellion. Revolt. Parents everywhere would fight for their *children's right to be creative.*

And yet, here we are.

Childhood creativity has been steadily on the decline since the 1990s. Many children are consuming huge amounts of preprogrammed electronics and spending the majority of their time with electronic gadgets. Some child development experts worry that kids are getting the wrong idea about what it means to *be imaginative or creative,* with slick Hollywood productions and electronic games setting the standard. If you give a five-year-old child a giant cardboard box and a pack of markers and cheerfully ask, "Do you want to make something creative from this box?" that child may look at you like you've lost your mind.

Childhood creativity is under siege. Various societal (and marketing) trends have played a role in the decline of childhood creativity, but the good news is that we live in a free world. Each conscientious parent can effect change. We have the power to encourage creativity in our children's daily lives—where music; drawing; painting; building; tinkering; pretending; dancing; writing stories, songs, jokes, and poems; and imagination have tremendous value.

And before you start thinking, "Yes, but only some children are *creative kids*," let me say loud and clear that it's a myth to believe that creativity is simply "talent." All children are curious and creative if given a chance.

The latest research about creativity is in sync with what successful creative adults know from real life: creative habits and creative skills can be learned. And when children have opportunities, materials, and encouragement to create, then creativity becomes an expected and accepted part of life. Creativity is an essential ingredient for a happy childhood.

Each parent (or caring adult) can do what it takes to open the door on childhood creativity—and our children will do the rest. So go ahead. Make a stand. Say YES to childhood creativity.

Why I Wrote This Book

I cannot imagine childhood without a daily dose of creative, imaginative activities. When I think about my childhood, filled with many hours of drawing, inventing songs, building forts, and writing stories at home, I know that these experiences greatly shaped who I am today in my personal life and my professional life. I've discovered that there is an extra layer of life to be experienced through individual and collaborative creativity. No one should miss out on this bonus. The door to that creative realm of life can be opened wide in childhood with long-lasting significance.

> *We need creativity in every area of life. We need creative people in medicine. We need creative people in industry and in banking. We need people who look at a problem and solve it in a new and refreshing way that no one else has thought of.*
>
> **—SUSAN STRIKER,** author of *Young at Art*

I've witnessed the power of childhood creativity from several angles. First, in my professional life, I produced and hosted a nationwide public radio series on child development, called *The Parent's Journal,* for twenty-four years. I interviewed many leading child development experts about the importance of imagination, curiosity, and creative activities for children. (You'll see many of these experts' comments throughout the book.)

> "Creativity is the ability to generate your own ideas. And, that's essential to knowing who you are as a person, to having a sense of identity, to really being able to think on your feet, to solve new problems.
>
> —**DR. STANLEY GREENSPAN,** author of *The Growth of the Mind*

Second, as a parent, I saw my own children dabble in all sorts of creative activities over the years, and these activities brought challenge, satisfaction, perseverance, and the ability to entertain themselves into their young lives. It was a pleasure to see each child develop their own passions and creative skills, and also to have so much fun doing creative activities with their friends.

Third, I learned from my own childhood that creativity helps develop creative thinking and problem-solving skills and makes life rewarding and full. I also discovered that doing creative activities is a wonderful way to find relief from the stress of everyday life.

I wrote *The Giant Book of Creativity for Kids* to help children (and parents) say yes to dabbling in creativity and discovering creative passions. When children say yes to more creativity, they increase their ability to shape their own destiny. That's the magical power of creativity.

THE SIMPLE PLEASURES OF BEING CREATIVE

Imagination and creativity bring so many good sensations and experiences to life for kids. There's something for everyone and the possibilities are limitless. Here are a few examples of the simple but meaningful ways creativity helps children live childhood to its fullest.

Create for Joy

- Squish your fingers in paint and make your first finger painting.
- Make your own musical shakers and play along to a favorite song.
- Design a pirate ship from a giant cardboard box with your parent.
- Make a puppet from an old red sock.
- Write a poem about the family pet.

Create for Intelligence

- Learn which pots and pans make the loudest sounds when you tap them with the spoon.
- Choreograph a dance routine for two or three dancers.
- Invent a tall tale from your imagination and tell it to a friend.
- Design a serpentine wall in the snow.
- Build a big fort indoors with blankets, pillows, and furniture.

Create for Connection

- Make a giant Hand-Print Mural with friends at your birthday party.
- Form a Family Band and put on a concert in the living room.
- Write a skit about the mishaps that happened at an imaginary barber shop and act it out.
- Have a freestyle dance party with friends just for the fun of it.
- Make a giant floor drawing with your mom or dad.

How to Use This Book

The Giant Book of Creativity for Kids begins with a "Parent's Guide to Childhood Creativity," offering practical suggestions to make creativity a priority in your child's life. You'll find parenting strategies, tips, and routines for each stage of childhood woven throughout each section. (And I've included ways to manage electronics and screen time—to free up time for more creativity.)

You'll find five hundred activities in *The Giant Book of Creativity for Kids*—divided into separate sections for each of the target age groups: toddlers, preschoolers, and grade-school children and older (ages six to twelve). To get started, flip to the section of *The Giant Book of Creativity for Kids* that matches your child's age. Pick an activity that seems like a good fit for your child. Assemble the materials, give a little demo if needed, and let the creative magic begin.

Creative dabbling is an important way that children find multiple ways to be creative and discover favorite creative activities too. This book presumes that a child who loves to paint might also like to write poems; a child who tinkers with gadgets might also want to sing; a child who likes to build forts might also want to learn to put on a puppet show. This open and authentic approach to creativity is woven into every page and encourages all kids to dabble in various kinds of creativity.

As your child gains confidence with materials and activities, he will invent his own variations and create brand-new ways of being creative. One idea leads to another. That's the beauty of imagination and creativity.

A Parent's Guide to Childhood Creativity

Childhood creativity is a rich blend of curiosity, imagination, and experimentation. For toddlers, creativity is mostly messing about with materials, supplies, instruments, and costumes to see what they can make or do in short, little spurts of time. Preschoolers and elementary-age children have a heightened awareness, more vivid imaginations, creative thinking skills, physical capabilities, and a longer attention span, so the sky is the limit on what they can imagine and create. (See more information about what to expect *creatively* in the Toddler, Preschool, and Grade-School activity sections of the book.)

Creative activities are beneficial for every child, no matter what their age. The American Academy of Pediatrics has been urging parents to include more non-electronic, active, and creative play in their child's routine for over a decade. It's a good thing to do in the short term and the long term too. Here are some of the splendid skills, habits, and experiences that children gain from doing hands-on creative activities. They learn to:

- Focus their attention on a project, idea, or activity
- Feel the joy and satisfaction from doing creative projects
- Problem solve, experiment, and analyze what works best
- Break a big project into little parts
- Be flexible
- Deal with complexity, ambiguity, and frustration
- Collaborate with others
- Improve specific skills (art, music, acting, writing, construction) and experience a sense of mastery
- Escape from daily stress by doing something creative
- Value their creativity (and see themselves as a creative person who can make and do imaginative and original things)

To add to this list, another terrific benefit of creativity throughout all the stages of childhood is the pleasure and social connection that comes from doing something imaginative with other kids or parents. The excitement of creating side by side with others provides a good motivation for trying something new.

> Some of the most important studies we have on creativity show that adults who still retain that capacity to play, to think up new ways to use objects—just original thinking of any kind—are the ones who really get ahead. And that type of creativity begins in childhood.
>
> **—JANE M. HEALY, PHD,**
> educational psychologist and author
> of *Your Child's Growing Mind*

Children experience a tremendous sense of freedom and competence as they create art and crafts, construct, dance, play music, pretend, act, tell stories, write creatively, and invent —creative thinking of any kind gives children a sense of independence. Childhood creativity at its best is not about coloring in the lines or being neat. It's not about producing something just because it pleases an adult. It's really much more open-ended and free; it's the process of experimenting with materials, ideas, and capabilities to see what you can do or make.

According to the latest neuroscience research, when people are innovative or creative, their brains function in a variety of ways. Part of the creative process happens in an intensely focused state of mind, concentrating on a challenge, activity, or problem. But another important part of the process happens when the mind is daydreaming or wandering.

If you look closely, you will see evidence of both of these aspects of the creative process in your child's creative routine. You may clearly see your child's intense concentration, for example, while he is creating buildings and roads with blocks, boxes, and toy cars. Or you might see a strong focus of attention as your child paints or draws or creates characters for a story. It's easy to see that this kind of creative focus is productive.

Look again and you might also see signs of creativity emerging from your child's daydreaming or mind-wandering. For example, your child might be playing a solo game of basketball, swinging on the swing set, or riding in the car and looking out the window and quite suddenly announce a clever idea for a story or project or a solution to a creative problem from yesterday. During these seemingly idle (but important) times of mind-drifting, children are processing ideas, and their creative

> *Kids learn so easily through creativity. It includes problem solving, sequencing, and letting your brain try new things.*
>
> **—CATHY FINK,** Grammy Award-winning musician, singer, songwriter

brains are doing fruitful pondering.

Creative thinking is woven into many creative activities: from making a painting to building a tower with blocks, from creating a puppet show to writing a story. Even young preschoolers generate ideas and figure out which ideas or solutions work best through trial and error and creative thinking.

Consider the four-year-old who wants to make a fort in the living room. First the child has to imagine what that fort might look like. Then as he starts building, small problems develop. The blankets and pillows keep slipping and the coffee table is not high enough to crawl under. So, other ideas are pursued. Eventually the little fort builder will pick a solution or a plan that seems to work best.

When researchers mention creativity, they often talk about two types of thinking: divergent thinking and convergent thinking. Divergent thinking is coming up with multiple, alternative ideas or solutions rather than believing there is just one answer. And convergent thinking is evaluating all the possible ideas to pick the one that works best.

Of course creative children aren't talking about divergent and convergent thinking (thank goodness!), they are just having fun and experiencing the creative process. But in truth when children practice creative thinking, they learn powerful skills and techniques that will carry over to other aspects and times in their lives.

THE SMALL SEEDS OF CREATIVITY

When my children were in preschool, I splurged on a real glockenspiel for them to play around with. I picked this musical instrument because it was simple to use (like a xylophone) and it was easy on the ears too. That glockenspiel sat on the coffee table and my children and their friends tapped and experimented with making music for many years.

$\longrightarrow$

When my daughter was in second grade, she asked to take piano lessons with her best friend. I agreed, and she took lessons from a fun-spirited teacher named Miss Dorothy. This talented teacher taught the basics of playing the piano and she encouraged the children to create their own songs, to practice performing them, and to put on short recitals for their families.

When my daughter was in fifth grade, she began singing in the school choir. One day she came home from school and asked if she could take voice lessons. I agreed, and found an upbeat and lively voice teacher who was a retired opera singer. Miss June provided weekly voice lessons for my daughter for several years that offered training and great enthusiasm for music.

The years went by and my daughter's interest in music continued to blossom. At age nineteen she learned to play the guitar. At age twenty-two she began writing songs, and singing and performing at small venues. At twenty-four she attended a summer program at Berklee College of Music to improve her piano skills. At age twenty-eight she recorded (and coproduced) her first professional album of original songs, called *A Mind of Your Own*. She went on tour with her band to promote her album, and along the way a newspaper reporter inquired about what inspires her songwriting. Here is a quote from Livy: "Always for as long as I can remember, I have loved to sing. I would say that was the seed."

I offer this glimpse of real life and musical creativity in our family simply as an example of the parenting mantra: *trust the creative process*. Not one of the individual moments of musical creativity in my daughter's childhood was particularly extraordinary. Instead she was just having fun with music. Her imagination, her determination, and her skills grew quietly and steadily over time. This is what the path to creative accomplishment often looks like.

It's hard to predict exactly where your child's creative activities are going. You can't go wrong, however, if you focus on fun in the present moment, follow your child's lead on what is most fascinating, and let things blossom naturally from there.

Seven Principles of Childhood Creativity

Encouraging your child's creativity is more of a privilege than it is a responsibility. It is so much fun to be around a happy, exuberant child, fully engaged in doing something imaginative and creative. If truth be told, watching your child's creativity blossom right before your eyes gives a surge of positive energy and satisfaction to you too. It's a gift that reveals itself in tiny moments of life with your child.

You have a very important role to play in supporting your child's creativity, and I believe it's beneficial to have a basic plan of action to help. With this said, here are seven principles offered to nurture, support, and promote your child's imagination and creativity.

1. BELIEVE IN THE GOODNESS OF YOUR CHILD'S CREATIVITY

Creativity has been the engine behind amazing discoveries and incredible works of art since the beginning of time. Tremendous innovations and marvelous expressions of creativity started from someone asking, "I wonder what would happen if I tried this?"

It's hard to say where the next remarkable innovation or brilliant work of art might come from. I believe there are curious, creative children at play right now who will change our world in incredible ways in the future with their clever ideas and innovations.

There are three big reasons why creativity matters to your child at whatever age he or she happens to be right now. First, creative activities can add happiness and entertainment to your child's routine. (And the truth is that life is busy and stressful at times even for kids, so a little extra dose of daily joy is always welcome.)

Second, your child is likely to discover something creative that he or she loves best of all by creative dabbling. It might be painting, drawing, or printmaking. It might be theatrics, or creating costumes, or dance. It might be building and tinkering with construction materials. It might be writing stories, jokes, or poems. It might be creating original melodies with a musical instrument or singing. Every child will find excitement and enjoyment from something different.

The other big benefit of doing creative activities is that your child will realize that he or she is an imaginative and creative person. "I made that! I created it from my imagination! I kept working at it until I got it the way I wanted it!" These statements and realizations that pop into your child's mind build creative confidence and competence that set the stage for a lifetime of creativity. Your child's creative development is worthy of your support, right along with his physical, social, emotional, intellectual, and spiritual development, simply as a way of nurturing your *whole child*.

Our lives are shaped by what we believe in. When you believe in the goodness and importance of your child's creativity, you will find many ways to support and encourage it throughout all the years of childhood.

2. BE A CREATIVITY MENTOR

Parents can be powerful promoters of childhood creativity. They are in a unique position of knowing their child best of all, seeing special interests and observing abilities.

Child development experts and researchers have written extensively in recent years about the creativity (and imaginative playtime) crisis for children. The vast majority of children today have few hours in the day devoted to spontaneous, hands-on creativity and playtime. Many children today are spending much of their free time (outside of school) with electronics: watching TV, playing video games, or spending time on the Internet, tablet, smart phone, or cell phone. Another factor in the creativity crisis is the lack of focus (and budget) in many schools for art, music, theatrics, dance, and other activities essential to a child's creative development. Also, our culture places a high value on digital content. (Even toddlers are surrounded by slick, commercial-grade apps on tablets and smart phones that can set a misguided standard in place for what it means to be creative.)

But the truth of the matter is that parents are powerful. They can write their own rules for their children. They can say no to the cultural pressures they do not agree with. Parents can put their own rules in place to manage electronic games and activities in order to allow more time for being creative! Here are some tips to support your child's creativity every day throughout each stage of childhood from two to twelve years:

- Keep the focus on fun.
- Set time aside for your child's creative activities on a regular basis. (Even 10 minutes of creativity is positive.)
- Expect childlike artwork, projects, and performances.
- Have assorted materials, supplies, costumes, kid-style musical instruments, and recorded music on hand for spur-of-the-moment creative activities.
- Don't micromanage projects.
- Tolerate a little mess. (Set up a casual cleanup routine—with your child helping—when creative activities are over.)
- Encourage your child to take a break when a project gets too frustrating.
- Don't get hung up on "creative talent." (See *Talent Is Overrated* on page 21.)

- Take your child to creative events in your community to experience the creativity of others.
- Be creative yourself. Find ways to express your own creativity; with solo projects that you enjoy doing alone, and collaborative projects that are fun to do with your child and with your family.

3. INTRODUCE YOUR CHILD TO THE CREATIVITY OF OTHERS

Take your child to community art, music, dance, theatrics, and storytelling events and shine a spotlight on what's possible with creativity. It gives your child ideas, often sparks new interests, and it makes life exciting. What's more, *creativity is contagious*!

Look around in your community, region, or state for creative events that are child-friendly. (Find creative events and performances when your family is traveling or on vacation too.) Outdoor events are especially good because young children can move and still soak up the creativity. Here are a few tips to find child-friendly events in your area.

> It's the nod of recognition, the smile, and the response of the parent that indicates to the child, the parent's belief in the goodness of that child.
>
> **—DR. ROBERT COLES,** professor emeritus at Harvard University and Pulitzer Prize–winning author of *The Moral Life of Children*

Experience Art

- Children's art shows at local schools, preschools, and art centers (that feature children's artwork)
- Outdoor community art events (with group graffiti, group or individual painters' painting, silhouette artists, sketch or portrait artists, and so on)
- Arts and crafts festivals (with finished artwork and crafts on sale)
- Craft demonstrations at community events (wood, metal, fabric, jewelry, leather, pottery)
- Art and photography museums or exhibits (that are appropriate for children)

See Building and Construction

- Traditional-building craft events and demonstrations (blacksmiths, timber construction, stonework, brickwork, carving, and using hand tools)
- Trips to the city to see incredible architecture and skyscrapers
- Trips to historic cities and towns to see homes, businesses, and cobblestone streets built many years ago
- Local or regional events during the annual Global Cardboard Challenge, where children of all ages create imaginative things with cardboard (go to http://cardboardchallenge.com to check events worldwide)

Attend Music Performances

- Outdoor community concerts
- Children's classical music concerts (short and typically affiliated with community orchestras)
- Music performances at school, church, or community arts centers that feature children playing music
- Music competitions, talent shows, and regional recitals featuring children or adults
- Holiday music performances
- Community or church sing-alongs
- Join (or start) a caroling group for the holiday and sing for your neighbors

> *Kids are having all these stories brought to them so vividly on the screen that they're not playing imaginatively themselves; and this is a great loss in terms of the future of creativity.*
>
> **—JANE M. HEALY, PHD,**
> educational psychologist and author
> of *Your Child's Growing Mind*

Attend Dance Performances

- Local talent shows at area schools and arts organizations
- Broadway musicals that come to town
- Square dancing and clogging groups, events, and competitions in your area
- Contemporary dance or ballet troupe performances
- Local festivals that include ethnic dancing (Greek, Latino, African, Hungarian, Polish, and so on)
- Preschool, elementary, middle school, or high school dance recitals (or at private dance schools)
- Holiday dance performances (professional groups traveling through town or community or school groups)

Attend Theatrical Performances

- Puppet shows
- Street fairs with mime or theatrics
- Improvisation or comedy events tailored to children
- Holiday plays for children (with professional actors)
- Local school or church plays or pageants

Attend Storytelling and Word-Creativity Events

- Poetry readings for kids (or school events where children recite original or traditional poems)
- Storytelling events for children at schools, libraries, preschools
- Regional storytelling festivals (select the storytellers who specialize in child-friendly tales)

> " Every child longs to be able to communicate his thoughts, his feelings, his capabilities, to put his thumbprint on the world and to say, I'm here!
>
> —FREDELLE BRUSER MAYNARD, author of *Raisins and Almonds*

One last tip: When you take your child to creative events in your community, give yourself permission to leave early whenever necessary so that you can end on a positive note before your child gets fussy, or overtired or hungry. It's perfectly fine to quietly leave midway through a concert, children's play, storytelling event, or arts and crafts demonstration with young children in tow!

4. ALL KIDS ARE CREATIVE

Creative dabbling helps all children discover their own unique interests and passions. Some children love drawing and painting and making crafts right from the start. Others love everything musical: making instruments, tapping a beat, inventing silly songs, or shaking a tambourine. Some children are drawn to tinkering, building, or assembling and disassembling gadgets to see what's inside and how they work. Other children adore costumes and dress-up and plays and charades. Some love digging in the earth best of all and building with twigs and mud. Other children love writing poems, stories, and riddles. Some love to dance.

Children need exposure to a wide assortment of activities to see what grabs their attention and revs their creativity. What's more, most children discover multiple favorite ways to be creative, with each stage of childhood ushering in new possibilities. Here are four tips to encourage creative dabbling:

- Select a few age-appropriate activities in each category (art, building, music, dance, pretend, words) and try it out *with* your child. Even 10 or 15 minutes of shared creativity can be satisfying for kids and spark an interest in something new she might choose to do on her own in the future.

- Realize that your child's creative passions or interests may change or expand over time. Resist the urge to label your child with one main interest or talent such as "musical" or "theatrical" or "artistic." Instead keep things flexible so your child feels the freedom to continue to dabble and make new discoveries.
- Accept the fact that your child may prefer different types of creative activities from you. This may be especially true as she gets older and more assertive or independent.
- Consider scheduling "Family Creativity Night" once a month and let everyone pick a creative activity for the group to try together. This is a terrific way to introduce some new activities that your child might not try on his own.

5. FUN IS THE MAGIC INGREDIENT

Some of the most important things you know about childhood creativity you likely learned years ago when you were a child. Perhaps you remember the belly laughs, silliness, and excitement of doing imaginative, musical, or theatrical activities with other kids. Maybe you recall the satisfaction of creating a song, a building project, dance routine, or painting a giant mural inside your garage. Chances are that you recall these specific childhood projects because of the positive emotions that surround these memories.

Children put their very best curiosity, experimentation, thinking skills, problem solving, and creative expression into projects when they are having fun. Joy is the magic ingredient and renewable resource that makes kids want to be creative again and again.

HAPPY TIMES OF CREATIVITY OPEN THE DOOR FOR DOING MORE

I remember creating a song while swinging on my backyard swing at about six years of age. (That experience took place over fifty years ago and I can recall it with great clarity.) I sang that new homemade song at the top of my lungs as I went swinging higher and higher. On that particular day I suddenly realized that anyone could create a whole new song from their own imagination. I was awestruck by this discovery!

When I look back on my creative dabbling in childhood, this particular moment stands out as being a pivotal experience. I was astounded to realize that musical creativity was available to everyone. After that, I understood that other kinds of creativity were open to everyone too! *The sky is the limit when it comes to being creative,* I concluded.

This childlike enthusiasm and belief that *everyone* can create their own amusing songs did not fade away. I am not a trained musician, but when I was thirty-three years old and starting a nationally syndicated public radio program, I decided it would be enjoyable to try to write the theme song for the show. So I created a simple, upbeat tune and wrote some lyrics and recorded it on a small recorder. Then I hired a musical arranger, found musicians to record it, and I even had the pleasure of singing backup vocals on the original version of the song.

I tell this story not because the theme song was an extraordinary work of art (trust me, it was not) but because my childhood discovery that everyone could sing their own song gave me the creative gumption to try this musical project at work many years later. I've had many exciting work projects over the years, but this experience of writing a song and recording it in a studio with professional musicians stands out as one of my most memorable and rewarding days on the job. I am ever so glad I took a chance on writing that song.

6. TIME IS OF THE ESSENCE

One of the most important things you can do to nurture your child's creativity is to set aside a little extra free time (or downtime) in your child's schedule for creative activities. This might mean finding a few minutes each day, or perhaps more, setting aside time on the weekend for a variety of creative activities. There are also little hidden moments in your family routine that are perfect for small but meaningful bursts of creativity too: dinnertime (add some creative word games at the dinner table), bedtime (invent stories together), long car trips and daily commutes (perfect for singing or creating new verses to familiar songs).

> "You want to be sure not to overschedule your child's free time, because those moments when kids just get together on their own and do what they want are the most joyous.
>
> **—DR. DANIEL GOLEMAN,** psychologist, author of *Emotional Intelligence* and *Focus*

Once you find pockets of time for your child's creative activities, it's best to eliminate electronic distractions so your child can truly engage his full attention toward his creative projects. This means the TV, computer, tablet, smart phone, cell phone, and electronic games are turned off and out of sight for a while. (I love the idea of designating a "nap basket" for all handheld electronics during time of creative activities, because even young kids get the concept of giving electronic gadgets a "nap" or a break for a little while.)

When I see a child spending long hours of time sitting in front of an electronic screen, I wonder if children aren't becoming adultlike a little too soon. I can visualize that same child, sometime in the future, all grown up and sitting at a desk, looking at a screen, tapping on a keyboard, and earning his living this way. I can't help but wonder to myself, "What's the hurry?" There will be so much time later in life for looking at screens to process information and do work. But there is only one time for being a child and grabbing onto all that childhood has to offer.

Children are wired to be active: to play, to follow their curiosity and imagination, and to see what they can create, invent, and do in the three-dimensional, physical world. This is the natural order of things. And all that exuberance for living life

> *It's kind of that inner wisdom that children have—an inner curiosity, their creativity, their spontaneity—their sense of wonder toward the world that every child is born with. I think there's a biological guarantee of this so that we can survive as a species. The trick is how to keep that alive as they grow.*
>
> **—THOMAS ARMSTRONG, PHD,** learning specialist and author of *In Their Own Way*

large as a busy, creative, active child is worthy of great encouragement and protection too.

No long lectures about the importance of creativity are needed for your child. No guilt trips about too much time spent on video games—just you initiating a confident and friendly plan to set aside a little extra time each day or each week for your child to get creative.

The beauty of setting aside a little extra time for childhood creativity is that once your child discovers something creative he or she really likes to do, the concept of giving up electronics for a while gets easier because your child is onboard and having fun with unplugged creativity. In the beginning, however, parents need to take the initiative and hold firm with a friendly, matter-of-fact attitude about setting limits on TV, video games, tablets, smart phones, and all things electronic. Make a plan that helps you manage electronics and promote creative activities. Here are some tips to get you started:

Manage Electronics and Screen Time

- Hold off from introducing your baby and toddler to screen time and high-tech toys. Note: the American Academy of Pediatrics recommends that children two years of age and younger have no screen time.
- Set an electronics plan in place about how much screen time is allowed each day or each week for your toddler, preschooler, or elementary-aged child, and stick with the plan. Note: the American Academy of Pediatrics recommends that children three years or older get no more than 1 or 2 hours a day of *quality* screen time.
- Let grandparents, friends, and other gift givers know you prefer gifts that foster imaginative play and creativity rather than high-tech toys and gadgets.

Make Your Home a Creativity Place for Kids

- Have materials and props on hand for creative projects: art, music, dancing, building, creative writing, storytelling, pretend, and theatrics on a regular basis.
- Mix up the types of creative play and activities—include high-energy, exuberant creative activities sometimes (dance; silly musical games; charades; big, messy outdoor art projects) along with quiet, relaxed creativity (arts and crafts, singing, building forts, pretend, puppets, storytelling, creative writing) at other times.
- Make your home a creative, active, joyful place that other children love to visit. Let playmates experience the joys of creative dabbling at your home right alongside your child.
- Make time for Family Creativity Night once a month or once a week, and put it on your calendar so you don't forget. (See Family Creativity Night ideas on page 37.)

7. TALENT IS OVERRATED

It might surprise you to know that many of the world's most successful musicians, artists, inventors, actors, comedians, architects, dancers, and writers say that their hard work and passion for their craft set the stage for their success rather than talent. This comment, heard time and again from many accomplished creative people, confirms that creativity is not just available to a select few on the planet.

When we realize that talent is overrated, we can begin to examine the landscape of childhood creativity more clearly and simply. Here's how I see it: When kids spend time doing creative activities, two important things happen. First, they are happy and engaged; and second, they eventually discover something creative that is *extra fun* to do. Those extra-exciting activities are pursued with passion. Skills develop. Creative habits and expectations are put in place. Mastery (at a certain craft) begins to unfold.

> *Mastery is this wonderful, exciting feeling: I'm better at it today than I was last week. It doesn't mean I'm the best in the world; it doesn't mean I won the Nobel Prize; it means simply: I'm getting better—and that is the root of motivation and self-esteem, and it's really magical.*
>
> **—EDWARD M. HALLOWELL, MD,** psychiatrist, author of *The Childhood Roots of Adult Happiness*

I'm not saying that every child who pursues his or her creative interests will become a professional artist, photographer, designer, writer, dancer, musician, architect, actor, or comedian. (But some certainly will.) I am saying, instead, that when children are given time, opportunities, materials, and encouragement, their creative development unfolds, and talent is built from the ground up through experience.

FAMILY CREATIVITY

Doing creative activities as a family adds a big dose of fun to everyday life. What's more, children experience the freedom to experiment with new materials and spend lighthearted time with parents too. Along the way, everyone discovers favorite ways of being creative. Some families might enjoy group art projects best of all. Others are delighted with storytelling, musical creativity, or dance and theatrics. Some parents and kids love the challenge of making giant structures with cardboard.

Imaginative entertainment is one of the main benefits of family creativity, but it's also an excellent way to smooth out small tensions in the family. Yes, there may still be little tantrums at bedtime or hassles about homework, but when you share a laugh or invent a silly story together, everyone gets a boost of positive energy.

The secret to success for family creativity is keeping the focus on fun for everyone. No need to strive for perfection or stretch the activity out too long if someone in the group is tired. Keep the focus on playful, imaginative fun. Give yourself permission to soak up the simple pleasures of childhood creativity.

There are three easy ways to put more creativity in your family immediately. First, begin to weave creative activities into your daily routines with your child. Second, add creative traditions throughout the year to celebrate seasons, milestones, holidays, and events in fun, imaginative ways. And third, put Family Creativity Night on the schedule. Here are some tips to help get things moving:

Creative Family Routines

Look for small windows of time throughout each day and add imaginative activities to spark your child's imagination and engage his creativity. Here are a few daily or weekly routines and transitions with creative ideas listed below that are just right for short spurts of parent and child creativity.

DRIVING TO AND FROM SCHOOL, CHILD CARE, CHURCH, OR SYNAGOGUE

- Sing Traditional Children's Tunes (ages 3–12), page 87
- Song Sage (ages 3–8), page 179
- Song-a-Day (ages 3–12), page 172
- Half-and-Half Songs (5–12 and up), page 282
- Song Starters (ages 5–12 and up), page 283
- Grow-Grow-Grow Your Song (ages 5–12 and up), page 285
- Amazing-Vehicles Sketchbook (ages 6–12 and up), page 230
- The Happiest Pet on the Block sketches (ages 6–12 and up), page 230

AFTER SCHOOL

- Clay-Critter Challenge (ages 5–12 and up), page 256
- Mixed-Box Towers and Towns (ages 2–8), page 165
- Shoe Box Dollhouse (ages 4–12 and up), page 265
- Shake, Shake, Shake-Along (ages 2–4), page 100
- Three-Minute Dance Routine (ages 2–12), page 102
- Follow-the-Leader Dancing (ages 2–12), page 103
- Old MacDonald Dance-Along (ages 2–5), page 105
- Zoo Zomba (ages 3–8), page 189
- Make a Pretend Highway (ages 3–8), page 206

KITCHEN-TIME CREATIVITY (WHILE PARENTS PREPARE DINNER)

- Tabletop Scribble Art (ages 2–5), page 60
- Scribble-Art Lunch Bags (ages 2–5), page 61

family

- Curlicue Glitter-Glue Drawings (ages 3–12), page 141
- Mystery-Loop Drawing (ages 6–12 and up), page 236
- Make Paper-Bag Puppets (ages 3–8), page 210
- "Can You Believe It?" Tall Tales (ages 6–12 and up), page 329
- Explain It to the Alien (ages 6–12 and up), page 335

FAMILY WALK IN THE NEIGHBORHOOD

- Create Pet-Adventure Stories (ages 3–12), page 219
- Two-Friends Stories (ages 3–12), page 219
- Amazing Animal-Adventure Stories (ages 6–12 and up), page 329
- Fairy-Tale Twists (ages 6–12 and up), page 333

BEDTIME (OR NAPTIME) OR AWAKING IN THE MORNING

- Story Basket (ages 2–5), page 127
- Create a Silly Animal Song (ages 3–12), page 179
- Create a Fill-in-the-Pause Song (ages 3–12), page 180
- Musical-Echo Songs (ages 3–8), page 180
- Parent Puppeteer (ages 2–8), page 119

FAMILY BREAKFAST ON THE WEEKEND

- Guess-What-I'm-Doing Charades (ages 3–8), page 207
- Worker-Bee Acting Club (ages 6–12 and up), page 309
- Tall-Tale Beginnings (ages 3–12), page 216
- Story-Time Guessing Game (ages 3–12), page 217
- First-Sentence Stories (ages 6–12 and up), page 334
- Explain It to the Alien (ages 6–12 and up), page 335

CREATIVE FAMILY BREAKFAST DRAWINGS

Cover your kitchen table with large sheets of white butcher paper (or brown craft paper) before you begin making pancakes or eggs for your weekend family breakfast. Add a few pieces of invisible tape to hold the sheets of paper together. Now you have a giant space for a family mural or masterpiece. Provide crayons and markers, and encourage everyone to turn on their imagination to see what they can create. Some families like to pick a theme for their sketches, with everyone drawing animals, people, places, vehicles, buildings, creatures, nature scenes, or colorful abstract designs. Others prefer a freestyle approach, with everyone drawing whatever pops into their imagination. The finished family masterpiece can be hung in the hallway, or turned into a giant paper tablecloth for the next family picnic. This is a good way to weave creativity into a leisurely weekend breakfast of creating, eating, and chatting.

Creative Family Traditions

Make a plan to add creative traditions for holidays, seasons, and birthdays and soon your year will be filled with creative family projects! Consider Thanksgiving; Christmas; Hanukkah; Fourth of July; Labor Day; Memorial Day; the first day (or last day) of summer, fall, winter, and spring; Mother's Day; Father's Day; Grandparents' Day; and birthdays too.

HALLOWEEN POSTERS

Everyone in the family makes their own giant poster with Halloween creatures.

Materials
- One large sheet of poster board for each person
- Markers (or crayons)
- Glitter glue
- Optional: fabric scraps, yarn, photos

Get Creative Have a poster party on the living room floor with each family member drawing a Halloween poster. The posters might have Halloween characters or scenes that are silly or ghoulish, or perhaps just a drawing of one giant pumpkin face. Once the drawings are finished, tape them inside your windows or on the walls to celebrate the season.

THANKSGIVING-GRATITUDE TABLECLOTH

Everyone draws something or someone they are thankful for, and the next thing you know, the tablecloth tells a story about what matters most at this moment in time.

Materials
- One plain tablecloth or flat bedsheet
- Nontoxic fabric markers (such as Crayola)
- Newspapers (used to absorb possible fabric paint bleed-through)

Get Creative Spread newspapers on a hard surface such as a wooden or tile floor and place the tablecloth on top. Ask everyone in the family to write or draw something (or many things) they are thankful for this year.

(Follow the instructions on the package of fabric markers for setting the color before the tablecloth is washed.)

Thanksgiving-Gratitude Apron for the Family Cook

Purchase a plain cotton apron and let everyone in the family draw a picture or write words about something from the Thanksgiving feast that they love best of all. (Follow the instructions on the package of fabric markers for setting the color before the apron is washed.)

It's really a cookie-decoration party (with a parent baking the holiday-shaped cookies a day before), but the creativity comes when the kids and parents add colored frosting and sprinkles.

family

Materials

- Cookie sheets
- Sugar cookie dough (make homemade or buy premixed dough in the grocery store)
- Assorted holiday cookie cutters
- Easy homemade frosting (see recipe below)
- Assorted cookie sprinkles
- Paper plates
- Teaspoons (or butter knives) for applying the frosting
- One large tablecloth

Setup A day before the family cookie bake, a parent or grandparent rolls out the dough, cuts the shapes, and bakes the cookies. (Place them in an airtight container to keep them fresh.)

At Christmas, our three girls each stand on the fireplace and tell their version of the Christmas story. Some years they dress the part too. We started this tradition when the oldest was two years old. We videotape these little stories every year and they are hilarious to look at later. One year Ella said that after Jesus was born, they all went and played soccer.

—Lindsey from South Carolina

When it's nearly time to decorate the cookies, cover the table with a large (washable) tablecloth, put the cookie sprinkles, paper plates, platter of baked cookies, and spoons (or butter knives) all around the table. Mix up a large quantity of frosting (see recipe below).

HOLIDAY FROSTING (FOR SUGAR COOKIES)

This is the very basic but spreadable frosting I have used for twenty-five years of family cookie baking with excellent results!

Ingredients

- 2 cups powdered sugar (add a little extra sugar as needed to thicken just a bit)
- 4 tablespoons milk
- Food coloring

Directions For a small batch of frosting use this recipe above to get the correct consistency for frosting the cookies. (For a large batch of decorated cookies, double or triple the recipe as needed.) Pour the powdered sugar in a bowl.

Add the milk and stir until the lumps are removed.

Add a drop of the desired food coloring. (If you have a large crowd of cookie decorators, make a triple or quadruple batch of frosting and make duplicate bowls of each color so that all the decorators around the table have easy access to the colored frosting.) Note that if you mix the frosting and let it set about 10 minutes, you get a good consistency for spreading. And if it gets too thick during decorating time, thin with a wee bit of milk.

Get Creative Everyone spreads frosting on a cookie (using a spoon) and shakes sprinkles to decorate. Place the decorated cookies on plates or cookie sheets to let the frosting dry thoroughly. (Note: older kids and adults can experiment with swirling or dripping several colors of frosting to create unique designs.)

Birthday Cookie Bake
Several days before a family birthday celebration, gather everyone together to decorate sugar cookies that were baked (ahead of time) in the shape of the birthday girl or birthday boy's initials. (You can find a set of large alphabet cookie cutters with A–Z letters at Williams-Sonoma or other retail or online stores.)

GIANT SNOW SCULPTURE

Celebrate the first big snow day of winter with everyone in the family working to create a giant snow sculpture.

Materials
- Plastic buckets, cups, scoops, and snow tools (to gather and shape the snow)

Get Creative Let the children decide what to create and everyone works together to mound up the snow and begin shaping the snow into the imaginative object or creature. (Parents will need to take the lead on creating the overall shape and keeping the activity safe for all.)

PLANT A COLORFUL FLOWER COLLAGE

Rejoice in springtime and sunshine by creating color designs with assorted flowers.

Materials
- Assorted spring plants and flowers
- Flower boxes or large outdoor planters
- Soil
- Small gardening hand tools

Get Creative Let each family member make their own colorful design created by flowers and plants. Some flower artists might alternate colors in a row in their containers. Others might create shapes or clusters of colorful designs. When you are done planting, take a family walk around the neighborhood or nearby park to admire other beautiful flower collages growing all around your community.

Flower and Fabric Color Collage

Add more colorful accents to your family flower creations by making multicolored fabric streamers to go inside your pots and window boxes. Start with a package of one-piece wooden clothespins. Cut medium-to-long pieces of tulle fabric in various colors (8 to 24 inches in length). Next, roll each piece of fabric tightly (jelly roll style) and thread it through the slit of the clothespin. Gather both ends of the fabric and tie a double knot around the rounded end of the clothespin. Place each fabric streamer firmly into the soil in the pots. Yes, the color will fade with the sun, but it adds a splash of extra color in early spring, and white or light streamers later in summer.

CREATE A SPRINGTIME SIDEWALK MURAL

Celebrate the simple pleasures of fresh air and creativity with everyone in the family getting creative with chalk.

Materials
- Giant sidewalk chalk in assorted colors

Get Creative Make a giant, colorful chalk mural on your sidewalk, with everyone in the family drawing something to celebrate springtime. Or, block off your entire driveway (for safety's sake) and turn the concrete surface into one giant drawing space for chalk art. Pick a theme that celebrates Mother Nature in springtime.

Sidewalk Art Day in Your Neighborhood (to Celebrate Spring)
Send out an e-mail or print a flier inviting all your neighbors to participate in a Springtime Sidewalk Art Day on an upcoming Saturday or Sunday this spring! Children, parents, and grandparents make colorful creations on the walkway and then everyone tours around to admire the neighborhood creativity. This is a good way to get outdoors to celebrate springtime, creativity, and neighborhood connections.

MOTHER NATURE COLOR TOUR

When spring and summer flowers are in full bloom, the color combinations and variations can be a feast for the eyes. This is a perfect time to pack up the family and head out to local parks and gardens in your community to appreciate the vibrant colors of nature. Some kids will enjoy taking photos and others may just like being outdoors with parents. Either way, this Mother Nature Color Tour is a marvelous way for a child artist to soak up the splendor of beautiful colors and perhaps even pick favorite color combinations to explore in next week's artwork too.

family

BUILD A GIANT SAND CASTLE

Celebrate the sunny days of summer with the whole family going to the beach to create a giant sand castle together.

Materials
- Small buckets
- Sand tools (plastic scoops and shovels)

Get Creative Use sand tools and buckets to dig and dump the sand into a big mound to get started. Next decide the shape or design of your castle and use hand tools and small containers to form the walls and shapes of the castle or building from the wet sand. (A friendly can-do attitude from parents helps keep this sand project moving along positively.)

Build a "Creatures of the Sea" Sand Sculpture

Ask your child to think of a giant sea creature or animal you can make together at the beach. Perhaps it's a giant turtle, mermaid, dolphin, fish, or octopus. Work with buckets, small plastic containers, and sand tools to create the large creature with the wet sand. Use small hand tools to create texture and details on the giant sculpture when the shape is finished.

CREATE FUNNY-FACE PIZZAS

Celebrate fresh vegetables in summertime with each family member creating silly faces on small homemade pizzas with fresh veggies from the garden.

Materials
- Small pizza crust (already baked) or large pita bread (already baked) for each person
- Tomato sauce
- Grated cheese
- Assorted fresh vegetables (sliced by parents and ready to use as decorations for the pizza)

Setup Chop or slice assorted shapes and sizes of fresh veggies such as green, red, or yellow peppers, kale, spinach, zucchini, tomato, and broccoli. Or offer or any of these veggies partially cooked or steamed: asparagus, carrots, beans, Brussels sprouts, purple or green cabbage, and so on. Place each vegetable on a plate or bowl (with a spoon) and put the assorted veggies in the middle of the table. Parents put a little tomato sauce and grated cheese on each crust of pita. Place it on a cookie sheet.

Get Creative Give each child their own pizza and let them create a face on the pizza with the veggies. When the creations are done, bake the pizzas in a 350-degree oven (approximately 8–10 minutes) or just long enough to melt the cheese and warm or cook all the veggies.

Create Fruit-Face Pancakes
Celebrate the spring, summer, or fall harvest of fruits in your community with a special Fruit-Face Pancake breakfast for your family. Everyone gets a big warm pancake and creates a face on the pancake using fresh fruits and berries. (Fruits to consider: strawberries, bananas, pineapple, melon balls, apple, peach or pear slices, or blueberries.) Take photos of these tasty creatures before they are eaten. (Add a little syrup— yum-yum!)

CAPTURE YOUR FAMILY CREATIVITY WITH PHOTOS, VIDEOS, AND AUDIO RECORDINGS

Once you get creative traditions going, be sure to take photos of some of your special artistic creations and make videos (or audio recordings) of the music, dance, storytelling, and theatrical productions your family group creates. You'll enjoy looking at or listening to these creative projects in the future in photos and video, and it's also a good way to honor and preserve some of the temporary projects that were created with sand, snow, and cardboard.

Family Creativity Night

Another exciting way to mix creativity into family life is to host a Family Creativity Night once a month. Creating an event that revolves around doing imaginative projects together—such as art, building and construction, music, dance, theatrics, and creativity with words—is a wonderful way to get everyone in the family on board with creativity. Here are a few ideas to make your Family Creativity Night enjoyable for everyone:

- Start off with a festive meal—but keep it extremely simple: sandwiches, or pizza, with fruits and veggies. You don't want to get overwhelmed making an elaborate meal at the same time you are gathering up materials for creativity.
- Consider a picnic (with paper plates and cups) on a blanket spread out on the living room floor, or take the picnic outdoors if the weather is good.
- Set aside just the right amount of time for your children's age and attention span—somewhere between 30 and 90 minutes of creativity typically works best—depending on the mix of ages in the family.
- Be sure to include activities that each age can participate in.
- Mix and match types of activities and keep them short. For example, start with everyone doing a silly follow-the-leader dance routine (or Zoo Zomba, page 189). After that do a group art activity or collaborative storytelling for 15–30 minutes. Then, end with a laugh. Pick a short, theatrical activity (such as Worker-Bee Acting Club, page 309) or create new, silly verses for an old familiar tune (such as "Old MacDonald," page 92).
- On special occasions invite your extended family members (grandparents, cousins, and aunts and uncles) or close family friends to join in your Family Creativity Night too.

Children like familiar routines and traditions and they like novelty too. With this in mind it's a splendid idea to find a few family favorites or traditional creative activities to be included again and again in your Family Creativity Night throughout the year. Then add new and exciting ways to be creative in each Family Creativity Night as well. Here are a few of my family favorite activities that might become familiar favorites for your family too:

ONE BIG LIST OF FAMILY-FRIENDLY ACTIVITIES

There are hundreds of creative ideas in the Toddler, Preschooler, and Grade-School sections of *The Giant Book of Creativity for Kids* that will be a perfect fit for your group during Family Creativity Night. Here are some activities to consider.

Art-and-Craft Activities for Family Creativity
- Scribble-Scrabble Art Portfolio (ages 2–5), page 63
- Paint-Dabber Creations (ages 2–5), page 65
- Colors-and-Shapes Collage (ages 2–5), page 68
- Torn-Paper Collage (ages 2–12), page 72
- Burlap Circle Prints (ages 2–5), page 159
- Sponge Prints (ages 2–10), page 75
- Hand-Printing on Burlap (ages 2–4), page 78
- "George the Giant" Mural or Poster (ages 3–12), page 139
- Water-Bottle Printmaking (ages 2–12), page 143
- Painted-Wood Collage (ages 3–12), page 150
- Burlap Squirt Painting (ages 6–12), page 250
- Painted-Cardboard Collage (ages 3–12), page 146
- Burlap-and-Button Collage (ages 3–12), page 147
- Wavy-Water Collage (ages 3–12), page 148
- Creepy-Critter Beanbag Box (ages 3–12), page 152
- Squeeze-Bottle Painting (ages 3–12), page 159
- Comic-Strip Creativity for Two (ages 6–12 and up), page 233
- Letter Art (ages 6–12 and up), page 236
- Mystery-Loop Drawing (ages 6–12 and up), page 236
- Curlicue-Circle Collage (ages 6–12 and up), page 240
- Snowflake Collage (ages 6–12 and up), page 239
- Mountain Collage (ages 6–12 and up), page 242
- Doodle Painting (ages 6–12 and up), page 245

$\longrightarrow$

family

- Sound-Effects Theatrics (ages 6–12 and up), page 325

Storytelling and Creative Word Activities for Family Creativity

PROGRESSIVE PAINTING

Start with one shape painted on a giant piece of paper, and everyone adds more shapes to create a group painting.

Materials
- Child's art easel
- Tempera paint (or assorted colored markers)
- Paintbrush
- Small bucket of water
- One large sheet of heavy drawing paper (or newsprint paper)

Get Creative Put a sheet of paper on the easel and select one artist (child or parent) to make one shape of any kind on the paper using a paintbrush. A second artist in the group goes to the easel and creates another shape or line to continue the painting. A third artist approaches the easel and creates another shape or mark or adds color to the prior shapes. (Please be very loose about the rules for Progressive Painting; just let each artist take his or her time adding the next strokes of the painting. Some children may add three or four lines or shapes when it's their turn and it really doesn't matter.) At some point when the painting is quite developed and it is your turn to paint (parent), ask for a consensus whether the painting is now finished or should the group just keep painting. (Do this when it's your turn so you don't inadvertently eliminate one of the children's turns to paint lest he or she feels slighted.)

> *One of the things that families are doing is instituting a day or a night where all the screens are turned off and all the cell phones are off. Then the families are playing together; cooking, making art, singing, or doing something together.*
>
> **—SUSAN LINN,** author of *The Case for Make Believe*

FAMILY CHARADES

This family favorite never goes out of style and it's enjoyable for children, parents, and grandparents to play together!

Materials
- Charades Party Game—Family Charades-in-a-Box (optional, see note)

Get Creative Each child or adult acts out the word or phrase (or picture) on the game card without saying a word, and the others in the group try to guess what is being acted out. Children can use facial expressions, movements, and gestures, and many unexpected or silly things happen along the way.

Note: Charades Party Game—Family Charades-in-a-Box Compendium Board Game by Outset Media is available online or in your local toy store. This boxed set of Charades includes six different games (including picture charades), suitable for all ages of children and adults from age four years and up.

STORY JAR

Everyone in the family writes down any good story ideas that pop into their mind throughout the week and a tall tale is created by the group during Family Creativity Night.

Materials
- One large plastic jar with a lid (or a shoe box)
- Small pieces of paper
- Pencil with eraser

Get Creative Cut small pieces of paper and put the papers and a pencil inside the Story Jar. Encourage the children (and parents) in the family to write down any ideas that might make a good story later in the week. The person then folds the paper in half and tosses it in the jar. (For example, someone in the family might write: "A puppy named Sam," or "A monster who likes ice cream," or "A friendly lion," or "A contest to make the biggest doughnut in the world.") Then when it's Family Creativity Night, parents (or older children) pick a paper from the Story Jar and invent a short story to tell to the group. Toddlers and preschoolers will likely want to have parents or grandparents telling the story while they listen, or they may want to make one-word suggestions about what might happen next while the story is under way. Older kids (ten and up) may love to create their own tall tales from start to finish.

> *We clean up the porch really well in the spring, put white Christmas lights all around, and move some speakers outside. Then we have spring and summer dance parties with our kids on the back porch. Whenever the kids are fighting and we need a game-changer, we just turn up the Laurie Berkner music and start dancing around. Our girls love to dance and this has become a fun family activity.*
>
> —Lindsey from South Carolina

Progressive Family Storytelling
One person in the family picks something to create a story about (for example, a penguin). The storyteller tells the beginning of the story for a short time, perhaps telling the penguin's name, where he lives, and what he likes to do. Then the storyteller pauses and the next person in the circle continues telling the story in his own way. Everyone takes a turn for a short time and then someone is selected to end the story.

Being creative with music can be as simple as playing pots and pans or inventing games and dances to music while you are listening.

—CATHY FINK, Grammy Award-winning musician, singer, songwriter

FAMILY KARAOKE

Find some family-friendly recordings (songs) and make your own version of karaoke singing!

Materials
- Familiar recorded songs (that are appropriate for children)

Singing is such a great human expression of togetherness; in joy and in sorrow. It's an outlet for so many emotions.

—JOHN FEIERABEND, artistic director of the Feierabend Association for Music Education and author of *The First Steps in Music*

- Music player (CD, MP3, and so on)
- Pretend microphone (ice cream scooper or cardboard tube, and so on)
- Optional: karaoke music system (CD or music player, microphone, and speakers)

Get Creative Each singer selects a song and sings along to the music! Add hats, costumes, or props to give it more theatrics. (Use a kid-karaoke sound system with a microphone—or just select familiar songs, turn on the music, and add a pretend mic for the singers.)

Set the rules before the singing begins: keep this fun for everyone; no put-downs or negative comments—only clapping and positive comments for all.

OLD-TIME TEEN DANCING

Have a few laughs and show your children or grandchildren some of your favorite dance steps from your teenage years!

Materials
- Recorded music with a good rhythm and beat for dancing

Get Creative Parents or grandparents, play some music from your teenage years and try to teach your children the dances you did when you were a child or teenager. Then let the kids take a turn and play their music and you try to learn their dance moves too.

"For the past two years during the Christmas holidays, our family has created its own music recital in our living room and everyone in the family performs something for the group. (We even print up a program.) Some of the adults play a song on the piano. My daughter sings or dances, my nephew played the drums last year. Any talent goes! We didn't practice or prep; it was more about just being together and playing around for fun. The best part was listening to my usually quiet forty-five-year-old brother giggle and joke around with his nieces and nephews.

—Angie from South Carolina

Creative Birthday Traditions

When a parent or child has a birthday, it's a good time to introduce a creative activity that might become a family tradition. You have a chance to celebrate the birthday and each family member's unique way of being creative too. You might expand this tradition to include extended family members too: cousins, grandparents, godparents, aunts, and uncles. Here are some birthday traditions to add to your family celebration:

SOMETHING-SPECIAL BIRTHDAY DRAWINGS

Everyone in the family draws a picture of something special about the birthday boy or girl!

Materials
- Drawing paper
- Markers or crayons
- Glitter glue
- Drawing pens or pencils
- Optional: Notebook with plastic sleeves (or small file folder) to save the annual birthday drawings

Get Creative Several days before the next family birthday event, gather everyone around the table and encourage them to create a drawing for the birthday boy or birthday girl (or for mom or dad). These drawings might feature something special that the artist likes to do with the birthday person or perhaps they will just be a special drawing to give as a birthday present. It's a lovely tradition, with a whole collection of artwork created over time. Save these drawings and create a special Birthday Drawing notebook for each member of the family.

BIRTHDAY ARTWORK BOOK

Start a new book-making tradition around your child's birthday!

Materials
- Card stock
- Markers or crayons
- Stapler or hole punch and ribbon

Get Creative Sometime around your child's birthday collect your child's recent drawings (or scribbles) and create a keepsake book of the artwork he has made this year.

BIRTHDAY ARTIST POSTERS FOR TODDLERS

Create a Birthday Poster tradition each year!

Materials
- Washable markers
- One sheet of poster board

Get Creative Provide nontoxic markers and a giant sheet of colorful poster board and encourage your child to create one giant drawing. When the drawing is finished, parents write a few words to tell the story of your child's birthday festivities or jot down a few highlights of your child's creative life this year on the poster. Hang the Birthday Poster in a place of honor, and make another one next year that reflects your child's preschool stage of drawing!

Highlights of My Year Birthday Poster
Right before your child's next birthday, encourage your preschooler, kindergartner, or six- to twelve-year-old child to think of something special that happened this past year, and create a giant poster with drawings, photos, and text to celebrate that milestone or memory.

PARTY POSTERS

After the birthday cake has been eaten and the party is over, encourage your child to create a colorful poster that captures the excitement of the day in words and photos!

Materials
- Rubber stamp set with all the letters of the alphabet
- Nontoxic ink pad
- Colored poster board
- Nontoxic white glue, such as Elmer's
- Photos from your child's most recent birthday celebration
- Kneaded eraser
- Pencil

Get Creative Your child assembles favorite birthday photos onto a giant poster board and glues them in place

family

in any pattern she likes. (Just be sure to encourage your child to leave about 1 or 2 inches of space between each photo for captions or words.) Ask your child to look at each photo and say one word or a couple of words that describes each photo.

Use a pencil to lightly print the suggested captions near each photo. Then help your child to select the appropriate rubber-stamp letters to create these words with the ink pad and rubber stamps. (Or help your older child to hand print these letters in order to create words.) When the giant Birthday Poster is finished, place it in an inexpensive poster frame and hang it in your child's room to admire and enjoy his or her creativity and birthday-party memories.

MUSICAL BIRTHDAY MARCH

Try this lighthearted tradition that requires grown-ups to act like kids, have a few laughs, and create fond memories too.

Materials
- Party hats
- Magic wands for kings and queens (see page 203 for directions on making your own)

- Preschool-friendly percussion instruments, such as harmonicas, kazoos, triangles, cymbals, maracas, and so on

Get Creative The birthday child becomes the leader of the Birthday March and stands at the head of the line. She calls out "one-two-three" and on the count of *three* the marching begins around the house or lawn with all the other partygoers marching behind. Everyone is singing "Happy Birthday" of course, with the verses repeated several times. For added excitement, add party hats and magic wands for all!

Family Birthday Band
Start another Happy Birthday tradition with percussion instruments for all! When it's time to sing "Happy Birthday," give everyone a small percussion instrument—musical shakers, tambourines, clackers, and any other preschooler-friendly instruments—to embellish the song. For added entertainment, encourage family members to invent new (positive or funny) verses to stretch out the song. Examples might include: "How old are you?" "Cake and ice cream for you!" "What wishes have you?"

Creative Birthday Parties

family

When your child's birthday rolls around this year, consider hosting a creative event to celebrate.

A creative-activities party celebrates the joyous spirit of imagination. Your child's party can include art, music, dance, theatrics, building projects, and creativity with words. Delightful and amazing things can happen when a group of children creates spontaneously together or side by side.

With a little advance planning, you can put on a special party that your child will remember for years to come. The main secret to success is to tailor the party to your child's age, abilities, and personality. Select an assortment of activities that match up with your child's interests. Tailor your event to your child's physical and social capabilities too. For children who are less comfortable with groups, keep the party very small, with only two or three other children in attendance. In this scenario you can focus the activities around individual creative projects, with the children side by side doing their own individual projects.

Check out the Toddler, Preschooler/Kindergarten, and Grade-School sections below to help you plan your party. A basic structure (or list) of activities and a loose schedule can help organize your time and keep the party moving along at a good pace. Then, once your basic plan is in order, allow for spontaneity, keep a flexible attitude, and adapt to the circumstances that present themselves as the children arrive.

HAVE A CREATIVE BIRTHDAY PARTY FOR YOUR TODDLER

You can host a superb toddler birthday party for your child that is creative and entertaining for everyone (even parents)! All it takes is a few minutes of preparty planning, realistic expectations about toddlers' interests and abilities, and a few parents to help during the party.

Here are a few tips for a successful creative birthday party for your toddler:

- Keep the party short (60–75 minutes is about right).
- Invite only a handful of other toddlers (and invite the parents to stay at the party too).
- Plan and host the party with safety as your top priority.
- Select a few toddler-friendly creative activities (and materials, supplies, and props) that are tailored to toddler abilities.
- If the idea of a group of toddlers with art supplies is overwhelming, then take the party outdoors or stick with music, dance, pretend, and block-building creativity instead.
- Have an entertaining, low-key *arrival activity* under way at the start (so children join in easily).
- Keep a friendly attitude and step in to divert or distract if small meltdowns happen.
- Appoint one or two parent or teenage helpers to make the party happy and manageable.

Itinerary for a Creativity Party for Toddlers
(for a 60- to 75-minute party)

- **Activity 1** (5–10 minutes): Select one creative arrival activity, such as Tabletop Scribble Art (page 60), Scribble-Art Lunch Bags (page 61), or Scribble-Art Gift Boxes (page 61).
- **Activity 2** (15 minutes): Select one to three art, building, music, dance, pretend, or word activities, such as Paint-Dabber Creations (page 65), Mixed-Box Towers and Towns (page 165), Sing Traditional Children's Tunes (page 87), Three-Minute Dance Routine (page 102), Make Paper Animal Ears (page 106), or Creative Rhymes with Your Toddler (page 123).
- **Activity 3** (10 minutes): Select one of the freestyle creativity activities, such as Tabletop Scribble Art (page 60), Block-Builder (page 80), or Sand Building for Toddlers (page 85).
- **Activity 4** (10 minutes): Cake time.
- **Activity 5** (15 minutes): End the party with another freestyle creativity activity.

HAVE A CREATIVE BIRTHDAY PARTY FOR YOUR PRESCHOOLER OR KINDERGARTNER

Having a creative birthday party is an outstanding way to celebrate your preschooler's special day. Children three, four, and five years old are enthusiastic about art, building, music, dance, pretend, and story time. You can easily mix and match activities to keep everyone entertained. Here are a few tips for hosting a successful creative birthday party for preschoolers:

- Plan the party to last approximately 90 minutes (keep it short and action-packed).
- Invite a small group of playmates and friends (and invite their parents to stay at the party).
- Appoint one or two adults to keep the party happy, manageable, and safe.
- Select a few creative activities that your child (and friends) will enjoy and create a basic itinerary to help organize the party time. (See sample preschool party itinerary below.)
- Gather all the needed supplies and props well in advance to avoid last-minute stress. (And have a few extras on hand.)
- Think of yourself as a friendly camp counselor helping to direct the party.

Be positive, give easy instructions, encourage sharing and inclusion for all, and have lots of patience.

° Have a short arrival activity under way so the children have something fun to do immediately and to allow a little extra time for latecomers.

° Incorporate guessing games during cake time to keep everyone engaged.

° Have paper bags prepared ahead with each child's name to send artwork home at the end of the party.

Itinerary for a Creativity Party for Children 3-5 Years (for a 90-minute party)

° **Activity 1** (10–15 minutes): Select one arrival activity, such as Glitter-Glue Drawings (page 141), Make Paper-Bag Puppets (page 210), or Create a Picnic (Picture) Tablecloth (page 142).

° **Activity 2** (15 minutes): Select two to three song or dance activities, such as Sing Traditional Children's Tunes (page 87), Create a Silly Animal Song (page 179), Zoo Zomba (page 189), or Magic Dancing Beans (page 192).

° **Activity 3** (30 minutes): Select one art, pretend, or building activity, such as "George the Giant" Mural (this activity needs lots of space; page 139), Mixed-Box Towers and Towns (page 165), Sand Building for Toddlers (page 85), or Guess-What-I'm Doing Charades (page 207).

° **Activity 4** (15 minutes): Cake time. Possibly include Story-Time Guessing Game (page 217) during cake time.

° **Activity 5** (15 minutes): Select another art, pretend, or building activity, such as Bubble-Wrap Printing (page 156) or Giant Drizzle Posters (page 154).

HAVE A CREATIVE BIRTHDAY PARTY FOR YOUR 6–12-YEAR-OLD CHILD

Children six to twelve are at a fabulous age for creative birthday parties. An exciting party can be planned around all of the activities your birthday boy or girl loves best of all. (Your child can select favorite activities that he or she has done many times and add in a few new ideas too.)

Here are a few tips for hosting a successful creative birthday party for elementary-age children:

- Plan the party for outdoors or an indoor space that can get a little messy.
- Schedule the party to last 90–120 minutes. (This is enough time for a lot of creativity.)
- Let your child select the creative activities for the party. Here are two approaches: (1) Plan a party with one special theme, such as art, music, dance, or theatrics, and select party activities in advance that all match up with that theme; or (2) plan a "mixed creativity" party that includes favorite dance, music, theatrics, and art activities blended together for a lively party.
- Consider having everyone come in a costume for a certain theme, for example: mismatched outfits; rainbow costumes (crazy color combinations); dress up as an artist, rock star, opera star, actor, clown, animals; and so forth. You can even tie the costume theme in to some of the activities.
- Create a basic itinerary ahead of time, with a list of activities and their order. (See sample party itinerary below.)
- Gather all the needed supplies and props in advance to avoid last-minute stress. (Have a few extras of all essential materials.)
- Have a short arrival activity under way so the children have something fun to do immediately when they walk into the birthday setting.
- Ask several other parents, grandparents, or older siblings to be party assistants to help with activities, manage materials, and keep things friendly.
- Have large paper sacks labeled with the children's names so each partygoer can easily carry artwork and creative projects home when the party is over.

family

Itinerary for a Mixed-Creativity Party for Children 6-12 Years (for a 90- to 120-minute party)

- **Activity 1** (15 minutes): Select one arrival activity, such as Letter Art (page 236), Clay-Critter Challenge (page 256), or Mystery-Loop Drawing (page 236).
- **Activity 2** (15 minutes): Select two to three song or dance activities, such as Half-and-Half Songs (page 282), Copycat Dancing (page 300), or Monster Shuffle (page 302).
- **Activity 3** (30 minutes): Select one art, pretend, or building activity, such as Amazing-Vehicles Sketchbook (page 230), Downtown Cityscape (page 263), Worker-Bee Acting Club (page 309), or Amazing-Animal Adventure Stories (page 329).
- **Activity 4** (15 minutes): Cake time.
- **Activity 5** (30 minutes): Select another art, pretend, or building activity.

TODDLER CREATIVITY

Ages 2–3

Toddlers are curious all day long. When they walk into a room, they survey the situation to see what they can get into. When they see something appealing, their little brains say, "Hey, what is this?" and they instantly touch it, shake it, or tip it upside down. Then, after a moment, something else catches their eye and off they go.

All of this curiosity and experimentation primes the pump for creativity. While toddlers are oozing with curiosity, they will typically sit only for short stretches of time. But these short moments of focused creative activities are packed with importance. What's more, the older-toddler stage (two to three years) is a perfect time to introduce all different types of creativity: art, music, dance, pretend, building-block creations, and storytelling and creativity with words.

When you set aside time in the family schedule and provide art materials, offer simple musical instruments, play music for dancing, offer dress-up clothes, tell stories, sing songs, and provide blocks for building you boost your child's creative development. You also infuse your child's routine with joy.

You are an influential creativity mentor. This means when your child sees you happily singing songs, inventing stories, drawing, dancing, or pretending, it sends a clear, strong message that being playfully creative is joyful and important. And when all is said and done, it is the joy that creativity brings to your child that is the very best reason to say yes to creative activities.

Art Activities

Children two to three years old are thrilled to experiment with simple art materials. Crayons, markers, paper, play dough, and tempera paints might seem basic to you, but from your toddler's perspective, these supplies are new and exciting.

Toddlers are naturally driven by the *process* of making art rather than the hope of creating a masterpiece, and this is a perfect perspective for your budding artist. The pace of art is often, fast, and fleeting—with your toddler focused for a few minutes of artwork, then off in an instant to explore something new.

Some of the most successful art activities may be short projects done with parents, caregivers, or side by side with other toddlers, with each artist doing their own work and glancing at the other from time to time to see what's going on. Yes, there may be a few interludes of working "together" on a joint project, but much of the time will be spent with your child enjoying his own creative process just because toddlers are very focused on their own activities and actions.

Some toddlers especially love the tactile experience of sticking hands in finger paint or play dough, or the excitement of paint and brushes. Others don't like gooey stuff on their hands, but they are pleased to create with markers, crayons, paper, and possibly glue sticks (under adult supervision). As toddlers scribble, paint, pinch clay, and manipulate toddler-safe tools, they begin to develop small-muscle control (and hand skills) too.

Your job is to provide opportunities for your toddler to dabble with art materials and art activities just for the pleasure of seeing what he or she can create. From this humble beginning your child's art creativity will grow with each delightful new project.

ages 2-3

SCRIBBLE ART

Never underestimate the power of the scribble! Toddlers circle round and round or zigzag back and forth or up and down on the paper with crayons

PARENTS' BEST APPROACH TO ENCOURAGING TODDLER ART CREATIVITY
(2-3 years)

- Have a variety of toddler-safe materials on hand for art projects.
- Create a little place for toddler artwork. (The kitchen table, play table, picnic table on the patio, or wooden, tile, or vinyl floor are fine places to create.)
- Expect a bit of mess and plan for it. (Use an oilcloth or vinyl tablecloth or newspapers under your child's art projects. Take art projects outdoors whenever possible.)
- Show a thumbs-up attitude for your child's art projects and creative process, but don't get too focused on a finished masterpiece!
- Encourage art activities for times when you and your child are both in good humor (and able to tolerate a little mess).
- Keep a watchful eye on your child at all times to keep everything safe and secure.
- Expect a short attention span for toddler art projects. Adopt the "it's fun for a few minutes" approach to making art!
- Include toddler-friendly art activities in Family Creativity Night and in your child's birthday party too.

or markers in a wonderfully spontaneous way! Half the fun is the physical process of scribbling freely. The other half is watching a colorful design emerge on the paper almost magically. This is freestyle art at its best. As an added bonus, toddlers are learning to grip and control a crayon in a way that will also come in handy for writing letters and making shapes in the preschool stage.

Materials
- Crayons or nontoxic, washable markers for toddlers (My First Crayola)
- Newsprint paper

Get Creative Provide paper and crayons or nontoxic markers for drawing and let your child do the rest: fat lines and skinny lines, circular strokes and straight lines. Celebrate the scribble!

You'll find art activities in this section that use nontoxic tempera and watercolor paints, washable (and nontoxic) colored markers, crayons, and nontoxic white school glue. But the assumption with offering these art materials is that parents (or other adults) will supervise diligently to make the creative experience safe for older toddlers. Yes, it's true that many children who are two, two and a half, and three years old already understand a few basics about safety ("Don't put things in your mouth"), but your child's safety is a higher priority than creativity. Be watchful at every turn to keep things safe, and delay introducing your child to these projects if he is not yet ready to keep paint or markers on paper rather than in his mouth. (Be careful, when using glue or markers, to keep small lids or caps in your hands only, to avoid any possibility of choking.) When you stick to these and other safety rules for toddlers, you can provide a happy introduction to some of the art activities (such as painting and gluing) that young kids get so excited to try.

Tabletop Scribble Art

Cover your entire kitchen table with white butcher paper. Use clear packaging tape to connect the long pieces of paper into one giant table drawing surface. (Use tape to wrap it around the corners of the table and hold securely in place too.) Give your child a box of crayons and let the freestyle creativity flow in a big way!

Scribble-Art T-shirts

What could be better than turning one of your toddler's first drawings into wearable art by creating a one-of-a-kind T-shirt! Materials needed are: one sheet of drawing paper and a package of eight fabric crayons (for example, Crayola-brand fabric crayons). Let your child create a colorful scribble drawing on a sheet of paper. Then later, you use a hot iron to transfer your child's drawing onto a small T-shirt for your child to wear her artwork! (Just follow the directions on the package of the fabric crayons for ironing and transferring the design. Note: according to Crayola if you want the design to be permanent, use 100 percent synthetic fabric such as polyester for this project.)

Scribble-Art Greeting Cards

Provide colorful markers for drawing on sheets of card stock. Then turn the drawings into greeting cards by folding the paper in half. Purchase booklet-style envelopes (6-by-9 inches) at an office supply store. (Grandparents and family will be thrilled to receive these lovely homemade cards.)

Scribble-Art Party Invitations

Provide a stack of 8½-by-11-inch card stock (white or colored sheets) for toddler scribbling. Then turn these drawings into customized birthday party invitations. (Save one birthday party invitation for your scrapbook.)

Scribble-Art Gift Boxes

Purchase two-piece apparel gift boxes at your local paper-supply store. (These two-piece boxes are made of shiny white cardboard and are in a flattened position when purchased—which is perfect for drawing on.) When the artwork is finished, pop up the lids to create fancy gift boxes.

Scribble-Art Lunch Bags

Purchase a package of fifty to a hundred white paper lunch bags (available at Walmart or online at paper-product websites). Let your toddler draw on the bags and use them for artsy lunches for mom, dad, and siblings.

Scribble-Art Mailers

Purchase giant white or manila mailers for this project. Bring out the markers and crayons and let your child scribble to create fancy mailers to use at holiday and birthday times to mail gifts.

Black-and-White (Contrast) Drawings

Start with black construction paper and white (or yellow) crayons for distinctive toddler drawings (scribbles) that can be posted on the fridge or turned into greeting cards or wrapping paper!

> *When I give children chalk, I don't expect them to make beautiful, wonderful drawings. I expect them to try the chalk and see all the different things they can do with it, and maybe even discover some things that I haven't thought of being able to do with chalk.*
>
> **—SUSAN STRIKER,**
> author of *Young at Art*

Here's an easy, organized way to promote drawing when you are on the go:

Materials

- ½-inch-thick three-ring binder with a clear plastic sleeve on the cover
- Notebook paper for three-ring binder
- Plastic zip-style pencil pouch with three holes to fit inside three-ring binder
- Toddler-sized crayons
- One 8½-by-11-inch favorite drawing by your child

PAINTS, PENCILS, INK PADS, MARKERS, AND ART DOUGH DESIGNED FOR CHILDREN 2 YEARS OF AGE

The majority of paints, markers, art dough, and ink pads that are available are listed as appropriate for children three years and up, but here are some good products I've found designed for children two years and up that you might consider:

- My First Crayola Washable Markers—these nontoxic markers have a secure tip on the end that can't be crushed or removed by little fingers. Check local arts and crafts stores in your area or order online at www.crayola.com or www.amazon.com.
- Lakeshore Washable Finger Paints—these nontoxic paints are listed as appropriate for children ages two and up, have vibrant colors, and can work in other toddler painting projects besides finger painting too.
- Lakeshore Giant Washable Ink Pads—giant ink pads (6 inches in diameter), big enough for printing with large objects.
- Lakeshore Jumbo Colored Pencils—chunky colored pencils designed for little hands.
- Lakeshore Wheat- and Gluten-Free (Art) Dough—good colors and easy to use. All Lakeshore products are available online at www.lakeshorelearning.com.

Setup Fill the notebook with paper, put the crayons in the plastic pencil pouch, and put one favorite drawing from your child into the outer plastic sleeve to create the cover for the notebook.

Get Creative This little artist drawing book can be filled with scribbles and drawings by your child whenever you are on the go. (It's a perfect activity during doctor's-appointment wait times.) Keep it in the car as an ever-ready notebook for your child to express a little creativity.

SCRIBBLE-SCRABBLE ART PORTFOLIO

Help your child create an artist container for storing her artwork.

Materials
- One cardboard file storage box with handles and lid—available at office supply stores (look for a box without logos, or just use colored construction paper and tape to cover any printing or logo)
- Nontoxic markers or crayons

Setup Remove the plastic wrap from the box and lid. Leave both pieces of cardboard in the flattened position. Use the markers to write your child's name and age on the lid or along the sides of the flattened box.

Get Creative Give your child markers to decorate the flattened art-storage box. When the drawing is finished, pop up the lid and pop up the box. (Once your child gets the idea, he can make his own artistic portfolio every year!)

TODDLER ART GALLERY

Here's an easy way for your toddler to make colorful frames to create a gallery of recent artwork in the hallway.

Materials
- A collection of your child's recent scribble art, printing art, and collages

NINE CRAFTY WAYS TO SHARE
AND USE YOUR CHILD'S SCRIBBLE ART

- Turn newsprint paper with scribble art (drawings) into wrapping paper for gifts.
- Create gift tags from your child's drawings on card stock (for birthdays and holidays).
- Make place cards (for family or holiday dinners) from scribble art on 4-by-6-inch note cards. (Fold the cards in half, write the names on one side, and prop them on the table.)
- Create placemats for the table from scribble art on colored construction paper. (Wrap each drawing in clear contact paper to "laminate" it and protect it from spills.)
- Make original journal or book covers from scribble art on butcher paper. (Cut the paper to size, fold it around the book, and use tape to secure it.)
- Create a colorful oatmeal-can cover from scribble art and turn it into a cookie jar. (Cut paper to the approximate size and wrap the oatmeal container with a drawing, securing with tape.)
- Help your child make a pencil holder from scribble art on colored construction paper. (Wrap a drawing around an empty frozen-orange-juice container; remove one end from the can.)
- Create artful stationery for thank-you notes to grandparents from scribble-art drawings. (Use colored copy paper for drawing, then run it through the printer to type the note.)
- Create a set of colorful artist spice jars from scribble art on construction paper. (Use a set of empty spice jars; cut drawings to size, wrap, and tape.)

- Large (11-by-17-inch) colored construction paper
- Nontoxic white glue, such as Elmer's (careful parent supervision needed)
- Paintbrush
- Small disposable plate or bowl
- Paper cup and water (for brush cleanup at the end)
- Invisible tape

Setup Pour a small quantity of the glue on the disposable plate.

Get Creative Let your child select colored sheets of paper for the "frames." Encourage your child to look through his recent drawings and collage work and select favorites he would like to frame. Help your child dip the brush in the glue and place small dabs of glue on the backside corners or edges of the artwork. Carefully position the artwork on the colored paper and ask your child to apply a little pressure in each area. Let the glue dry. A short time later help your child position her framed drawings along the walls of a hallway, with your child applying small pieces of invisible tape to "hang" each piece on the wall to create an art gallery. (Make this gallery toddler-friendly by hanging the work at eye level for your child.)

PAINT-DABBER CREATIONS

A delightful painting-on-burlap activity for older toddlers and parents!

Materials
- 1-inch foam paintbrush
- Nontoxic finger paint (two or three colors), such as Lakeshore Washable Finger Paints for children 24+ months
- 3 disposable plastic or paper plates
- White or cream-colored burlap fabric
- Scissors (for adult use only)
- Cardboard or card stock
- Painter's tape
- Nontoxic white glue, such as Elmer's (parents use or supervise carefully to keep things safe)
- Mat board, for finished presentation
- Vinyl tablecloth (to contain the mess)

Setup Cut an 8-by-8-inch (or 10-by-10-inch) piece of burlap. Place the burlap on top of the cardboard and secure both to the tablecloth with two long pieces of tape along the left and right edges.

Get Creative Pour a little of three different colors of paint on the plates.

CREATE A MINI ART PACK FOR KITCHEN-TABLE CREATIVITY

You can't leave a toddler to his own devices, so supervision is always needed, but you can set up your home so your child is free to do some "solo art" at the kitchen table while you are nearby cooking dinner or doing chores and supervising too. Designate a small, portable carrying case, with easy-to-use (and safe) art materials for solo art activities at the kitchen table or art while the two of you are on the go in waiting areas. Here are some tips on creating a mini art pack for your toddler.

1. Pick a container:
- Small canvas tote bag or book bag with handle. (Personalize this art bag with fabric markers as a parent-and-child art project when you have creative time together!)
- Canvas shopping/grocery bag with carry handles.
- Small basket with handle.

2. Stock it with toddler-friendly (and safe) art supplies:
- Crayons
- Jumbo colored pencils for toddlers (for example, Lakeshore Jumbo Colored Pencils)
- Large colored dot stickers
- Assorted drawing paper: newsprint, drawing pad, colored construction paper, scraps of poster board, card stock, blank note cards, corrugated cardboard
- White or manila envelopes or mailers
- Small pack of white paper lunch bags

3. Bring out the art pack regularly (and provide supervision):
- While you are making dinner (your child sits at the kitchen table to make art)
- While you are doing quick chores (your artist is creating happily nearby)

Dip the foam brush in the paint and give a little demo of how to press the paintbrush on the burlap to create a dab of color. Let your child experiment with layers of paint dabbed on the burlap to create a multicolored design. (Supervise carefully to be sure no paint is put in the mouth.)

Let the paint dry thoroughly. Place the burlap painting on a sheet of mat board (slightly larger than the burlap). Remove several strands of the burlap around the edges to create a frayed border. Put four dabs of glue in the corners of the burlap (on the back side) and glue it to the mat board for a finished frame-like presentation.

SCRIBBLE WASH PAINTINGS

Here's an activity that offers freestyle coloring or scribbling, then adds a dose of painting with a brush:

Materials
- Heavy drawing paper
- 1 white crayon
- 1-inch paintbrush
- Nontoxic watercolor paint set (parent's supervision)
- Painter's tape
- Plastic cup with water
- An old cookie sheet

Setup Flip the cookie sheet upside down and place a sheet of paper on top. Run painter's tape along all four edges of the paper to hold it firmly in place on the cookie sheet so that it will not buckle or move when water is applied.

Get Creative Give your child a white crayon and encourage him to scribble on the paper. Once he's finished scribbling, hand him the paintbrush (soaked with paint and water) and let him paint on the paper and watch the

- In the waiting room at your doctor's office
- At restaurants (while waiting for the food)
- When drawing together for a quiet transition before bedtime
- During family meetings (kids love to draw while listening)
- While waiting for Sunday family brunch (a perfect time to scribble)
- While parents are preparing for a party, packing for a vacation, or at other crunch times (when your toddler needs a little self-entertainment)

Toddlers simply love to put pieces of tape on paper—pure and simple. Here's an easy way to create a toddler-friendly tape dispenser. Start with one 8- or 9-inch round cake pan made of metal and a roll of invisible tape. Tear about ten to twenty 1- or 2-inch pieces of tape from a traditional tape dispenser. Turn the cake pan upside down and stick all of the small pieces of tape around the outer edge of the pan with about ½ inch of tape extending over the edge. Give your child a little demo of how to grab a piece of tape and stick it on paper. Supervise to keep it safe.

scribble design emerge like magic. Let the paper dry thoroughly and remove the tape.

COLORS-AND-SHAPES COLLAGE

Here's a good way to start collaging in the early years with a little help from a grown-up:

Materials

- Colored construction paper (assorted colors)
- Large sheets of drawing paper (or card stock)
- Scissors (for adult use only)
- Nontoxic glue stick or nontoxic washable school glue (supervise carefully to keep things safe)

Get Creative Parent uses scissors to cut twelve to twenty shapes from colored construction paper—circles, half circles, quarter circles, squares, rectangles, triangles, ovals—before the project begins. (Make these shapes big enough for your child to handle. Older toddlers may be able to cut freestyle shapes on their own using preschool

ages
2–3

safety scissors.) Help your child apply glue to the large sheet of drawing paper, and then let your child create a collage design with the shapes on the sticky surface.

STAMP-IT PRINTMAKING

Toddlers love the satisfaction of pressing stamps in ink and on paper to reveal colorful designs.

Materials
- Nontoxic children's ink pads, such as Lakeshore giant colored-ink pads for 24+ months
- Big rubber stamps for young children in an assortment of shapes, such as a circle, square, triangle, letters, numbers (available at craft stores)
- Assorted papers

Get Creative Your child can create a colorful design overlapping and stamping shapes, letters, and numbers in a purely freestyle way. Have a variety of paper and card stock on hand for artsy experimentation, and turn the artwork into cards, gift bags, and invitations.

Safety note: Supervise carefully to keep things safe. This project is only appropriate for children who will not put ink or ink pad in their mouths.

PLAY-DOUGH CREATIONS

Squishing and squeezing shapes is a marvelous beginning for making three-dimensional art.

TIP FOR MESS-FREE PLAYING WITH PLAY DOUGH

Provide a giant cookie sheet for your child to use as the surface for creating play-dough art to contain the mess. Or simply cover the kitchen table with a piece of vinyl or oilcloth. When the creativity is done, gather up the largest pieces of play dough and return them to the container and take the tablecloth outside for a good shake-out.

MAKE HOMEMADE PLAY DOUGH

Sure you can buy ready-made play dough in containers, but you can make your own excellent version at home. Here's an easy recipe that will keep for months in an airtight container!

Ingredients
- 1 cup flour
- 1 cup water
- ¼ cup salt
- 1 tablespoon vegetable oil
- 2 teaspoons cream of tartar
- 1–2 teaspoons food coloring

To make Add all the ingredients to a saucepan and cook over low heat for about 5 minutes, stirring continuously to avoid lumps. When the mixture clumps together into one big ball of dough in the pan, remove from the heat. Pour the dough onto a cookie sheet to cool. Once cool, add the food coloring and knead the dough lightly with your hands. Store this dough in a ziplock bag or plastic container with a lid.

Materials
- Play dough
- Assorted safe kitchen tools or play-dough tools, such as a small (toy) rolling pin and a fork and spoon (to make impressions)

Get Creative Freestyle pinching, pounding, and shaping is the toddler-friendly way to get creative with play dough.

Safety note: Supervise carefully to keep things safe. This project is only appropriate for children who will not put play dough in their mouths.

ages
2–3

COLORFUL ART RUBBINGS

To your child's eyes these colorful designs appear like magic with a bit of rubbing over a textured surface!

Materials

- One 10½-by-13½-inch plastic needlepoint canvas (This is an inexpensive, thin, gridlike plastic sheet with square holes, typically used for needlepoint. Available at craft supply stores.)
- A large tablet of newsprint, or large sheets of (legal-sized) pastel-colored copy paper
- Optional: roll of painter's tape
- Assorted colored crayons (preschool size) with paper wrapper removed

Setup Place the plastic canvas on the work table. Put one sheet of paper over the top. (Use the tape to secure the paper to the table if needed.)

Get Creative Give a short demo of how to use the side of a crayon to rub over the paper to create a design from the textured plastic underneath. Your child selects a color and begins rubbing the crayon over the paper. When he rubs with more colors, multicolored designs appear, with overlapping colors emerging quite naturally.

Black-and-White Rubbings
Try the art-rubbing idea above, but this time your child uses a white crayon on large black construction paper placed over the plastic grid (above) for a nice black-and-white design. (Save these rubbings in your child's Scribble-Scrabble Art Portfolio, page 63, to be used in other creative projects in the future.)

Colorful Sidewalk Rubbings
Take paper, painter's tape, and crayons outdoors and find a safe section of sidewalk for your child to experiment with sidewalk rubbings. Simply place the paper on the sidewalk and rub with crayons and watch a colorful textured (sidewalk) pattern emerge. Supervise each moment during this activity to keep your child safe from bikes or traffic nearby.

TORN-PAPER COLLAGE

A good first collage activity providing the simple pleasure of tearing paper and smearing glue around!

Materials
- Colored construction paper
- Nontoxic white glue, such as Elmer's (supervise carefully to keep things safe)
- Card stock or heavy drawing paper
- Newspapers or vinyl tablecloth (to contain the mess)
- Wet paper towels (when fingers get gooey)

Get Creative Work together to create a few piles of color-coded paper scraps by tearing pieces of the construction paper. Each artist (parent and child) gets one sheet of card stock. Spread a little glue on an area of the card stock and begin placing paper pieces on the sticky surface to create a design. (Help your child with a bit of the gluing as needed.) Gently use hands to apply a little pressure to the papers to flatten the pieces to the card stock.

Please supervise your child so the glue doesn't create a safety hazard.

CREATE A COLLAGE BOX

Get a medium box or plastic container with a lid for a collage box. Inside this box, save your child's small scraps of paper or partially finished work. Then, when it's time to make a new collage, ask your child to select some of these lovely colorful papers for part of the collage design. Here are some of the small works or scraps that might end up in the Collage Box:
- Rubbings on paper (including sidewalk rubbings)
- Scraps of fabric leftover from fabric collage projects
- Small pieces of your toddler's recycled scribble art
- Watercolor dabs on watercolor paper
- Small pieces of sponge prints (or other prints on paper)

COLLAGE GREETING CARDS

These handmade greeting cards are a beautiful expression of a toddler's creativity.

Materials
- Scraps of lightweight, solid-color fabrics (cotton, silky, or shiny fabrics)
- Scissors
- Nontoxic white glue, such as Elmer's (supervise carefully to keep things safe)
- Paper plate
- Several sheets of 8½-by-11-inch card stock
- Small paintbrush

Setup Fold one sheet of card stock in half to create an 8½-by-5½-inch card. Parents cut narrow scraps of fabric of various lengths (between 2 and 3 inches in length and ½ inch wide) and put a small dab of glue on the paper plate.

Get Creative Spread the glue over part of the front area of the paper card. Let your child select scraps of fabric and place the fabric firmly on the glued surface. (No need to fill the entire card.) Give a brief demo of how to press the fabric pieces onto the glued surface. Let the glue dry thoroughly before touching the finished cards.

Fabric Collage Art
Use the same materials to create a larger collage with fabric on an 8½-by-11-inch piece of card stock. For added contrast, start with black card stock or construction paper. These lovely designs can be displayed in a frame or shadow box and hung on the wall for all to admire.

JUNK-MAIL COLLAGE

At long last, a fine way to make junk mail into something colorful and creative!

Materials
- Nontoxic markers (and/or crayons)
- 1 sheet of card stock
- Assorted junk mail (envelopes, flyers, ads)
- Nontoxic white glue, such as Elmer's (supervise carefully to keep things safe)
- Preschool safety scissors

Get Creative Work side by side with your toddler, with each artist (you and your child) creating his or her own collage with little scraps of colorful junk mail, markers, and crayons.

BLOBBY PRINTS

Help your child drop some blobs of paint on the paper and watch a lovely organic design emerge.

Materials
- Sheets of card stock (various colors)
- Scissors (for adult use only)
- Nontoxic, washable tempera paints in squeezable containers (supervise to keep things safe)

Setup Fold each sheet of card stock in half, then use scissors to cut in two.

Get Creative Help your child squeeze three or four different colored dollops of paint onto one of the cards. Place another piece of paper on top of the painted paper and use a hand to apply pressure to the top paper. Carefully peel the top sheet of paper away, starting at one corner. Lay the paper on the table to dry (with the painted side faceup).

CIRCLE PRINTING

Use a small tomato-paste can for an easy, colorful first printing project.

Materials
- A few drops of water
- Three or more colors of nontoxic solid tempera paint in a plastic holding tray (supervise to keep things safe)
- One or more small cans of tomato paste (6-ounce)
- Paper
- Optional: nontoxic ink pads and shape, letter, or number stamps, colored markers, or crayons
- Newspaper or vinyl tablecloth (to contain the mess)

Get Creative Pour a few drops of water onto each tempera cake. Place the can on top of one of the solid paint cakes and apply pressure or move it back and forth to absorb some of the paint. Let your child press the can firmly on the paper several times to create colored circles. Let your child repeat this paint process with more colors to create a colorful circle print that fills the paper. (Your child may wish to use other optional art supplies to add more color and designs to the artwork.)

Burlap Circle Prints

Your child can create a similar circle-print design with tempera paints using white burlap fabric instead of paper. Use a little painter's tape to hold the burlap in place on the tablecloth for easy printing.

Circle-Print Greeting Cards

Try the same printing activity listed above, but print on 8½-by-11-inch sheets of card stock or colored construction paper. When the paint is dry, fold the papers in half to create greeting cards.

Circle-Print Wrapping Paper

Follow the instructions for Circle Printing, above, but print on long sheets of brown craft paper, white butcher paper, or newsprint to create handmade gift wrap.

SPONGE PRINTS

Kids love the idea of making art from a simple old kitchen sponge and paint or nontoxic printing ink.

Materials
- Scissors (for adult use only)
- 1 or 2 old kitchen sponges
- Nontoxic, washable ink pads or finger paints, such as Lakeshore Giant Washable Ink Pads or Lakeshore Washable Finger Paints
- Disposable plate
- Heavy paper (drawing paper or card stock)

Setup Use the scissors to cut the sponge in half (create easy-to-handle sizes). Wet the sponge and wring out the excess water. Pour the paint into the disposable plate.

Get Creative Dip one end of the sponge into the paint and press it onto the paper. Let your child experiment with overlapping colors on the paper to create freestyle designs.

ONE-COLOR PAINTINGS

Most toddlers love the experience of dipping a big paintbrush into paint and moving the brush around on the paper (parent supervision needed)!

Materials
- Large sheets of newsprint or drawing paper
- Large, 1-inch-wide toddler-sized brush (short handle is best)
- Artist smock or apron
- One color of tempera paint or finger paint
- Vinyl tablecloth (to contain the mess) or a child's easel

Get Creative Set up the materials and supervise to keep things safe. Toddlers are thrilled to have one color of paint

and simply enjoy the sensation of spreading colorful paint around on paper!

FREESTYLE FINGER PAINTING

Here's a gooey but enjoyable outdoor painting activity for messing about with paints—with a bit of parent supervision needed:

Materials
- Nontoxic, washable finger paint, such as Lakeshore Washable Finger Paints for children 24+ months
- Paper
- Newspaper or vinyl tablecloth (to contain the mess)

Get Creative If this is your child's first time finger painting, give a quick demo of how to dip fingers into paint and smear on the paper. (After that, just supervise to keep things safe and let your child have the pleasure of creating.)

Finger Painting on a Cookie Sheet Outdoors
If your child loves the excitement of smearing goopy paint around and around and watching the swirls change, then let him finger paint on

Every day can be art day for toddlers, but only some days are worthy of messy art projects. (Let's face it, messy art projects can add stress to the day!) So ask yourself, "Can I handle a little unexpected spill or extra mess right now?" Be honest. If the answer is no, then make it an easy art day, with crayons and paper at the kitchen table.

an old (recycled) cookie sheet instead of paper. I highly recommend that you take this activity outdoors. First because it's messy, but also because you want to establish a new environment (away from the high chair or kitchen table) so your child does not think this goopy stuff is for eating! Be sure to have a wet washcloth ready for a quick cleanup as soon as the painting is done.

Thumbprint Painting

Select two or more colors of nontoxic, washable finger paint for this project. Use 6-by-9-inch sheets of colored or white construction paper (or 4-by-6-inch white, unlined note cards). Help your child dip thumb or fingers into paint to create a series of thumbprints and fingerprints on the paper. (Supervise to keep things safe.)

> When your children are building with blocks, using finger paints, or making up a story—anything where they're using their imaginations—they're actually building connections inside those little brains. You can almost look at them and see those synapses growing and all those neurons reaching out to make important connections!
>
> **—JANE M. HEALY, PHD,** educational psychologist
> and author of *Your Child's Growing Mind*

You can buy inexpensive washable vinyl or plastic toddler-sized artist's smocks in long sleeve or short sleeve at school supplies stores. You can also create easy, homemade smocks from any of these recycled items: adult T-shirts or men's or women's dress shirts or blouses (cut the sleeves shorter), kitchen aprons, or a child's nightshirt.

HAND-PRINTING ON BURLAP

Just like the traditional toddler hand-print art—but this time printed on burlap instead of paper.

Materials
- Nontoxic, washable finger paint, such as Lakeshore Washable Finger Paints for children 24+ months
- Disposable paper or plastic plate (paint palette)
- 10-by-10-inch piece of burlap fabric
- Paper or cardboard
- Vinyl tablecloth (to contain the mess)
- Painter's tape

Setup Pour a little paint in the plate (add a few drops of water to thin it). Place the burlap over the paper or cardboard. Secure the burlap and paper to the vinyl tablecloth with a little painter's tape.

Get Creative Help your child dip one hand in the paint and make one or more handprints on the burlap. (Repeat with several other colors and overlapping handprints for a multi-colored design, or go traditional with one or two handprints centered on the burlap.)

BOX-PAINTING FOR TODDLERS

A happy and messy (outdoor or basement) painting activity for a toddler who loves the thrill of painting big!

Materials
- One large cardboard box (the size of a microwave or even bigger)
- Nontoxic, washable tempera paint or finger paint (supervise to keep things safe)
- Small paint roller (3 inches) and paint tray (or disposable plastic plate)

Get Creative Pour paint into the tray and give a little demo of how to dip the roller in the paint and roll it back and forth on the box. The finished art product might not look like much to art critics' eyes, but toddlers love this creative process. Let your child paint each side of the box and make a colorful creation. When the box is dry, your child can decide what the colorful box will be used for! (Supervise carefully to keep things safe. This messy project is only for older children who will not put paint in their mouths.)

TODDLER PAINTS AND BRUSHES

Here are a few suggestions for painting supplies just right for children ages two and up.
- Nontoxic, washable finger paints. These paints can be used both for finger painting and with a brush for other paint projects.
- Solid tempera paints. These 3-inch-round tempera disks look like giant watercolor blocks and they fit neatly inside an inexpensive plastic tray.
- Nontoxic, washable liquid tempera paints in squeeze bottles.
- Stubby, chunky brushes with a short handle and wide bristles (store them in a tall plastic cup, bristle-end up).
- Two small buckets for cleanup: one with cool, soapy water and another with just water for rinsing. (Toddlers love to clean up—let them help!)

Building and Construction Activities

Toddler builders come in all varieties. Some like to watch from the sidelines as older siblings or parents stack up blocks to create a tower, and eventually they warm up to the idea of creating structures of their own. Some jump right in and boldly start building. Other toddlers are most excited by demolition, offering squeals of delight when their towers come crashing down.

Most toddlers have a very short attention span, so their building playtime will be brief. Many of the happiest moments may be times when a parent or grown-up can join in the construction play, with the toddler doing her own building independently and glancing over from time to time to get some good ideas from the grown-up block-builder nearby.

You'll find blocks made of wood, plastic, interlocking plastic, cardboard, foam, and fabric. Tiny blocks pose a choking hazard, so be sure to avoid anything in this category. Small boxes and recycled containers from your kitchen are perfect for toddler building projects too. They can be easily covered with construction paper and tape to make colorful buildings, and they are free and recyclable.

These playful opportunities for construction and building projects are just right for stirring up a bit of excitement for construction and building creativity for your toddler.

ages
2–3

BLOCK-BUILDER

Freestyle building with blocks can be a splendid way of being creative.

Materials
- Safe toddler building blocks of wood, plastic, cardboard, or fabric
- Optional: small action figures, dolls, toy trucks, and people

Get Creative Gather up assorted blocks and let your child's curiosity and little hands do all the heavy lifting of building creativity! When you are in a creative mood, work alongside your child, building your own little habitats too. (Your child may sneak a peek and pick up a few tricks from you about balancing blocks and building towers.)

PARENTS' BEST APPROACH TO ENCOURAGING TODDLER BUILDING CREATIVITY *(Ages 2-3)*

- Have a collection of safe blocks and building materials that are easy to grab and handle.
- Keep blocks in plain sight (in tubs or baskets) to encourage freestyle construction play whenever your child is in the mood. (Let your child play independently as much as possible, but be available to offer brief help on an as-needed basis to deal with meltdowns.)
- Include building activities during playdates with other children. (Offer a pile of blocks for each toddler to use, since sharing is not perfected yet by the toddlers!)
- Do some of the parent-and-child building projects below, such as Mixed-Box Construction, Build a Rainbow Tunnel for Toy Cars, and Sand Building, whenever time permits.
- Include building activities in Family Creativity Night, and at your child's birthday party too.

BEST BLOCKS FOR TODDLERS

Here are some of my favorite toddler-friendly building blocks (available online and at local toy stores):

- Mega Blox First Builders (80 plastic blocks)
- PlanToys 50 Construction Set (wooden blocks with some colored blocks included)
- ImagiBRICKS Giant Building Blocks (16 blocks made of cardboard)
- Lego Duplo My First Construction Site

MIXED-BOX CONSTRUCTION

Help your child test out some easy cardboard stacking-and-building materials to see what he can create!

Materials
- Clear packaging tape
- 10 or more cardboard shoe boxes (you can often find free, recycled shoe boxes at your local shoe store)
- Scissors (for adult use only)
- Colored construction paper

Setup Tape the lids closed on most of the boxes to create building blocks. Leave a few lids untaped. You may want to color-code the boxes with loose lids with colored construction paper taped to the sides so your child easily sees which boxes have lids that come off.

Get Creative Dump the boxes on the floor; give a ten-second demo of stacking a few of the boxes the first time around, then let your child experiment and build. (For easy out-of-the-way storage, just toss these boxes into large mesh laundry bags or king-sized pillowcases. Secure with rubber bands, and store them under beds.)

TODDLER CREATIVITY

ages 2–3

BIG-BOX CONSTRUCTION

There's something extra special about a toddler and parent building with really giant boxes!

Materials
- 4 to 6 medium or large cardboard boxes (check your neighborhood grocery store for clean, recycled boxes)
- Optional: colored construction paper and tape (to cover logos or printing if you like)
- Optional: action figures and dolls or stuffed animals (for the people living in the buildings your child is about to create)

Get Creative Bring the boxes into a large room (or outside) and see what your child wants to build. Some kids like to stack, others line them up end to end or turn them upside down or sideways for a creative hut.

BUILD A RAINBOW TUNNEL FOR TOY CARS

Parent and child work together to create and decorate a simple, multi-colored tunnel just right for zooming toddler-friendly cars and trucks from end to end.

Materials

- Crayons or toddler-safe markers
- Colored 9-by-12-inch construction paper
- 2 cardboard shoe boxes
- Scissors (for adult use only)
- Duct tape
- Invisible tape

Setup Encourage your child to draw or scribble on the colored paper while you are doing the initial setup. Remove the lids from the boxes and parents use scissors to cut a huge, upside-down U-shape on each of the two widest sides of the shoe boxes. When finished cutting, there will be a total of four upside-down U-shapes in these two boxes. (Be sure to leave about 1½ or 2 inches of cardboard along the edges for added structural support.) Place the shoe boxes side to side so that two U-shapes are lined up together to create a big, wide tunnel. Press these sides firmly together and use a few pieces of duct tape to hold in place temporarily. (Note: in order for toddlers to easily zoom their cars through the tunnel, it must be very wide. Hence, this project uses the widest side of a shoe box to cut

---

TODDLER TOOL TIME

Plastic or wooden toy tools let toddlers experiment with pretend hammering, sawing, and turning giant plastic tools. These play tools whet the appetite for building projects:

- Melissa & Doug Deluxe Wooden Pound-A-Peg
- Fisher-Price Drillin' Action Tool Set (plastic)
- Kidoozie Little Builder Tool Belt
- Little Tikes Little Handiworker Workhorse

out the shape for the cars to pass through.) Parent cuts the colored construction paper in half to create strips of paper 4½ by 12 inches long to decorate the tunnel.

Get Creative Let your child assist by pressing more strips of duct tape to help fasten the two boxes together more firmly. Next let your child help create a rainbow-colored exterior of the tunnel by placing strips of colored paper (with decorative scribbles) over the top and sides of the tunnel. (Use invisible tape to attach the colored paper to the tunnel.) When your creation is finished, place the tunnel on a hard floor and give a quick demo of how to zoom a toddler-friendly toy car through it.

> " *Stacking blocks or playing in clay or mud—all of those things are teaching toddlers important principles about the three-dimensional physical world.* "
>
> **—JANE M. HEALY, PHD,**
> educational psychologist and author
> of *Your Child's Growing Mind*

SAND BUILDING FOR TODDLERS

Digging, dumping, and forming wet sand is a fabulous way to begin to get a feel for building creativity. This activity is best for older toddlers who won't put sand in their mouths. Supervise carefully.

Materials
- Sand
- Water
- Plastic sand toys and tools, or plastic margarine or yogurt containers and recycled spoons
- Sandbox or giant plastic tub with lid (see note)

Get Creative Toddler sand building is really parent-and-child time, working side by side to press, form, and dig in the sand. This is the very beginning of sand building, with your two-to-three-year-old gaining a little excitement for what he or she can do with sand and water.

Note: If you don't have a backyard sandbox, create a mini sandbox using a medium or large plastic utility tub with a lid and fill it with clean play sand (available at toy or hardware stores).

BUILDING WITH SNOW

Make some happy memories building a little structure in the snow with your toddler!

Materials
- Snow
- Toy bucket with handle
- Plastic (toy) garden tools for digging.

Get Creative Fill buckets and containers with damp snow and dump them on the ground to make snow bricks. Build a little wall (or simple miniature building) from the snow and use hands or tools to smooth and shape the structures. Add twigs at the end to decorate your structures.

Music Activities

Parents and caregivers are important music mentors for toddlers. If parents show that they enjoy singing and being playful with music, their toddlers will want to be creative with music too. Singing favorite children's songs, inventing lively or silly songs for your child, and experimenting with toddler-friendly musical instruments together is part of the plan. All of these musical activities set the stage for your child's interest in music, and musical creativity too.

It's hard to know just how much your child notices the rhythm, the melody, the words, and even the emotion of the song that he hears at two years of age. But when you keep the focus on fun and let your child dabble in musical activities, a good foundation is put in place. Every toddler will approach these musical activities in his or her own way. Some will join in by singing a few memorable words to each song and some will prefer to listen. Most toddlers will be enthusiastic about playing toddler-friendly musical instruments: wooden clackers, maracas, conga shakers, rhythm sticks, and hand drums. They may even enjoy shaking and tapping their instruments as you sing or play the piano. All of these musical activities and experiences will help set the stage for musical creativity for your child.

SING TRADITIONAL CHILDREN'S TUNES

Parents, grandparents, and caregivers can be marvelous musical-creativity mentors by singing to their child!

Get Creative Create a repertoire of children's tunes and sing them to your toddler during your daily time together. (Select songs you remember from

PARENTS' BEST APPROACH TO ENCOURAGING TODDLER
MUSIC CREATIVITY *(Ages 2–3)*

- Sing to your child during your daily routines together: rise-and-shine songs in the morning, songs in the car while running errands, perhaps a song before dinner, and lullabies at naptime or bedtime.
- Invent your own playful songs and sing them to your child.
- Play a collection of toddler-friendly children's music and see what your child likes best. (See page 94 for playful recorded music for young children.)
- Invite your child to sing along or join in musical activities, but realize that every child becomes comfortable with singing or music making on their own schedule. (One big tip: sometimes the silliest songs, wackiest "animal" voices, or funniest refrains provide an extra invitation for reluctant toddlers to participate in the musical fun.)
- Have toddler-safe musical instruments at home and let your child experiment. Keep a positive and accepting attitude and realize that music skills will develop slowly over time. (See the list of toddler-friendly music makers on page 97.)
- Include music-making activities in your child's playdates with other toddlers, and be sure to have enough instruments for each child to experiment with, since sharing is still a foreign concept to toddlers!
- Expect very brief moments of musical activities at this stage in your child's life due to your toddler's short attention span and desire to be constantly on the go.
- Include toddler-friendly musical activities in Family Creativity Night and in your child's birthday party.

ages
2-3

your childhood, or find new songs that grab your attention and add these to your song list.) Following are ten traditional children's songs that are just right for toddlers and parents to get you started. Sing a song in the morning to greet the day. Sing in the car when you are driving to child care and work.

Sing a song before bath time. Sing a lullaby at bedtime too. Your toddler will soak up these melodies and eventually become sufficiently comfortable and familiar with music to begin to sing and make music himself.

> *If I could get one message across to people in my lifetime, it would be that every parent should sing lullabies to their baby.*
>
> **—JOHN FEIERABEND,** artist director of the Feierabend Association for Music Education and author of *The First Steps in Music*

It's Raining, It's Pouring

It's raining, it's pouring,
The old man is snoring.
He went to bed and he
Bumped his head
And he couldn't get up in the morning.

Mary Had a Little Lamb

Mary had a little lamb,
Little lamb, little lamb,
Mary had a little lamb,
His fleece was white as snow.
Everywhere that Mary went,
Mary went, Mary went,
Everywhere that Mary went,
The lamb was sure to go.
It followed her to school one day,
School one day, school one day,
It followed her to school one day,
Which was against the rule.
It made the children laugh and play,
Laugh and play, laugh and play,
It made the children laugh and play,
To see a lamb at school!

Action to Go Along with the Song
Create a simple lamb puppet using construction paper, markers, a craft stick (or popsicle stick), and glue. Give your child the paper puppet and let her bounce the puppet to the beat of the music.

Baa, Baa, Black Sheep

Baa, baa, black sheep,
Have you any wool?
Yes, sir, yes, sir,
Three bags full.
One for my master,
One for my dame,
And one for the little boy,
Who lives in the lane.

Action to Go Along with the Song
Use black construction paper, white pencil (for the eyes, the smile, and the outline), glue, and a craft stick (or popsicle stick) to create a black-sheep puppet that your child can move to the beat of the tune as you sing.

Jack and Jill

Jack and Jill went up the hill,
To fetch a pail of water,
Jack fell down and broke his crown,
And Jill came tumbling after.
Up Jack got and home did trot,
As fast as he could caper,
He went to bed and bound his head
With vinegar and brown paper.

Rock-a-Bye, Baby

Rock-a-bye, baby,
On the treetop,
When the wind blows,
The cradle will rock.
When the bough breaks,
The cradle will fall,
And down will come baby,
Cradle and all.

Hush, Little Baby

Hush, little baby, don't say a word,
Papa's gonna buy you a mockingbird.
If that mockingbird won't sing,
Papa's gonna buy you a diamond ring.
If that diamond ring turns to brass,
Papa's gonna buy you a looking glass.
If that looking glass gets broke,
Papa's gonna buy you a billy goat.
If that billy goat won't pull,
Papa's gonna buy you a cart and bull.
If that cart and bull turn over,
Papa's gonna buy you a dog named Rover.
If that dog named Rover won't bark,
Papa's gonna buy you a horse and cart.
If that horse and cart fall down,
You'll still be the sweetest little baby
in town.

I'm a Little Teapot

I'm a little teapot
Short and stout,
Here is my handle,
Here is my spout.
When I get all steamed up,
Hear me shout.
Just tip me over and pour me out.

Action to Go Along with the Song

As you sing the line "Here is my handle,"
put your left hand on your hip, with
elbow bent (to create the handle for the
teapot). And as you sing, "Here is my
spout," then put your right arm up in the
air (to create the spout for the teapot).
Then, with hands still in place to create
the handle and the spout, sing, "Just tip
me over and pour me out" while you
bend at the waist to the right to imitate
the action of pouring tea out into a cup!

Twinkle, Twinkle Little Star

Twinkle, twinkle little star,
how I wonder what you are?
Up above the world so high,
like a diamond in the sky.

When the blazing sun is gone,
when he nothing shines upon,
Then you show your little light,
twinkle, twinkle all the night.
Then the traveler in the dark,
thanks you for your tiny spark,
He could not see which way to go,
if you did not twinkle so.
In the dark blue sky you keep,
and often through my curtains peep,
For you never shut your eye,
till the sun is in the sky.
As your bright and tiny spark
lights the traveler in the dark,
Though I know not what you are—
twinkle, twinkle little star.

> *Singing is one of the most wonderful things you can share with your child.*
>
> **—STEPHANIE STEIN CREASE,**
> author of *Music Lessons*

Eensy-Weensy Spider

The eensy-weensy spider
Climbed up the waterspout.
Down came the rain
And washed the spider out.
Out came the sun
And dried up all the rain.
So the eensy-weensy spider
Climbed up the spout again!

Action to Go Along with the Song
As you sing the first two lines of the song, place tip of your right thumb on the tip of your left forefinger; while these fingers are joined, swivel both hands so that the left thumb joins up with the right forefinger; release the bottom pair of fingers and swivel them back to the top; continue to alternate joining and releasing each pair of fingers. As you sing the third and fourth lines of the song, hold your hands in the air and wiggle your fingers to imitate rain. As you sing the fifth and sixth lines of the song, hold your arms in the air in the shape of a circle (the sun). As you sing the last two lines of the song, create a brief climbing action with your fingers and thumbs.

Ring around the Rosy

Ring around the rosy,
A pocket full of posies,
Ashes, ashes,
We all fall down.

Action to Go Along with the Song
Several children (or parent and child) hold hands and go around and around in a circle, then all fall down on cue at the end.

LAST-WORD SINGING

Here's a way to get older toddlers to sing along.

Get Creative Sing a song that your child has heard many times before, such as "Old MacDonald Had a Farm." In this "Last-Word" version, you sing each line of the song, but omit the last word, leaving a long pause in its place, and encourage your child to sing the missing word. (In the beginning you may need to pause and then softly sing that last word if your child is hesitant.) This is an easygoing way to promote singing together. Once this singing routine becomes familiar, this routine often becomes a favorite musical activity.

ages 2–3

HOMEGROWN SILLY SONG

Create your own clever, silly, or sentimental songs to capture your child's attention.

Materials
- Lyrics (and/or recorded music) for favorite children's songs

Get Creative Borrow some familiar melodies (such as "It's Raining, It's Pouring," "Mary Had a Little Lamb," or "Rock-a-Bye, Baby") and then add your own words or verses to change it up!

CREATE A NURSERY RHYME SONG

Get creative with a familiar rhyme and invent your own song to delight your child.

Materials
- Words from a familiar nursery rhyme
- Traditional children's song you know

Get Creative Select a favorite children's nursery rhyme that does not traditionally have a melody

behind it and blend it with a familiar tune. Here's an example of the "Hey Diddle, Diddle" nursery rhyme turned into a song using the melody of "Jack and Jill":

> *Hey, diddle, diddle,*
> *The cat and the fiddle,*
> *The cow jumped over the moon.*
> *The little dog laughed*
> *To see such sport,*
> *And the dish ran away with the spoon!*

Add your own extra verses to extend this song too. Here's a sample:

> *The spoon got mad,*
> *The cow was sad,*
> *For all the eggs were broken.*
> *The cat ran home,*
> *And locked the door,*
> *And no more words were spoken.*

Everybody can learn to sing. If children are in a home where the parents are singing, they are going to assimilate that singing as a natural part of life.

— JOHN FEIERABEND, artist director of the Feierabend Association for Music Education and author of *The First Steps in Music*

Here are three award-winning collections of children's songs that bring a playful, creative sound of music into your toddler's routine:

- *Baby Beluga* by Raffi. Raffi is an award-winning singer/songwriter who has entertained two generations of children. This collection of playful, original songs is perfect for young children and a big hit with parents too. (Available in CD, MP3, and vinyl.)
- *Storytime Favorites* by various artists (produced by Music for Little People). This collection presents lively renditions of familiar nursery rhymes and traditional children's songs. (Available in CD and MP3.)
- *American Playground* by various artists (produced by Putumayo Kids). This CD presents a collection of ten classic children's songs reinterpreted by some of the country's top children's music performers. (Available in CD and MP3.)

CREATE YOUR OWN "DADDY AND ME" (OR "MOMMY AND ME") SONG

Delight your child with a customized song about something special you do together!

Materials
- A familiar tune (and lots of imagination)

Get Creative Create lyrics about some of your favorite activities with your child and borrow a melody to put beneath it. Here's a sample of a simple song I wrote about going to the beach, sung to the tune of "Mary Had a Little Lamb." This is not a musical masterpiece. But it shows how you can create a simple song that will have special meaning for your child.

Going to the Beach Today

Going to the beach today,
Beach today, beach today,
Going to the beach today
To dig in the sand.
Waves will chase us back and forth,
Back and forth, back and forth,
Waves will chase us back and forth
As quickly as they can.
Going to the beach today,
Beach today, beach today,
Going to the beach today
For Daddy and me to play.
Birds will circle overhead,
Overhead, overhead,
Birds will circle overhead,
This sunny day in May.

WRITE A SONG ABOUT YOUR FAMILY PET

Use humor and imagination to invent a whimsical tune about the mischief or endearing qualities of your family pet.

Materials
- A familiar tune and lots of imagination

Get Creative Let your imagination soar and invent a silly or adventurous song about your family pet. Pick a familiar tune and add your new lyrics to create an original song. Here's a sample song I wrote called "Treats for Peetie." This song can be easily sung to the tune of "Do Your Ears Hang Low."

Treats for Peetie

Peetie eats tasty treats that we drop
from table,
And he thinks no one can see.
He wags and wiggles, and snorts
and giggles,
And he barks to say, "More please."
But Mama gets cross if we drop
more food,
And she says, "Go away now, Peetie."
But he wags, and wiggles, and snorts
and giggles
He is hungry and a wee bit greedy.

WRITE A WAKE-UP SONG

Add a dose of creativity to your child's routine with a whimsical, homemade song.

Materials
- A familiar tune and lots of imagination

Get Creative Create your own rise-and-shine song to sing in the morning. Find a poem or nursery rhyme about morning time or make up your own lyrics and borrow a tune to sing about the start of the day. Here is an old-fashioned children's rhyme I borrowed for a wake-up song that can easily be sung to the tune of "Here We Go Round the Mulberry Bush."

Wake the World This Sleepy Morn

Donkey, donkey, old and gray,
Old and gray, old and gray,
Donkey, donkey, old and gray
   so early in the morning.
Open your mouth and gently bray,
Gently bray, gently bray,
Open your mouth and gently bray
   so early in the morning.
Lift your ears and blow your horn,
Blow your horn, blow your horn.
Lift your ears and blow your horn,
So early in the morning.
To wake the world this sleepy morn,
Sleepy morn, sleepy morn.
To wake the world this sleepy morn,
So early on this day.

(Add more verses using your child's name and favorite play activities to look forward to.)

FIND RECORDED CHILDREN'S MUSIC AT YOUR LOCAL LIBRARY (CDS)

Visit your local library to borrow (free) copies of children's music collections. You'll find CDs and digital copies of favorite children's songs from many different artists. You can typically borrow these for two, three, or four weeks, so you'll have plenty of time to enjoy the music and learn the melodies and lyrics to expand your repertoire of songs to sing to your child.

ages
2–3

TODDLER-FRIENDLY MUSICAL INSTRUMENTS

Try these easy-to-use instruments for some toddler music making:

- Wooden clackers
- Rhythm sticks
- Toddler-style maracas
- Hand drums
- Wooden train whistle
- Toy piano
- Baby rattles
- Triangle
- Conga shakers

Some of these instruments can be found at your local toy store (in sets), others can be ordered from music stores or suppliers. Hearthsong (www.hearthsong.com), Little Hands Music (www.littlehandsmusic.com), and Music in Motion (www.musicmotion.com) are three terrific online sources for instruments for children ages two and up.

SONGWRITING FOR TWO

Here's an easy way for your toddler to give a wee bit of help inventing a silly song along with you.

Materials
- Colorful magazine photos

Setup Tear out any of the photos from magazines in the following two categories: photos of pets and critters of every kind (insects, snakes, zoo animals, dogs, cats, fish, and so on), and photos of vehicles (bicycles, cars, trucks, wagons, skateboards, boats, tractors, airplanes, and so on). Arrange these photos faceup on the floor—with all the animals in one area of the floor and all the vehicles in another.

Get Creative Ask your child to select one photo from each pile so that you can create a silly song that mixes the two objects/critters together. (For example, fish + bicycle.) Ask your child to give the critter in the photo a name, and work that into the song too. Try using the tune of "Old MacDonald Had a Farm" or "Mary Had a Little Lamb," or pick another traditional song you can borrow.

EXPERIMENT WITH TODDLER-FRIENDLY MUSICAL INSTRUMENTS

The excitement your child feels tapping or shaking a simple instrument can open the door to musical creativity.

Materials

- Toddler-safe music makers (see suggestions that follow)

Get Creative Offer a small collection of toddler-friendly (and safe) music makers for your child to try. These toddler-style music makers are perfect for spontaneous music making, with your child simply experimenting with each sound. These are all relatively inexpensive, and your child only needs a few to get started with the joy of music making.

NOODLE SHAKERS

These little shakers are simple to make and pleasing to listen to! Safety note: for this shaker and the variations that follow, secure the lids carefully with clear packaging tape to avoid any possibility of choking on the beans, rice, or pasta.

Materials

- 2 to 3 tablespoons of dried (uncooked) elbow macaroni
- One empty plastic spice jar with lid
- Nontoxic markers
- Colored construction paper
- Safety scissors (for adult use only)
- Clear packaging tape

Get Creative Put the uncooked macaroni in the plastic jar, put the lid on, and put clear packaging tape along

ages 2–3

the bottom edge of the lid to firmly hold the lid in place. Let your child use markers to scribble a design on the colored paper and wrap the paper around the spice jar, using tape to hold it in place.

Big Pasta Shakers
Use a larger plastic container such as an empty Parmesan cheese container, filled with uncooked pasta (ziti or rigatoni) to create a different variety of toddler-friendly percussion instrument. Seal up each container with the packaging tape, and decorate with colored paper and scribbles. Add more clear packaging tape around the paper decoration to keep sweaty hands from making the paper bleed.

Beany Shakers
Make a whole set of musical shakers (with empty plastic spice jars) with each one filled with a different variety (and size) of dried beans and creating its own unique sound. Possible dried beans to consider: split peas, navy beans, and kidney beans. Put the lid in place and tighten it, then use clear packaging tape or duct tape all around the shaker to keep the ingredients safely locked inside.

Rice Shakers
Make a similar plastic shaker filled with dried (uncooked) rice, or add a mixture of rice, dried beans, and pasta to create a slightly different percussion sound. Put the lid in place and tighten it, then use clear packaging tape or duct tape all around the shaker to keep the ingredients safely locked inside.

POTS-AND-PANS DRUM SET

Bring this makeshift drum set out whenever you can tolerate a little racket, and let the wild rumpus begin!

Materials
- Assorted metal pots, pans, mixing bowls, and lids
- Large wooden spoons
- Spatula

Get Creative Arrange an assortment of unbreakable pans, pots, and mixing bowls on the floor—turned upside down. Give your child a few safe large spoons and spatulas to be used as makeshift drumsticks.

SHAKE, SHAKE, SHAKE-ALONG

Get a family Shake-Along started with a simple musical instrument and a happy tune to follow along to.

Materials
- Familiar (classic) children's songs
- Assorted toddler-friendly shakers

Get Creative Let your child play a clacker, maracas, baby rattle, conga shakers, or any of the homemade shakers (above) to her favorite recorded tunes. Her rhythm may not match the beat of the music, but it is a fine way to get the idea of playing along with music.

TODDLER CLAPPING SONGS

Share the simple pleasure of clapping and singing in your everyday routines together.

> *The parent has to encourage the child to patty-cake their hands or fill in the last word of a song. Eventually if they hear enough songs, they'll start singing some simple songs themselves.*
>
> —**JOHN FEIERABEND,** artist director of the Feierabend Association for Music Education and author of *The First Steps in Music*

Materials
- Traditional children's rhyme (see next page)

Get Creative Clapping (or tapping) to the beat of a nursery rhyme is a good way for your toddler to begin to learn about beat. Invent your own rhymes and clap along, or share favorite rhymes from your own childhood and add a bit of clapping.

ages 2–3

100

Here are four good clapping and tapping rhymes for parents and toddlers:

Peas Porridge Hot
Peas porridge hot,
Peas porridge cold,
Peas porridge in the pot
Nine days old.
Some like it hot,
Some like it cold,
Some like it in the pot
Nine days old.
My mamma likes it hot,
My daddy likes it cold,
But I like it in the pot
Nine days old.

Hickory, Dickory, Dock
Repeat this rhyme several times for extended clapping.

Hickory, dickory, dock,
The mouse ran up the clock.
The clock struck one

And down he run.
Hickory, dickory, dock.

One Potato, Two Potato
Repeat the rhyme several times and include clapping, then tapping.

One potato, two potato,
Three potato, four,
Five potato, six potato,
Seven potato more.

Miss Mary Mack
Miss Mary Mack, Mack, Mack
All dressed in black, black, black
With silver buttons . . .
All down her back . . .
She asked her mother . . .
For fifty cents . . .
To see the elephant . . .
Jump over the fence . . .
He jumped so high . . .
He reached the sky . . .
And he didn't come back . . .
Till the Fourth of July . . .

Dince Activities

All toddlers can have fun with dance. Parents and caregivers can encourage their child to experiment and get creative with dance by providing music, initiating some toddler-style dance activities, and keeping the focus on fun. It's a simple plan that helps each child get comfortable and excited about dancing in their own playful way.

Some children will bop, bend, wiggle, shake, or shuffle as soon as the music is turned on. Others need a bit of prompting to join in the fun. (A silly round of Fishy-Swimmy Dance or Follow-the-Leader Dancing with other children can often provide a boost of encouragement for reluctant dancers.)

There may be no other time in your child's life when he will dance in quite this same charming, innocent, spontaneous way. So grab your camera or turn on your video recorder and capture this unique first chapter in your child's dance creativity.

THREE-MINUTE DANCE ROUTINE

Turn on the music and let the dance magic begin!

Materials
- High-energy recorded music with a good dance beat

Get Creative This is a good activity to include in toddler playgroups. Some toddlers in the group may dance, others may stand and observe, and still others may choose to play with toys nearby! It's all good, because each child is soaking up the music.

Toddler Dance Party

Take the music and dancers outdoors! Place a tablecloth or beach
towel on the ground, and assemble
an assortment of toddler-safe
percussion instruments on the
tablecloth. (Toddler-style percussion instruments might include
conga shakers, wooden clackers,
toddler-style maracas, baby rattles,
and noodle shakers.) Start the recorded music and let the children
pick a shaker, and let the dancing
and shaking begin.

FOLLOW-THE-LEADER DANCING

There's a whole lot of happy wiggle-
waggle action going on when toddlers
follow the leader.

Materials
- Recorded music with a happy beat
  for dancing

Get Creative When the music starts,
the leader (parent) calls out simple
movements for others to follow: waving hands, wiggle-waggling, swaying

side to side, marching around the room, and so on. Afterward, each child takes a turn being the dance leader (with or without callouts), and all the other dancers follow his or her movements.

Fishy-Swimmy Dance

Turn on the music and give a little ad-lib demo of your very best Fishy-Swimmy dance move. Show hands and arms moving through the water, and wiggly-dancing around the room to the beat of the music.

MARCHING KINGS AND QUEENS

Bring out the crowns, wands, and streamers and get a group of toddlers marching as a merry group of royal dancers.

Materials

- Assorted props and costumes to make this march regal: paper crowns, hats, streamers, batons and magic wands, bells, and shakers
- Recorded music with a good beat for marching

ages
2–3

MUSIC AND MOVEMENT CLASSES FOR PARENT AND CHILD

If you're feeling like you'd enjoy a little company while you experience music with your toddler, check out the movement and music classes in your own community. Your town may offer local classes at arts organizations or at schools, or check out these national companies with music and movement classes for parent and child nationwide: Music Together (www.musictogether.com) and Kindermusik (www.kindermusik.com).

Get Creative Assemble the props, put on the costumes, and turn on the music. Ad-lib a little demo of big, bold marching steps around and around the room and see what sort of march the toddlers create to the beat of the music.

OLD MACDONALD DANCE-ALONG

This familiar children's tune, with its funny "Ee-I-ee-I-oh" refrain, inspires dance enthusiasm from toddlers on the dance floor.

Materials
- The "Old MacDonald" song—sing it or play a recording

Get Creative Explain that every time you sing "Ee-I-ee-I-oh" in the "Old MacDonald" song, each dancer will do a special little dance movement (like tossing their hands up in the air). Then sing a lively version of "Old MacDonald Had a Farm," and when you get to the "Ee-I-ee-I-oh," toss your own hands in the air while the children follow along. Sing this song three or four times through in this same way—with the children raising arms and shaking or dancing at each "Ee-I-ee-I-oh." For a little extra delight, sing extra "Ee-I-ee-I-ohs" at unexpected places in the song.

MAMA OR PAPA WALTZ TIME

This lovely classic dance step for parents and toddlers generates squeals of delight and enthusiastic requests for "more, more, more!"

Materials
- Recorded music with a waltz tempo

Get Creative Hold your child in your arms and dance a waltz around and around the room to your favorite tunes. This is a simple and much-loved way to introduce your child to the joy of gliding to the beat of a song.

Pretend Activities

Children two years of age are just at the very beginning stages of pretending. Much of their make-believe comes from playing with props and imitating what they see others do. When a two-year-old picks up a toy telephone and begins talking, he is imagining that he is a grown-up and he acts out a familiar or fascinating scene from real life. These pretend moments are very spontaneous and short-lived, but they are moving your child along the path of imagination and make-believe.

The main way to encourage toddler pretend is to offer toys, props, and costumes that are age appropriate and safe and let your child invent and act out her own imaginative scenes. It's also fun for parents and caregivers to join in the toddler pretend from time to time, with their toddler leading the way and grown-ups simply acting out a small part in the play.

Many toddlers also enjoy short, spontaneous puppet shows that parents or care-givers initiate. One hand puppet with a parent as the puppeteer inventing a silly animal voice and having a little conversation can be very entertaining. It also gives the idea that perhaps the toddler can slip his hand inside and wiggle the puppet around in his own version of puppet show too. These toddler-friendly pretend activities plant tiny little seeds to encourage your child's creativity to grow.

MAKE PAPER ANIMAL EARS

Make a simple pair of animal ears from colored construction paper and let your child's imagination and pretend play put it to good use.

ages 2–3

Materials
- Colored poster board or large sheets of construction paper
- Scissors (for adult use only)
- Tape
- Nontoxic white glue, such as Elmer's (supervise carefully to keep things safe)
- Furry fabric scraps, yarn, or felt for decorating

Get Creative Cut a 3-inch-wide strip of poster board or heavy construction paper long enough to fit around your child's head (approximately 24 to 26 inches long) plus an extra 2 inches for fastening. (If your paper isn't long enough, you may need to cut several pieces and tape them together.) Tape the ends of the strip together to create a basic hatband. Cut animal ears out of construction paper or poster board—create pointy ears for a kitten, rabbit ears that stand up tall, or dog ears that hang down low. Help your child use the fabric scraps or yarn to decorate the ears. Then staple the ears to the child's paper headband and use tape over the staples for safety.

PARENTS' BEST APPROACH TO ENCOURAGING TODDLER CREATIVITY WITH PRETEND *(Ages 2–3)*

- The basic parenting motto here is: Have props, dress-up clothes, and easy costumes available and let your child invent his or her own way to be creative with make-believe.
- Encourage pretend activities during playdates and playgroups, and have toys and props for all the children to experiment with.
- Older toddlers may enjoy trying on more elaborate costumes to become superheroes, knights, princesses, or ballerinas. (Some toddlers like this and others are reluctant, so follow your child's lead.)
- Expect only short spurts of interest in make-believe play during the toddler years. (Toddlers by nature are on the go and have a short attention span.)
- Include toddler make-believe activities in Family Creativity Night and your child's birthday party too.

HATS GALORE

Create a hatbox with a dozen or more interesting hats for spontaneous make-believe for toddler girls and boys. Toddlers enjoy putting hats on to act out small make-believe scenes; being a carpenter, a police officer, a firefighter, a mom, grandma, dad, grandpa, an artist, or any other worker they see in real life. It's quick, spontaneous, and satisfying pretend play. Here are some suggestions for fun hats.

- Assorted hats from your closet, yard sales, or secondhand stores
- Chef's hat (made of paper—available online or at party supply stores for under $3)
- Beret (artist)
- Ski hats
- Cowboy hats
- A bandanna (become a pirate)
- Visor
- Assorted baseball caps
- Plastic fireman's hat
- Policeman's cap
- Scarf (babushka for a grandma)
- Grandpa hats (anything a grandpa might wear)
- Toy hard hat (for construction play)
- Church-lady hat (fancy hat with flowers)
- Sailor hat
- Animal ears
- Assorted Halloween costume hats

ages
2–3

MAKE AN ANIMAL TAIL FROM TIGHTS

Make an easy animal tail from a child-sized pair of recycled tights and let the wiggle-waggle animal-pretend begin!

Materials
- One pair of little girl's nylon tights (stockings)
- Scissors (for adult use only)
- Tissue paper, waxed paper, or fabric scraps
- Duct tape

Get Creative Parents—use scissors to cut one leg off the tights. Stuff the remaining leg with tissue paper, waxed paper, or fabric scraps to create a puffy, long tail. Tie a knot at the top of that tail, where it meets the torso section of the tights. To attach the tail to your child's backside, simply tuck the torso section of the tights into your child's jeans or pants.

> *Free play, when children can exercise their imagination, is one of the richest learning experiences that children have.*
>
> **—DR. DANIEL GOLEMAN,** psychologist, author of *Emotional Intelligence* and *Focus*

MAKE A MAJESTIC CROWN (FOR A PRINCE OR PRINCESS)

Create a simple homemade crown and let the royal make-believe begin!

Materials
- A roll of butcher paper
- One pack of precut cardboard scalloped borders (available at teacher supply stores)
- Crayons or nontoxic markers
- Scissors
- Optional: colored dot stickers (available at office supply stores)

Setup Cut a 24-inch section of scalloped border and use a little tape to secure it to the paper table covering for easy coloring. Encourage your toddler to decorate his or her crown with crayons, markers, and dots. When the decorating is finished, peel the tape off from the crown and paper. Cut the scalloped border to crown length for your child. Use tape to fasten the two ends together to create a crown that fits your child.

Get Creative Put your child's crown on her head and add other royal props or dress-up clothes such as a cape, a mesh shawl, giant bead jewelry, or a magic wand, and let the royal pretend begin.

CREATE A DRESS-UP BOX (WITH TODDLER-STYLE COSTUMES)

Create a dress-up box with costumes that are easy to wear and comfortable enough to play in. The costumes and props really help your child imagine and invent the make-believe play. She may pretend to build something or repair something as she wears a plastic hard hat. Or she may pretend to cook or bake a birthday cake when she puts on a chef's hat or apron. Here are some ideas:

- A plastic tub with a lid (for the dress-up box container)
- Costumes to put inside the dress-up box, such as vests, mittens or gloves, hats, shirts, child-sized glasses frames (with the lenses removed), purses, wallets, backpacks, briefcases, tote bags, bangle bracelets, and giant plastic pop-beads for a toddler-safe necklace
- Add recycled toddler-safe (and nonscary) Halloween costumes too, such as wigs and headgear in small sizes.

LITTLE BALLERINA

Put on a dance costume, twirl around, and let the fantasy play begin.

Materials

- Tutu (see directions on the next page to make a super-easy no-sew tutu)

- Leotard or lightweight sleeveless or long-sleeve T-shirt
- Child-sized tights
- Doll or favorite stuffed animal (for a pretend dance partner)

Setup Make one or two homemade, no-sew tutus (one for your child and one for her doll or stuffed animal)

Get Creative Help your child put on her ballerina outfit (and put the tutu on her doll or stuffed animal) and let your child invent her own pretend dance scenario.

ages 2-3

MAKE A NO-SEW TUTU

Here's a super-easy way for parents to make an excellent tutu with no sewing involved!

Materials
- 60 inches of grosgrain ribbon (5/8 or 1¼ inches wide)
- Approximately 25 yards of 12-inch-wide tulle fabric (100 yards available for approximately $12. One supplier to check is www.efavormart.com)
- Scissors (for adult use only)

Directions Cut a piece of ribbon approximately 54 inches long. (This will be the waistband of the tutu. Use approximately three to four times the length of your child's waist and trim excess later.) Cut fifteen to twenty pieces of tulle fabric, each piece approximately 24 inches long. Lay the ribbon on the work table stretched out end to end. Tie a knot in the ribbon approximately 12 inches from one end, to keep the tulle bunched up in the midsection of the ribbon as you create your tutu. Grab one piece of tulle and fold it in half lengthwise (so that it is now 18 inches long, with double thickness). Create a loop at the midpoint (fold) of the tulle, position it under the ribbon, and make a slip knot in the ribbon. Repeat this slip-knot process with the twenty or more cut pieces of tulle. Tie a knot about 12 inches from the other end of the ribbon to keep the tulle from slipping off the end. If the tutu seems too long for your child, use scissors to trim the length of the skirt. Tie the tutu around your child's waist with a bow and she's ready for dance time.

LAUNDRY BASKET SAILBOAT

A plastic laundry basket makes a good sailboat for all sorts of pretend on the high seas!

Materials
- Laundry basket or large cardboard box
- Bandanna (for pirate's hat) or sailor's hat
- Optional: two cardboard (mailing) tubes for oars

Get Creative Put on a sailor or pirate hat, step inside the laundry basket, grab your oars, and say, "Ahoy, mate!" (This is a little demo to show your toddler how this make-believe sailing begins!) Then come ashore, hand the oars to your child, and let his imagination launch his own version of pretend sailing play.

TEDDY BEAR TRAIN

Make a simple little shoe box train and your child becomes the Teddy Bear Train conductor!

Materials

- 2 or 3 cardboard shoe boxes
- Hole punch
- One roll of 2-inch-wide clear packaging tape
- A ball of yarn
- Scissors
- Train conductor's hat
- Stuffed animals

Setup Remove the lids from the shoe boxes and use the hole punch to create a small hole at the two ends of the box. Cut a 12-to-14-inch-long piece of yarn and thread it through the punched hole on the end of one shoe box. Tie a triple knot and tape the knot and end of the yarn securely inside the shoe box. Punch a hole in both ends of the next shoe box to create the second train car. Cut a short piece of yarn about 10 inches long and thread that yarn through the rear of the first shoe box and the front of the second shoe box. Tie triple knots in both ends and use tape to securely fasten each knot-ted end inside the shoe boxes. Add one more train car with a third shoe box if you like, following the same plans to hook the last car to the second car with yarn and tape.

Get Creative Put several small stuffed animals inside the Teddy Bear Train. Put the conductor's hat on your child's head, shout out your best imitation of a train whistle, and hand over the train to your child and let his version of Teddy Bear Train make-believe begin!

CLASSIC PRETEND PLAY

Toddlers are happy to imitate everyday scenes from the world around them. They notice what goes on in the coffee shop, library, grocery store, and other familiar places, and these scenes get woven into their pretend play, with a few basic props to inspire the action. Some toddlers develop favorite pretend scenarios that they like to play over and over again. Some might be enthralled with fix-it pretend, for example, imi-tating a mechanic or repairman. Others love kitchen and cooking make-believe. Some toddlers love to pretend to be parents working on the computer, doing chores, or caring for a doll baby.

Get Creative Encourage your child to invent spontaneous pretend-play sce-narios by providing toys and props that can be used in a variety of imaginative ways by your child. Here are eight classic make-believe play activities that toddlers will love to do again and again. Bring out the props, offer a small challenge or invitation that might help start the pretend play, and let your child's imagination do the rest.

Kitchen-Table Fort and Camp-Out Pretend

Use a king- or queen-sized sheet to build a fort. Put the sheet over a table so the edges reach the floor on all sides. (If you are using twin sheets, overlap them on the top of the table and tape them together to hold the table fort in place.) Gather up a few props and toys (such as a sleeping bag, pillow, back-pack, books, and so on) and put them inside the fort and let your child invent his or her own make-believe fort play with dolls or stuffed animals or action heroes inside.

Cook's in the Kitchen

Start with a paper chef's hat (available at paper or party supply stores) to jump-start this cooking pretend. Use a clear packaging tape (3 inches wide) placed around the hat to adjust the size for your child. Gather up safe, unbreakable kitchen props (muffin tins, pie pans, spatula, empty plastic spice jars, pots, pans, and giant spoons). Bring out a toy kitchen appliance, or simply use a small table or large cardboard box turned upside down to serve as the pretend stove or kitchen counter.

Teddy Bear Picnic
Spread a blanket or tablecloth on the floor or lawn. Gather up a few props, such as a shoe box (for the table), stuffed animals, and toy tea set or plastic coffee cups and spoons. Add some snacks to turn this make-believe playtime into a real picnic. Both boys and girls will enjoy this pretend activity with their favorite stuffed animals.

Pretend Bookstore or Library
Provide a collection of books and props (book bag, table and chair, magazines) and bring out a collection of stuffed animals. Jump-start the pretend by saying, "Let's have a story hour for the stuffed animals (or dolls)." You read the story and let your toddler show the pictures to the animals as you go. Then bow out and let your child do the talking and pretend reading and showing pictures.

Pretend Telephone
This is a classic pretend-play activity that never goes out of style. The main prop needed is a toy cell phone or telephone. Add a few stuffed animals too, so your toddler can chatter on the phone, pretending to be mom or dad and sometimes passing the phone to the stuffed animals. It's simple but much-loved make-believe play for toddlers.

TOYS AND PROPS FOR SPONTANEOUS PRETEND PLAY

Gather up an assortment of safe household items and toys and your toddler will invent her own freestyle make-believe. Your toddler's curiosity will create this play with little help needed from parents except a little supervision to keep things safe. Here are some ideas to get you started:

- Barn and farm animal sets
- Blocks
- Books
- Cardboard boxes (small or medium-sized)
- Cars and trucks
- Dolls and accessories
- Dress-up hats, clothes, purses, wallets, backpacks
- Giant Legos
- Kitchen set and pretend food
- Laundry basket
- Miniature wagon (for transportation of animals and dolls on the go)
- Noah's ark (wooden set with boat and animals)
- Plastic animals
- Plastic lawn mower
- Plastic or wooden tool set
- Play grocery cart and pretend groceries (empty containers and boxes)
- Pots and pans and cooking toys
- Pretend money
- Pretend picnic set (plastic or wooden)
- Puppets
- Ride-on toys (without pedals)
- Safe kitchen gadgets and utensils: colander, cookie sheet, ice cream scoop, muffin tins, plastic cookie cutters, plastic plates, rolling pin
- Sandbox and clean play sand

$\longrightarrow$

- Sandbox toys
- Sprinkling can
- Stuffed animals
- Tea set
- Toddler-sized cleanup toys (little broom, dustpan)
- Toddler tool set (plastic hammer and saw)
- Toy phone
- Toy camera
- Wooden or plastic people and animals
- Wooden or plastic toy train (plastic shopping cart, dolls, trucks, stuffed animals, toy tool set)

Pretend Grocery Store

Gather up some empty food boxes and let your child invent a little grocery store in your living room! Gather a few grocery store props: shopping bag, canned goods, empty plastic food containers and boxes, toy shopping cart (or plastic laundry basket), toy cash register. Assemble the props on a small table (or the floor) to create the grocery. Play along for a few moments of selecting food items and tossing them in the basket and going through the checkout line. Once your child is happily inventing his own pretend grocery store scenario, leave the store and let him make believe on his own.

Pretend Coffee Shop

A coffee shop is a fascinating place that inspires a good round of toddler make-believe play. Gather up props (toy coffee pot, plastic cups and spoons, small notepad and crayon for taking orders, and stuffed animals for the customers). Add a medium-to-large cardboard box (turned upside down) or a table, and place the props on the table to get the coffee shop make-believe under way. A parent or caregiver can be the customer and your child is the coffee server, taking orders and pouring coffee. (Lighten up and have a little pretend play along with your daily cappuccino!) Then, when it's time for you to move out of the scene, the dolls and stuffed animals are the next round of customers for this pretend coffee shop.

Puppy Parade

Assemble the puppies in a big parade float (aka wagon) and let make-believe begin. Help your child gather up a collection of stuffed animals (all the stuffed dogs and puppies available), bring out the toy wagon, add a few party hats, turn on the music, and let the Puppy Parade begin.

MAKE MINI PARTY HATS

Make colorful party hats to add a little drama to the Puppy Parade. Here are the easy directions to make miniature party hats with your child.

Materials
- Scissors (for adult use only)
- Colored construction paper
- Stapler (for adult use only)
- Streamers
- Invisible tape

Get Creative Cut one sheet of construction paper into a square and roll it into a cone-shaped party hat that is the correct size for one of the stuffed animals.

Use the stapler to hold the paper in the cone-shape. Parents cut some paper streamers and let your child assist in taping them onto the tip of the hat. Make enough mini party hats for all the stuffed puppies in the parade.

MAKE A CARDBOARD TRUCK FOR YOUR CHILD

Hey, it's time to get this big rig moving!

Materials
- One large cardboard box (about the size of a microwave oven, or bigger)
- A roll of brown craft paper or butcher paper
- Invisible tape
- Assorted colored markers
- 4 colored plastic disposable plates (for the tires)
- Scissors (for adult use only)
- Baseball hat or other "trucker" hat
- Wooden blocks (for the load for the truck)

Setup If you are using a cardboard box with lots of printing or logos, cover it with sheets of craft paper and secure it with tape. Let your child decorate the truck. Place one of the plastic plates upside down on the side of the box at the front to create the front wheel. Use long pieces of tape to attach the wheel to the box. Place the other three plates on the box as the remaining tires. Your child can dump the wooden blocks inside the truck so there's a big load to haul!

Get Creative Once the truck is made, ask your child to find a truck driver for the big truck! (It might be your child, or perhaps a big stuffed animal.) The truck can be easily pushed along the carpet or wooden floor (with stuffed animals inside) for lots of big-rig make-believe.

> I would say that creative play actually helps children learn great life skills that will serve them their whole life long; how to become problem solvers, how to become risk takers. They learn to build on what they already know and that there isn't just one way to do things.
>
> **—SANDI DEXTER,** preschool teacher and author of *Joyful Play with Toddlers*

MAKE A CARDBOARD KITCHEN SET

Turn medium to large boxes into a pretend refrigerator, stove, dishwasher, and sink for your toddler's kitchen pretend play!

Materials

- 3 medium-to-large cardboard boxes
- 1 roll of brown craft paper or white butcher paper
- Markers
- A large roll of clear packaging tape
- Scissors (for adult use only)
- 2 large and 2 small red plastic disposable plates
- Assorted toy (or real) small pots and pans for pretend kitchen play

Setup Gather up three boxes to create the following kitchen: 1 medium box (turned upside down) to create a stove (remove the four bottom flaps); 1 large box (standing vertically) to create a fridge; 1 medium box (standing vertically) to create a dishwasher. If the boxes have printed logos or writing on the outside surfaces, cover each box with craft or butcher paper and use tape to hold the paper in place. (This provides a clean surface to draw upon.) Draw handles and dials and doors to make

ages 2–3

these kitchen appliances resemble the real things. Tape the plastic plates to the stove top to make four burners on the cook surface. Gather up toy pots and pans or safe, real kitchen gadgets and pans.

Get Creative Once the cardboard kitchen appliances are made, put a couple of pots and wooden spoons on the cardboard stove and let your child's imagination create the kitchen-play make-believe, cooking up a meal or making a dessert for you!

CREATE A FINGER-PUPPET STAGE

Turn a shoe box on its side, do a little cutting and gluing, and voilà—you've created a terrific finger-puppet stage!

Materials
- Shoe box
- Scissors (for adult use only)
- Nontoxic white glue, such as Elmer's (supervise carefully to keep things safe)
- Construction paper

Get Creative Remove the lid from the shoe box. Use scissors to remove a center square section from the lid that is about 5 inches by 3 inches. (When this cardboard section is removed, the lid will resemble a frame.) Next cut a section of colored construction paper that resembles a curtain with a scalloped edge, and glue it along one edge of the lid with the scalloped edge facing down toward the open space in the lid. Use the scissors to cut a 4-by-4-inch hole in the bottom of the shoe box. Place the shoe box on its side.

PARENT PUPPETEER

Put on a one- or two-minute puppet show to entertain your child and have a few laughs together!

Materials
- Finger-Puppet Stage (see above)
- Two finger puppets

Get Creative To put on a puppet show, place the finger-puppet stage on its side (on the kitchen table) with the curtain/lid facing outward toward your audience. Put one or two finger puppets on your hand and gently slip your hand through the back opening in the box and into the front of the stage area so the puppets can clearly be seen by your child. Invent two characters and create a simple back-and-forth conversation between the two puppets. Keep the conversation simple, easy to understand, and toddler-friendly. And above all else, ham it up for a few laughs.

ages
2–3

"IF YOU'RE HAPPY AND YOU KNOW IT" PUPPET SHOW

Parents become silly-theatrics mentors in this whimsical little song-and-dance routine for a puppet!

Materials
- One finger puppet
- Finger-Puppet Stage (see previous page)

Setup Place the shoe box on its side (on the kitchen table) with the curtain/lid facing outward toward your audience. Put one finger puppet on your hand and gently slip your hand through the back opening in the box and into the front of the stage area so the puppet can clearly be seen by your child.

Get Creative Introduce your puppet character to start the show, for example, "Hello, my name is Gina and I'm a singing giraffe!" Then do your very best rendition of "If You're Happy and You Know It!" (Ask your audience to clap along every time you sing, "Clap your hands.")

If You're Happy and You Know It!

If you're happy and you know it,
Clap your hands.
If you're happy and you know it,
Clap your hands.
If you're happy and you know it,
Then your face will surely show it,
If you're happy and you know it,
Clap your hands.

Create more verses as you go, substituting "clap your hands" with other shout-outs, such as "wave your hands," "twirl around," "take a bow," "shake a leg," "stomp your feet," and "wiggle-waggle"!

TODDLERS' OWN PUPPET SHOW

Older toddlers can try their hand at putting on a simple finger-puppet show for parents.

Materials
- One or more finger puppets
- Kitchen table and chair
- Music (or you sing a familiar children's song)

Get Creative Your child becomes the puppeteer, making the finger puppets dance upon the stage (kitchen table) while you sing a familiar children's song. (This is a good way to learn to manipulate puppets on the stage.)

Hand Puppets on the Kitchen Table
Provide one hand puppet for your toddler and one for you. Position yourselves across the kitchen table from one another with a puppet on your hand and another on your child's hand. Ad-lib a little conversation back and forth between the puppets, or sing a familiar song (or play music) and watch both puppets dance upon the stage (table)!

Creativity with Words

Parents and caregivers have many opportunities to introduce toddlers to the joys of creativity with language. You can recite playful nursery rhymes and create your own customized rhymes to delight your child. You can read aloud from imaginative children's books that make the words upon the page sound musical and captivating to your child's ears. You can create your own "I Spy" rhyming books to read to your child and create "Mommy (or Daddy) and Me" picture books with your toddler. These activities are easy to incorporate into everyday routines and they offer brief moments of fun that match up with a toddler's attention span.

When you share these entertaining and imaginative experiences, you show your child what creativity with words and language is all about. This is a terrific way to help your child develop enthusiasm and interest, and before you know it, he will be participating imaginatively with his own style of creativity with words.

PARENTS' BEST APPROACH TO ENCOURAGING TODDLER CREATIVITY WITH WORDS (*Ages 2–3*)

- Read books to your toddler that have a playful approach to language. (For suggested books, see Playful Read-Alouds for Toddlers, page 127.)
- Be a lively storyteller who invents silly voices, creates sound effects, and makes storytelling an art form to entertain your toddler with words!
- Give yourself permission to invent new verses and change the words to traditional nursery rhymes and poems just for the fun of it.
- Create customized books for your child, and let her help with illustration, gluing, and putting books together.
- Include toddler-friendly story-time and language activities in Family Creativity Night.

ENJOY CREATIVE RHYMES WITH YOUR TODDLER

Reading or reciting playful-sounding rhymes is a splendid way to introduce your child to creative fun with language!

Materials
- Favorite classic children's rhymes

Get Creative Introduce your child to some of your favorite rhymes from childhood or from a cherished nursery rhyme book. Here are eight favorites for toddlers to help you get started. These rhymes set the stage for using words, voice, and storytelling in entertaining and imaginative ways.

Higglety, Pigglety, Pop!

Higglety, pigglety, pop! (clap hands)
The dog has eaten the mop.
The pig's in a hurry, (roll hands)
The cat's in a flurry,
Higglety, pigglety, pop! (clap hands)

Hey Diddle, Diddle!

Hey diddle, diddle,
The cat and the fiddle,
The cow jumped over the moon.
The little dog laughed,
To see such sport,
And the dish ran away with the spoon!

Three Little Kittens

Three little kittens lost their mittens,
And they began to cry,
"O mother dear, we sadly fear
Our mittens we have lost!"
"What, lost your mittens?
You naughty kittens!
Then you shall have no pie!"
"Meow, meow, meow!"
The three little kittens found their
*   mittens,*
And they began to cry,
"O mother dear, see here, see here,
Our mittens we have found."
"What, found your mittens?
You good little kittens,
Then you shall have some pie!"

Hickory, Dickory, Dock

Hickory, dickory, dock,
The mouse ran up the clock
*   (use two fingers to walk up your*
*   child's arm).*

The clock struck one
And down he run
    (use two fingers, to walk down
    your child's arm),
Hickory, dickory, dock.

Little Boy Blue

Little Boy Blue, come blow your
    horn,
The sheep's in the meadow, the cow's
    in the corn;
But where is the boy that looks after
    the sheep?
He's under a haycock, fast asleep.
Will you wake him? No, not I;
For if I do, he'll be sure to cry.

It's Raining, It's Pouring!

It's raining, it's pouring,
The old man is snoring,
He went to bed and bumped his head,
And he couldn't get up in the morning.

Mary, Mary

Mary, Mary, quite contrary,
How does your garden grow?
With silver bells and cockle shells,
And pretty maids all in a row.

Teddy Bear, Teddy Bear

Teddy bear, teddy bear, turn around.
Teddy bear, teddy bear, touch the
    ground.

Teddy bear, teddy bear, touch your
    shoe.
Teddy bear, teddy bear, say "How'd
    you do."
Teddy bear, teddy bear, go up the stairs.
Teddy bear, teddy bear, say your
    prayers.
Teddy bear, teddy bear, turn out the
    light.
Teddy bear, teddy bear, say good
    night!

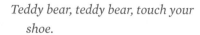

CREATE YOUR OWN RHYMES

Create short rhymes and new verses for classic children's rhymes as a delightful way to mix imagination and language together.

Materials
- Familiar children's rhymes
  (see page 123) and imagination

Get Creative Give yourself permission to be imaginative and silly and to borrow ideas and verses from classic children's poems and rhymes and see what you can create for your child! Here is a sample of a homemade rhyme I created using the classic "Higglety, Pigglety, Pop" (see previous page) as my inspiration and guide.

Many times the little songs we sing to kids have rhyming. And the brain is a pattern-seeking organ and so it is fun for a child's brain to be able to hear those repeated rhythms, repeated tonal patterns, and repeated words.

—JILL STAMM, PHD, associate clinical professor in psychology and education at Arizona State University and author of *Bright from the Start*

Lickety, Luckity, Lam

Lickety, luckity, lam
The cat got in the jam,
She licked her toes,
And wiped her nose,
Lickety, luckity, lam.

Lickety, luckity, loo
The mice are nibbling too.
They took the cheese,
They ate the peas,
Lickety, luckity, loo!

CREATE A NURSERY RHYME WITH YOUR CHILD'S NAME OR NICKNAME

Parents, grandparents, and caregivers can be fabulous creativity mentors when they invent customized nursery rhymes for their child.

Materials
● Familiar children's rhymes and poems (to borrow or use as a guide) plus your imagination

Get Creative Write one short opening line about your child. Then add a second line that rhymes and fits. Be spontaneous and jot down ideas quickly as they pop into your head for best results.

Here is a sample of my homemade rhymes using the classic "Higglety, Pigglety, Pop" (see page 123) as my inspiration and guide.

Momo Builds His Towers High

Momo builds his towers high,
Blocks are stacked up to the sky.
Some fall down and some do crash,
Momo likes to hear them splash.
Towers are strong and towers are true,
Build them up like builders do.

CREATIVE STORYTELLING

Appoint yourself to be the family story-teller (and storytelling mentor too).

Materials
- A favorite children's book or nursery rhyme or poem

Get Creative Your storytelling voice is the magic ingredient that makes words seem special to your toddler. What's more, when you read words and rhymes, poems and stories that you enjoy, your child will warm to the idea of creativity from words in a very natural way too. This is how it all starts, and you will be truly amazed at the tiny little steps that happen from this humble beginning of experiencing word creativity together.

ages 2–3

PLAYFUL READ-ALOUDS FOR TODDLERS

Here are ten terrific books that have a special rhythmic, playful use of words perfect for toddler read-alouds:

- *Goodnight Moon* by Margaret Wise Brown
- *Moo, Baa, La La La* by Sandra Boynton
- *Blue Hat, Green Hat* by Sandra Boynton
- *Brown Bear, Brown Bear, What Do You See?* by Bill Martin, Jr., and Eric Carle
- *Chicka Chicka Boom Boom* by Bill Martin, Jr., John Archambault, and Lois Ehlert
- *Peek-a Who?* by Nina Laden
- *Each Peach Pear Plum* by Janet and Allen Ahlberg
- *Sputter, Sputter, Sput!* by Babs Bell and illustrated by Bob Staake
- *Perfect Piggies! A Book! A Song! A Celebration!* by Sandra Boynton
- *The Baby Goes Beep* by Rebecca O'Connell and illustrated by Ken Wilson-Max

Book-Box Read-Aloud

To add a little surprise to your daily read-aloud routine, assemble a collection of favorite books in a basket or box. Tie a little blindfold (handkerchief or scarf) loosely over your child's eyes and ask him to reach into the basket and pick a mystery book to read.

STORY BASKET

One little scrap of paper (with one word), and a clever story begins!

Materials
- Paper
- Pencil
- Basket

Setup Think of ten individual words (or themes) that would be good for storytelling and write each of them on a piece of scrap paper. For added enjoyment, include a small photo, clip art, or drawing that illustrates the word on each paper. Fold the papers in half and toss all the papers into the basket.

Get Creative Ask your child to select a story idea from the story basket. Create a short (2-to-3-minute) toddler-friendly story about the word, character, or theme on the paper. Make your story silly or entertaining, with actions that your child will understand or relate to from real life! Use finger and hand motions or gestures to accentuate the action in the story. Use your voice to create added interest, with nonscary sound effects, whispers, high-pitched or low-pitched voices, and so on.

CREATE YOUR OWN BOARD BOOKS FOR YOUR TODDLER

Make your own toddler board books with simple text and colorful drawings or photos. Some books might just have one word and a familiar object on each page, while others might have one line of a toddler-friendly story.

These books are easy to make and fun to read aloud to your child.

Materials
- Paper and pencil
- Card stock
- Hole punch
- Ribbon or twine

Directions Create a book cover by hand lettering (or printing text of) the title of the book in bold, colorful letters on one sheet of card stock. Perhaps create a little sketch on the cover as well. On a second sheet of card stock, write the first word or line of your book across the top of the page and leave room for a simple drawing or photo. On the back side of the above page, write your second word or line of text and leave more space below for a drawing or photo.

Continue in this same way, creating as many pages (with drawings) as you like. Create a back cover for your book that is either blank or that has a drawing or design related to what's inside.

Now line up all the pages (card stock) in the correct order and use the hole punch to punch three or four holes along the left side of the book.

ages 2-3

Use twine or ribbon threaded through each hole to create a simple binding for the book.

CREATE AN "I SPY" RHYMING BOOK

This little homemade version of an "I Spy" book can be tailored to your child's favorite objects or daily routine.

Materials
- Your own board book (see page 128)
- Paper and pencil

Setup Brainstorm a list of rhyming words (objects) in your toddler's vocabulary (or world); for example, *cat* and *hat*, *car* and *star*, *truck* and *duck*.

Get Creative Before you start writing, give your book a title—perhaps something with your child's first name included, such as "Susie's 'I Spy' Rhyming Book." Write (or type) a short four- or five-word opener for your book, such as, "Susie said, 'I spy . . .'" This opener will be repeated throughout the book, on the pages that contain the rhyming words. You might end the book with one special "I Spy" object on the last page.

Here's a sample.

Title: "Susie's 'I Spy' Rhyming Book"

Page 1: Susie said, "I spy . . . a dog and a frog." (*Do a simple drawing of a dog and frog*)

Page 2: Susie said, "I spy . . . a duck and a truck."

Page 3: Susie said, "I spy . . . a cat and a hat."

Page 4: Susie said, "I spy . . . a chair and a bear."

Page 5: Susie said, "I spy . . . a goose and a moose."

Page 6: Susie said, "I spy . . . a spoon and a moon."

Page 7: Susie said, "I spy . . . a clock and a sock."

Page 8: Susie said. "Oh my, I do spy, a cuddly little teddy bear, just for me!"

CREATE A "MOMMY (OR DADDY) AND ME" PICTURE BOOK

Have a little fun creating words and simple drawings or funny photographs to make this a truly special book for your child. It's fun to read now, and can be tucked away as a keepsake for years to come.

Materials
- Your own board book (see page 128)
- Markers
- Optional: photos

Get Creative Write a book about the activities you enjoy doing with your child and illustrate it with photos or simple but colorful drawings. Write easy, clear captions for each photo or illustration in your book.

Create a "Grandma (or Grandpa) and Me" Book

Ask grandparents to take photos of the times spent with your child and ask them to create their own little handmade books for you to read to your child. (These books become lovely keepsake books over time, and are entertaining to read in the kindergarten and preschool years too.)

Create a "My Friend and Me" Book

If your child has a cousin or playmate or sibling he or she plays with, why not create a special book of photos of happy moments of playtime or creative time together. Photos might include outdoor play, painting, making music, water play, trucks, dolls, block play, and other activities that provide the backdrop for memorable photos with friends. Use the same materials (card stock, ribbon, markers, and so on) to create a customized "My Friend and Me" book.

Create a "My Pet and Me" Book

If your family has a cat or dog, capture some spontaneous moments with your child and pet together in photos. Create silly or clever captions for each photo. Then create a book using the materials and layout described above in the "Daddy and Me" or "Mommy and Me" activity above.

CREATE A "MY BUSY DAY" BOOK

Create a clever book about a young toddler (or animal character) who has a busy day going to all the places your child goes to in real life!

Materials
- Your own board book (see page 128)
- Nontoxic markers
- Paper and pencil

Get Creative Think of a character for your story and give him a name. (Your character might be a clever little bear, or a mischievous goat or dog, or perhaps a two-year-old boy or girl.) Now create a list of some of the places your child visits in real life: a bakery, a coffee shop, a playground, a zoo, an art store, a farmer's market, and so on. Write simple (toddler-friendly) lines of text on each page telling the story of your character's busy day. Add some simple yet colorful drawings to make the story come alive.

CREATE A "WHAT'S INSIDE THE BOX?" BOOK

Create a little book with a big box drawn on each page. Lift the paper flap to see what's inside that box!

Materials
- Your own board book (see page 128)
- Nontoxic markers
- Paper and pencil
- Scissors
- Invisible tape or clear package tape

CREATE A "MY FIRST WORDS" BOOK

Create a little keepsake book by jotting down some of the new words your toddler acquires—with a date and any details to tell about using this word. This is a book to tuck away and bring out several years later when your child is old enough to take pleasure in looking back on his baby or toddler years.

Setup Assemble the supplies on the table.

Get Creative Write a list of ten to twelve things your child is familiar with. (Select easy-to-draw objects, such as a duck, a spoon, an apple, a kitty, a boat.) Think of a simple, upbeat (toddler-friendly) line that will be repeated on each page of your book, such as: "Jimmy asked Mamma, 'What's inside the box?'" (Consider using your child's name in this line to personalize the story.)

Now create the pages for this book. At the top of each page, write the repetitive line you created above. Use the markers to draw one different object, such as a kitten, a fork, and so on, on each page right under the line of text.

Draw a square box (or present with wrapping paper and a bow) on another sheet of card stock. (Make this box big enough to completely cover the object you just drew on the book page. Use scissors to trim any excess paper around the box so it just fits neatly over the object.)

This box is the paper flap that will be taped over each object in the book to hide it. Use a piece of invisible tape to position the paper flap in place over the top the drawing of the object.

Make more pages for your book in this same way. When finished creating the pages, draw a picture on the cover and write the name of the book (and your name as author at the bottom).

Create a "Who's Behind the Door?" Book

Create another personalized book similar to the one above, but in this book place small photos of family or friends on each page and cover the photos with a paper flap that looks like a door! (Make several of these on heavy card stock by drawing rectangles with a doorknob to create a door. Make them each large enough to cover one of the photos and then cut them out.) Use tape to position each door over the top of a photo throughout the book. When the door is lifted (or opened side to side), a familiar person is seen.

CREATE A CUSTOMIZED BEDTIME STORY BOOK

Make a comforting or silly bedtime book with familiar people, animals, or characters just right for your toddler.

ages 2-3

Materials

- Your own board book (see page 128)
- Nontoxic markers
- Pencil

Get Creative Make your own version of *Goodnight Moon*, creating a story that has favorite objects, toys, teddy bears, pets, and people that your child can say good night to as a comforting way to settle into sleep. (Add a few silly sayings or objects to add a little surprise to your text if it fits in with your story.) Add some simple drawings that match up with your story.

Create a "Teddy's Bath Time" Book

Create a book about your child's favorite stuffed animal getting a bath in the tub! Add short text and simple drawings or add photos of your child's snuggly friend at bath time.

Create a "One Special Day" Book

Create a handmade book with simple text and photos or drawings about a memorable day spent at the beach, visiting a farm, on a big ship, going to the zoo, visiting grandparents, or some other special outing that you would like to capture in a book and read aloud to your child.

CREATE A "MY FIRST COLORS" BOOK

Work together with your child to create a personalized book about recognizing colors.

Materials

- Your own board book (see page 128)
- Markers or crayons

Get Creative Use a marker to write the word for one color, such as "red," at the top of each page. (Be sure to pick colors your child might be familiar with: red, green, yellow, blue, purple, orange, and so on.) Give your child one color marker and ask him or her to decorate or color the pages to match up with the word on each page. Let your child create a colorful cover for the book, and put the title of the book on the cover too, for example, "Tammy's First Colors Book."

CREATE A "COLORFUL ICE-CREAM CONES" BOOK

Here's a simple and colorful book for parents (or grandparents) to make with their child on a cozy day indoors.

Materials

- Your own board book (see page 128)
- Scissors (for adult use only)
- Colored construction paper
- Pencil
- Soup can to use as a template
- Brown paper
- Tape or nontoxic white glue, such as Elmer's (supervise carefully to keep things safe)
- Markers
- Stapler

Setup Cut two round circles from each color of construction paper. (Use a pencil and soup can from the pantry placed on the paper as your guide for making a perfect circle.) Next cut a long triangle shape (from brown paper) to use as an ice-cream cone for each page.

Get Creative Work with your child to glue or tape a cone on each page and then stack (and tape or paste) two identical colored balls on top of the cone to represent the ice cream. Handwrite the word for each color on the pages, assemble the book, and enjoy reading it together.

ages 2-3

CREATE A "MY FAVORITE FOODS" BOOK

This colorful little book celebrates the familiar foods in your child's life.

Materials
- Magazine or catalog photos of food (for example, garden-seed catalog, cooking catalog, or ads)
- Scissors (for adult use only)
- Your own board book (see page 128)
- Markers
- Stapler

Setup Find food photos and cut them into manageable sizes before this activity begins.

Get Creative Help your child pick out photos of individual foods that you have already cut out and then glue or tape them, one to a page, to your board book. Now write in bold letters the name of that food—for example, "cheese," "apple," "sandwich," and so on. When you've created enough pages for the book, create a front cover (using more photos or markers) and write the title of the book on the cover in bold letters. Assemble the pages in order and use the stapler to make it into a booklet.

PRESCHOOL AND KINDERGARTEN CREATIVITY

Ages 3–5

Children three to five years old are enthusiastic creative dabblers! They have a great knack for exuberant theatrics and pretend. They love to try new art materials. They have fun with building and construction. They are keen listeners, delighted by silly or preschooler-friendly storytelling. They are naturally drawn to music and dance and will happily participate in all sorts of fun with movement, singing, and music making.

Preschoolers and five-year-olds are much more capable of using tools and materials than toddlers, so there are many extra projects to tackle. They can typically follow a few simple instructions and they can easily imitate what they see others doing too. The ages of three, four, and five are an excellent time to encourage your child to entertain himself with creative activities of all kinds. This puts an expectation and habit in place that will pay dividends for many years to come.

When you set aside time in your preschooler's schedule and provide materials for imaginative projects, your child's creativity will grow in leaps and bounds. When your child invites friends over to play, and they engage in art, dress-up, music, dance, and pretend play together, the children experience the joy and satisfaction of creating with others too.

You are an important promoter of imagination for your preschooler and kindergarten-aged child, with many opportunities in your child's life to encourage creative dabbling. And when you spend one-on-one time (or family time) enjoying music, storytelling, puppet shows, making art, and building projects together, you become an important creativity role model too.

Art Activities

Children three to five years old are eager to try all sorts of art projects. They have the skills and basic understanding of safety (keeping things out of their mouths) that allows them to dabble in a wide array of art activities, such as cutting and pasting paper, making collage, painting, drawing, creating mixed media projects, print making, and clay work. Most kids in this age range are thrilled to work with others, and they enjoy solo art projects too.

Children three to five move happily and easily from one painting or drawing to the next, with little regard for doing something perfectly. This is a fabulous mindset for an artist to have and worthy of encouragement. In fact, their "mistakes" (of paint drips or extra glue) often get incorporated into their artwork and accepted as part of the process. (Hooray for embracing the joys of making art!)

The youngest preschoolers will scribble or paint spontaneously with little regard for drawing "something real" (or representational). Typically at around age four and a half or five, children begin to try to draw a house or tree or dog or person in their own expressive style. But their abstract (or nonrepresentational) artwork is beautiful and satisfying and should never be discouraged as a good way to be creative with art materials.

You can give your three-to-five-year-old child a happy introduction to being creative with art by including art activities in his or her routine. Gather up a few materials, set aside a little time, and see what imaginative artwork your child can create!

DOOR MURALS OR POSTERS

Hooray for making colossal art to decorate your child's bedroom door!

Materials
- Scissors (for parent)
- Giant roll of white butcher paper or poster board
- Invisible tape
- Washable markers or crayons

Get Creative Cut a long piece of white butcher paper (7 to 8 feet long). Secure this paper to a hard-surface floor (wood, concrete, or tile) with invisible

138

PARENTS' BEST APPROACH TO ENCOURAGING PRESCHOOL
AND KINDERGARTEN ART CREATIVITY *(Ages 3–5)*

- The magic mantra for preschooler art is "Follow the fun!" Don't look for a highly polished masterpiece—look for an artist who is happy!
- Stock up on easy-to-use, inexpensive, child-friendly art materials, and make them easily available so your child can initiate art projects whenever he or she is in the mood. (See suggested art supplies on page 140.)
- Set aside time for art in your child's routine and consider art activities as an alternative to your child's screen-time activities for a part of each week or day.
- Encourage art activities during playgroup or playdate time with other children.
- Create a space for your child to do artwork. (The kitchen table is fine, or create a little art nook, but set up the space to allow for a little mess.)
- Supervise to keep your child safe. Preschoolers can typically use safety scissors, markers, paint, brushes, colored pencils, erasers, nontoxic print materials, clay, fabric, nontoxic glue, and tape, but they still need a watchful eye from adults.
- Do parent-and-child art activities when you have time and include art activities in Family Creativity Night and your child's birthday party too.

tape. Encourage your child to draw something gigantic and imaginative on the paper. When the drawing is finished, hang the giant mural on the bedroom door.

"George the Giant" Mural or Poster
Create a colorful George the Giant (or Greta the Giant) mural together! Draw the body of the giant, then

embellish the giant with colorful shoes, belts, clothing, and hats too. Hang the finished giant drawing over a door and admire your group creativity!

Monthly Mural

Encourage your child to create a big, imaginative, colorful poster once a month. Some children may incorporate holiday or seasonal themes into their drawing, while others may take a freestyle approach. This is an outstanding way to encourage big drawing projects throughout the year.

> *Children's imaginative play is like fingerprints or snowflakes; each child's play is individual and unique to that child.*
>
> **—SUSAN LINN,** author of *The Case for Make Believe*

MAKE AN ART KIT ON WHEELS

Put a portable supply kit together for solo art projects at the kitchen table so your child will always be able to shift gears into creativity mode! Here are some ideas for materials to include:

- 1 Small (recycled) child's suitcase with wheels and easy-to-open zipper
- Drawing paper, such as a tablet of newsprint paper, colored construction paper, or card stock (perfect for drawing then folding into homemade greeting cards)
- Drawing supplies (stored in individual ziplock bags) such as washable (nontoxic) markers, colored pencils, markers, crayons, or nontoxic water color pencils
- Small paintbrush and cup for water
- A set of washable watercolor paints (in a tray)
- Safety scissors
- Tape

ages 3–5

GLITTER-GLUE DRAWINGS

Preschoolers create colorful, sparkly drawings with glitter-glue pens and construction paper.

Materials
- Assorted glitter-glue pens
- Newsprint paper or colored construction paper

Get Creative Encourage your child to do any freestyle drawing or design she would like. Let the glue dry thoroughly.

CURLICUE GLITTER-GLUE DRAWINGS

These sparkly, colorful drawings are made on little pieces of felt using glitter-glue pens.

Materials
- Scissors (for adult use only)
- Felt (assorted colors, available in 12-by-12-inch squares for about 25 cents each)
- Painter's tape
- One sheet of cardboard
- Glitter-glue pens (assorted colors)

Get Creative Cut the felt squares into manageable sizes for drawing (4-by-4 inches or larger). Tape one fabric square to the cardboard using painter's tape. Give a little demo to start the project: squeeze one small circle of glitter glue onto the fabric. Pick another color of glue and draw a circle or squiggle around the first circle. Add a third or fourth color of glue and draw other curvy shapes around the last shapes. Let the glue dry thoroughly.

Glitter-Glue Fabric Poster
If your child makes a series of Curlicue Glitter-Glue Drawings (see above), help her glue these lovely drawings onto a sheet of colorful poster board in a design of her choosing using a little clear school glue, such as Elmer's.

Fabric-Pen Drawings
For another idea for drawing on fabric, start with small or medium-sized

ARTIST'S NOTEBOOK FOR CREATIVITY ON THE GO

Every artist needs a little book for drawing and coloring when inspiration strikes!

Materials

- Large ziplock bag
- Markers, crayons, or colored pencils
- 8-by-10-inch journal with unlined pages inside

Fill the ziplock bag with assorted crayons, markers, and colored pencils. Your child can use his artist's notebook at the kitchen table while you make dinner, or create artwork in the car or wherever waiting is part of the experience (doctor's appointments, and so on).

squares of muslin or cotton fabric and a pack of nontoxic fabric markers (Crayola, for example; follow the manufacturer's directions for setting the color before washing). If your child creates a series of fabric drawings, perhaps a family member with sewing skills can turn the drawings into a small quilt or wall hanging for your child's room.

CREATE A PICNIC (PICTURE) TABLECLOTH

ages 3–5

Start with a plain bedsheet that's ready to be recycled, and encourage your child to create a one-of-a-kind tablecloth for family picnics!

Materials

- 1 plain (recycled) twin or full-sized flat bedsheet
- Nontoxic fabric markers (Crayola brand, for example)

Setup Stretch the sheet over a picnic table outdoors (or on the patio floor) and put newspapers under the sheet to control bleed-through from the markers.

Get Creative Encourage your child to use the entire giant surface to draw on. Or work side by side, drawing together along with your child to create a colorful design or series of pictures. Follow the directions listed on the pack of fabric markers for setting the color before washing.

ARTISTIC TOY BOX

This is a super-easy way for your preschooler to create a colorful and imaginative toy box.

Materials

- One white cardboard file box with built-in handles and lid (available at office supply stores)
- Nontoxic markers and crayons

Get Creative When you purchase the cardboard file box, it will be collapsed, and in that condition it's a good flat surface for children to draw upon easily. Encourage your child to create a colorful design or freestyle drawing on all sides and top of the box. Then fold the box and voilà—you have a masterpiece that will hold toys or books or art supplies!

BOOK-BAG DRAWING

Your preschooler can create a lovely, artistic book bag (or cloth grocery bag) with a few fabric markers and lots of imagination.

Materials

- White or natural canvas book bags or tote bags (available from www.dickblick.com and other craft and art supply stores)
- Nontoxic fabric markers (for example, Crayola brand)
- Vinyl tablecloth or newspaper (to contain the mess)

Get Creative Encourage your child to create a drawing or design (or scribble) on all surfaces of the canvas bag. (Follow the manufacturer's instructions about care and washing.)

WATER-BOTTLE PRINTMAKING

Disposable water bottles make terrific printing tools, so grab some paint and give this a try!

Materials

- A set of 6 tempera paint cakes in a tray (Colorations brand, for example)
- Small plastic disposable water bottle (select a water bottle with ripples and indentations on the bottom)
- Paper (try newsprint, copy paper, or colored construction paper)
- Newspaper or vinyl tablecloth (to contain the mess)

Get Creative Add a little water to each tempera cake. Fill the water bottle with water if it is empty (you need a little weight to make this work). Place the bottom of the bottle on one of the wet paint cakes, apply a little pressure and wiggle the bottle around, then press the bottom of the bottle on the paper to create a design. (You'll notice the paint sticks to the ridges and indentations on the bottom of the bottle, making very interesting designs on the paper.) Repeat this same process using various colors of paint, then print designs on the paper.

Water-Bottle Print-Art Gift Bags
Use a water bottle and tempera paint in the same way as described above, but this time print on white-paper lunch bags to create colorful gift bags.

Water-Bottle Print-Art Gift Boxes
Do the bottle-art printing project described above, but start with a plain, collapsed (flat) gift box and create colorful circle designs on the top lid of the box using the supplies listed above.

Scribble-Art Cookie Bags
This is a perfect art project for Grandma or Grandpa's house, where cookies are sometimes in the cookie jar! Decorate white-paper candy bags with markers, crayons, or colored pencils. Encourage your child to create colorful freestyle drawings or scribbles on the paper bags to be used for birthday treat bags or holiday cookies or candies. (Make this art year-round to create a year's supply for celebrations.)

GIANT CATERPILLAR SIDEWALK DRAWING

Making sidewalk art never goes out of style, and kids love to make something truly colossal with you!

ages 3–5

Materials
- Jumbo (washable) sidewalk chalk (assorted colors)

Get Creative Parents (or caregivers) and preschoolers work together to create a giant colorful caterpillar or other giant creature of your child's choice on the sidewalk using colorful chalk! Make it silly or imaginative: "Hey, does a caterpillar wear shoes on all those legs?" (Supervise carefully to keep your child safe from traffic, bikes, or skateboards.)

WHEN KIDS ASK, "WHAT SHOULD I DRAW?"

Sometimes preschoolers have an immediate idea about what they want to draw and other times they seem stumped about where to begin. If your child asks, "What should I draw?" here are a few comments you can try to prompt your child to discover something in his or her own imagination:

- "Do you want to draw something from one of your favorite books?"
- "Is there a person (or animal) you know that you would like to draw?"
- "Do you want to make a colorful design with your favorite colors?"
- "Do you want to draw something from the outdoors?"
- "Do you want to draw something silly?"

These open-ended questions help your child generate his own ideas and ultimately find more satisfaction creating something in his own special way.

PAINTED-CARDBOARD COLLAGE

Preschoolers start with corrugated cardboard and tempera paints to create a colorful, textured collage.

Materials

- One sheet of corrugated cardboard
- One 11-by-14-inch piece of colored mat board
- Preschool (safety) scissors
- Nontoxic, tempera paint cakes (various colors)
- Nontoxic white glue, such as Elmer's
- Paintbrush
- Newspapers or vinyl tablecloth (to contain the mess)

Setup Parent removes the paper layer from the cardboard to reveal the corrugated ridges. Cut or tear 8 to 10 small rectangles or squares of the textured cardboard for this project. Offer a little help with gluing (see below), too, if needed.

Get Creative Your child squirts glue on the mat board and assembles the cardboard shapes on the sticky surface in any collage design he likes. Let the glue dry for 10–15 minutes.

When it is dry, your child paints the cardboard shapes to create a colorful, textured collage.

MIXED-PAPER COLLAGE

Preschoolers love to sort, cut, and paste different-colored and textured papers to see what they can create.

Materials

- Colored construction paper
- Magazine photos
- One sheet of mat board, poster board, or cardboard for the collage base
- White (nontoxic) glue or glue stick
- Preschooler (safe) scissors
- Optional: Fragments of your child's unfinished (or rejected) drawings or paintings

Get Creative Your child tears or cuts assorted pieces of paper and uses the

ages
3–5

glue stick to create a multicolored and multitextured collage. There are no rules, just a desire to make something original and artful with the materials. Some children enjoy overlapping the papers, some make a puzzle-piece design, and others create designs with a few pieces of paper and lots of empty space on the background. All these and other choices make lovely collages.

BURLAP-AND-BUTTON COLLAGE

Create an interesting artsy collage with scraps of burlap, buttons, clear glue, and mat board!

Materials
- Small scraps of burlap fabric (assorted colors)
- Nontoxic white glue, such as Elmer's
- Fabric scissors (for adult use only)
- One 11-by-14-inch piece of mat board or poster board
- Assorted buttons

Setup Parents use scissors to cut some small scraps of fabric for the project.

Get Creative Your child uses glue and assorted buttons and burlap to create a lovely collage mounted on a piece of mat board of any color. (Help your child apply a little pressure or pat the glued fabric and buttons to hold them in place if needed.)

Glitter-Glue-and-Button Collage
Start with a sheet of mat board. Your child uses glitter-glue pens to create a drawing on the board, and then presses buttons into the glue for an interesting design.

Silky-Fabric Puzzle Collage
Parents—cut small scraps of silky, smooth, or shiny fabric scraps into narrow rectangles (assorted colors). Encourage your child to glue the fabric to a black (or colored) sheet of mat board to create a small lovely collage. One challenge is to suggest that your child make a "puzzle-like" collage, with each little scrap of fabric touching the next. Or just keep the project completely open-ended! (My daughter created a 6-by-8-inch Silky-Fabric Puzzle Collage when she was four years old. We framed it and hung it on the wall many years ago. This delicate, colorful collage is as lovely today as it was twenty years ago. And it's a treasured part of our family art collection!)

WAVY-WATER COLLAGE

Cutting wavy pieces of paper is half the fun for newbie scissor users, and the other thrill for preschoolers is using lots of glue!

Materials

- Construction paper (multiple colors)
- Crayons
- Preschool-style (safe) scissors
- Glue stick or nontoxic white glue, such as Elmer's
- Large sheet of heavy drawing paper (or oversized card stock 11 by 17 inches)

Get Creative Work alongside your child to create your own Wavy-Water Collage while your child creates hers too. First, cut curvy strips of colored paper.

(Note: anything goes here as far as meeting the definition of "curvy." Some kids make choppy little cuts as they go—which is a terrific variation.) Next, assemble them in a design on the heavy paper. And glue the wavy water strips in place. (Experiment with overlapping some of the papers or leaving blank spaces between the waves to create an interesting and unique collage.)

RUBBING COLLAGE

Your child can create a distinctive, colorful collage using crayon rubbings made with a textured, plastic craft mat.

Materials

- One 10½-by-13½-inch plastic canvas for yarn crafts (inexpensive and available at craft supply stores)
- Assorted paper (construction paper, newsprint, colored copy paper)
- Large crayons with paper wrapper removed
- Preschooler (safety) scissors
- 1 large sheet of card stock
- Glue stick
- Optional: 2-inch-wide painter's tape (to hold the paper and plastic canvas while rubbing)
- Optional: foil gift wrapping paper

MAKE A COLLAGE KIT

If you create a little collage kit with supplies, your child will have instant access to collage supplies and will be more likely to make some artful collages when she's in the mood to create! For a preschool-friendly collage kit, designate a box or container (or expanding file case with a handle and pockets) and fill it with assorted papers, fabrics, and materials for collage. Here are some materials to put inside the Collage Kit:

- Assorted buttons
- Cereal and pasta boxes (flattened)
- Colored gift bags (recycled)
- Construction paper
- Corrugated cardboard
- Doilies
- Duplicate family photos
- Fabric scraps (try solid colors of felt, burlap, wool, corduroy, heavy cotton, canvas)
- Foil gift wrapping paper
- Glitter-glue pens
- Magazine photos
- Magazines
- Natural objects: leaves, bark, twigs, moss, small shells, etc. (in a plastic food storage bag)
- Old lace
- Recycled maps

Setup Place the plastic canvas on the work table. Put one sheet of paper over the top. Give a short demo of how to use the side of a crayon to rub back and forth over the paper to create a design. Try another colored crayon to briefly show the effect when two or more colors are rubbed on the same sheet of paper.

Get Creative Your preschooler uses scissors to cut small scraps of the textured rubbings to create a collage on a large sheet of card stock. (Use a glue stick to attach the papers to the card stock or mat board.)

PAINTED-WOOD COLLAGE

Here's a wooden collage project, with painting and gluing, too, for children ages three to five to do with a grown-up!

Materials
- Optional: small 3-to-4-inch foam paint roller and tray
- Paintbrush
- Children's acrylic (or tempera) paint
- 9-by-12-inch (or 11-by-14-inch) sheet of hardboard (available at art supply stores)
- Assorted precut wooden shapes (for example, Woodsies Wood Shapes—220 thin wooden shapes in the package—available from www.dickblick.com)
- Nontoxic white glue, such as Elmer's
- Vinyl tablecloth (place underneath the wood shapes while painting)

Get Creative Use the roller or brush to paint the hardboard, then let the paint dry. Paint an assortment of wooden shapes various colors and let the paint dry. Arrange the painted wood pieces on the hardboard in an interesting design. Glue each piece of wood in place and press firmly (or apply weight on top). Let the glue dry completely before moving your collage.

Painted-Sticks Collage

For a smaller-scale wooden collage, start with a 9-by-12-inch hardboard panel and a package of extra-wide craft sticks instead of wooden shapes. (Use all the other supplies listed above.) Half the fun is painting the sticks different colors and the other half is using the glue to arrange a design on the hardboard.

ages 3–5

ROLLER-PAINTING ABSTRACTS

This is a super-fun outdoor painting project for a child and parent to try together! Go big! Go messy! Go colorful!

Materials

- Outdoor picnic table (or floor of concrete patio)
- Newspaper or vinyl tablecloth (to prevent leaks on table)
- Large roll of butcher paper or brown craft paper
- Painter's tape
- Tempera paints
- Several 2-inch foam rollers and small paint trays (or disposable plastic plates)
- Artist smock (or old adult-sized T-shirt) for your child
- Bucket and water (for cleanup)
- Paper towels

Setup Cover the table with newspaper or an old vinyl tablecloth to contain leaks. Cover with giant sheets of butcher paper. (Use tape to hold in place.) Pour a little paint into the tray. Give a quick demo to show how to dip the roller into the paint and roll it back and forth on the paper.

Get Creative Let your child enjoy the fun of painting with a roller. No rules for this abstract painting, just lots of experimentation. Your child may be happy with one color of paint or he may want to create a design with two or more colors. (Dip the roller in the water bucket to rinse between each color. Use paper towels to dry the roller after its bath!)

Knotty-Roller Painting

Do the same roller-painting idea above, but this time cut two 6-inch pieces of twine or string and tie each one snugly around the foam paint rollers, leaving about ½ inch between each string. (Tie a double knot on each string and trim the ends so there is not excess string.) Now you have a striped roller with some knotty texture to create interesting designs on paper. Dip and dab this roller into the paint to saturate it completely. Then create a design on paper, rolling in any direction, crisscrossing, overlapping, or any other pattern you like. One good challenge is to try to make a complete painting with one soaking of paint; some areas will be full of paint and others will have light washes only. (Repeat the same roller process with a second color of paint if you like.)

RUBBER-BAND PAINTINGS

This painting activity is a little bit like doing batik in that the rubber bands preserve the color underneath!

Materials

- 10 to 12 assorted rubber bands (rubber bands must be ¼ inch wide or wider)
- Children's acrylic paints
- 3 small 2-inch foam paint rollers (available at craft stores)
- 3 disposable plastic plates or containers
- One 5-by-7-inch canvas panel
- Old vinyl tablecloth or newspapers (to contain the mess)

Get Creative Fill each plate with a different color of paint. Help your child put three or more rubber bands around the white canvas panel.

Each rubber band can be positioned diagonally, vertically, or horizontally. Next, dip a roller into the lightest colored paint (yellow, for example) and roll it over the canvas panel without disturbing the rubber bands. (Areas under the first rubber bands will remain white.)

Let this paint dry thoroughly. Next, add four or more rubber bands to the canvas in any configuration you like. Then add the next layer of paint (orange, for example). Let the paint dry. Next, add four or more rubber bands in any direction you like (diagonally, vertically, or horizontally) and add one more layer of paint (red, for example). When done, let the paint dry thoroughly and remove the rubber bands to see your unique design.

CREEPY-CRITTER BEANBAG BOX

Start with a giant cardboard box, add some paints, and encourage your child to create an artistic beanbag-tossing arcade game!

Materials

- Giant cardboard moving box
- Nontoxic tempera paint
- Paintbrush

ages
3-5

PLEASE DON'T ASK "WHAT IS IT?"

When young preschoolers (three to four years old) paint, they are usually just experimenting to see what they can do. Many preschoolers are a bit too young to paint realistic or representational objects, but they are most definitely making art! Don't bother asking, "What's that you're painting?" because it's a question that has no reliable answer. Here's a conversation between a preschooler and a mom who dared to ask:

Mom: "What are you painting, Tommy?"

Tommy (three and a half years old): "Something red!"

Mom: "But what is it?"

Tommy: "It's a red painting!"

Mom: "Is that a house you painted in the middle of the paper there?"

Tommy: "No, it's a picture."

Mom: "But what's that picture supposed to be?"

Tommy: "It's a red picture!"

Mom: "Is that little spot over on this side a tree?"

Tommy: "NO! That's a green picture!"

Mom: "Is that green picture supposed to be grass on the lawn outside?"

Tommy: "No! It's a green painting!"

Grandpa walks into the room

Grandpa: "Hi, Tommy, what a cool red-and-green painting!"

Tommy: "Here, Grandpa, this painting is for you!"

- Scissors (for adult use only)
- Pencil
- Newspapers and wet cloth (to contain the mess)
- Beanbags or socks rolled into tight balls

Get Creative Parents cut the flaps from the top of the box and turn it upside down. Let your child draw (and paint) a giant creature of any kind on the side of the box in any way he or she chooses. (The creature might look like a giant blob—which is perfect for your preschooler artist!) Encourage your child to draw a super-giant mouth on that critter. When the paint dries, cut a big circle from the cardboard to create an opening in the mouth your child painted. Gather up your beanbags or socks and turn this work of art into a beanbag-tossing game.

GIANT DRIZZLE POSTERS

Messy outdoor excitement for one or more preschooler artists!

ages
3–5

Materials

- Children's tempera paints or nontoxic acrylic paints
- Disposable plastic cups
- Large paintbrushes
- Poster board

Setup Select four to six different colors of paint. Pour a small quantity of paint in each cup. Add a little water to make the paints soupy and easy to drizzle.

Get Creative Dab a brush in one color of paint and soak up some paint. Now drizzle or dribble paint on the poster board to make a colorful design. Let the painting dry thoroughly before moving the painting.

SALT-AND-WATERCOLOR PAINTINGS

Shake a little salt on a really wet watercolor painting and a little magic design appears in the process!

Materials

- Children's watercolor paints (in a tray)
- Paintbrush
- Heavy drawing paper or watercolor paper
- Container of water

- Salt in a shaker
- Vinyl tablecloth (to absorb extra paints and contain the mess)

Get Creative Encourage your child to paint a quick watercolor design (one, two, or three colors only) on the paper. Use a little extra water on the brush so that the paper is quite saturated with wet paint. Then shake salt over the wet painting to create an interesting pattern.

COOKIE-SHEET PRINTING-PAINTINGS

These beautiful paintings are quick and easy to make, with your child swirling paint on a cookie sheet, then pressing a sheet of paper on top (with a little help from you).

Materials
- Heavy drawing paper (or water-color paper)
- Set of children's watercolor paints in a tray (or washable tempera paints)
- Chunky paintbrush (½ inch wide or wider)
- Recycled metal cookie sheet (or a sheet of Plexiglas from art supply store)
- Small bucket of water

Setup Parents give a quick little demo by making your own painting on the cookie sheet and pressing a piece of paper on top of it to make a print so your child gets excited about (and understands) this quick painting process.

Get Creative Turn the cookie sheet upside down. (You will paint on the underside of the cookie sheet.) Dip your brush in a liberal amount of water, then dip it in watercolor paint. Dab the brush on the cookie sheet to create a blob or circle of paint. Rinse the brush and dip it into another color and paint a swirl of color around that circle. Repeat with several other colors of soupy, wet paint to create a quick, colorful, circular design. (Be sure to use to use a liberal amount of paint so the cookie sheet is quite wet with color.) Place a sheet of paper on the cookie sheet and firmly rub your hand all over the paper to absorb the paint. Carefully lift one corner of the paper and peel it off to reveal your abstract painting. Now that your child sees the process, let her try her own Cookie-Sheet Paintings!

Salty Cookie-Sheet Paintings

Try the same process described above (Cookie-Sheet Printing-Painting), but this time let your child shake salt all over the painted cookie sheet before you apply the paper on top. (Be sure the paint is very wet and watery before shaking salt on top.) A lovely variation of color and shapes is created in this salt-and-watercolor process.

BUBBLE-WRAP PRINTING

Here's an artful way to get your child to recycle packaging material.

Materials
- Scissors (for adult use only)
- Plastic bubble wrap (with tiny bubbles)
- Approximately 8½-by-11-inch tagboard or hardboard
- 2-inch-wide clear packaging tape
- Newspapers or old tablecloth (to contain the mess)
- Tempera paint cakes (3 to 4 colors) in a plastic holder (or improvise with a disposable pie pan)
- 3 to 4 disposable cups (with water)
- 3 to 4 foam paintbrushes (1 to 1½ inches wide)
- Multipurpose drawing/sketch paper or newsprint paper
- Optional: old rolling pin (or brayer) that can be used exclusively for art

Setup Cut a sheet of bubble wrap a few inches larger than the tagboard. Place the bubble wrap on the table, place the tagboard on top of the bubble wrap, and fold edges over the back of the board. Use tape around the back side of the tagboard to hold the bubble wrap firmly in place. (The front side of this board will be your printing surface.) Place the tablecloth or newspapers on your work surface to contain the mess. Place a teaspoon of water (or slightly more) on each paint cake to create a soupy paint.

Get Creative Encourage your child to dip the first foam paintbrush into one color of paint and soak up as much paint as possible on the brush, then paint it upon any area of the

ages 3-5

PRESCHOOLERS LOVE ART EASELS

An art easel is not essential, of course, but it's a good art accessory (or gift) if your family budget has a little wiggle room. Some children's easels accommodate two artists standing up; other versions are for three or four artists. My favorite easels have a trough for paint containers, and I highly recommend purchasing spill-proof paint containers. (Check out the Melissa & Doug brand 4 Spill-Proof Paint Cups.) You'll also find designs that allow height adjustments to accommodate growing kids and children in wheelchairs too. Here are a few brands to consider: Melissa & Doug Deluxe Wooden Standing Art Easel, KidKraft Deluxe Wood Easel, Little Tikes Double Easel (plastic).

bubble wrap. Repeat this process with two or three additional colors of paint, encouraging your child to cover the entire bubble-wrap surface with random dabs and strokes of paint. (This is an abstract art process, so any spontaneous application of paint is perfect!)

Place the painted bubble wrap on a sheet of paper (painted side down) and use the rolling pin or brayer to apply pressure to the back side of the tagboard. Carefully lift the tagboard off the paper and let the artwork dry.

Rainbow-Stripe Bubble-Wrap Printing
Use the same basic art materials above in the Bubble-Wrap Printing project, but this time your child paints wide stripes of various colors across the

GIVE ABSTRACT ART A CHILD-FRIENDLY LABEL

Preschoolers are fabulous at making abstract art. They experiment with bold colors of paint, shapes, and designs with little concern for making something "real" (or representational). This spontaneous, free-flowing type of art is an important part of childhood creativity.

I'm in favor of calling this freestyle art "design" simply as a way of mentioning it in conversation and of encouraging this style of creativity. For example, a parent might say, "I love your colorful design!" Or a preschooler might announce, "I think I'll make a blue-and-yellow design," when beginning a new painting. This phrase, *making a design,* gives parents and preschoolers a child-friendly way to begin to talk about the process of making art that honors the many ways of being creative and eliminates the pressure to always create something "real," such as a tree, a house, an animal, or a flower.

bubble wrap before pressing the paper on the painted surface. Some children will alternate colors (for example, stripes of blue, then green, then blue, then green), while others will make color choices randomly. When the entire surface of the bubble wrap is filled with painted stripes, press the bubble wrap on the paper, wet-paint-side down, and apply a little pressure. Some children enjoy adding more stripes of paint and pressing on the paper a second time to see what happens.

Paper-Towel Abstract Printing
Use the same art materials listed in the Bubble-Wrap Printing project, but this time instead of bubble wrap, cover the tagboard with a sheet of paper towel as your printing surface. (Remember to place the paper towel upon the tagboard and tape it in place before beginning this project—see page 156 for details.) Encourage your child to fill the entire paper-towel surface with paint and press the printing surface on the newsprint or sketch or drawing paper, then apply

pressure with a brayer, a rolling pin, or your child's hands.

SQUEEZE-BOTTLE PAINTING (OUTDOORS)

Squeeze little blobs of paint from bottles to create a colorful design on paper.

Materials
- Washable (nontoxic) tempera paint in squeeze bottles (for example, Colorations brand)
- Paper or poster board
- Newspaper or vinyl tablecloth (to contain the mess)

Get Creative Put a painter's smock on your child. Give a quick demo on how to position the bottle over the paper and then squeeze the bottle over the paper to create a design. Then let your child get creative.

Giant Color-Blot Posters
Create an activity similar to the Squeeze-Bottle Painting above, but start with a large sheet of poster board placed on a hard floor (concrete or a wooden patio floor works well). Squirt (or drip) a generous amount of different colored tempera paints onto the paper using the squeeze bottle mentioned above. When satisfied with the colors, place another giant sheet of paper or poster board on top of the painted surface and have your barefooted child walk on it to press the colors on both papers in an interesting pattern. Carefully peel the top layer of poster board off to reveal the two designs just created.

BURLAP CIRCLE PRINTS

Here's a clever way to make artful prints with burlap!

Materials
- One 12-by-12-inch piece of burlap fabric (to make each printing can)
- One or more small (6-ounce) tomato paste cans
- One sturdy rubber band (or hair band)
- Washable (nontoxic) tempera paint
- Small disposable plate
- Sheets of drawing paper or colored construction paper

Setup Fold the burlap in half and place the tomato paste can on top. Use a rubber band to hold the fabric tightly in place around one end of the can.

This is your textured printing tool for this project.

Get Creative Your child dips the burlap-covered can in the paint and presses it firmly on the paper, repeating with various colors of paint. Part of the charm of this project is the variation of the prints, with some shapes barely noticeable and others full of intensity. New and unexpected colors can be created by redipping the burlap into different colored paint. Or if your child wants to keep colors distinct, use several burlap tomato cans, each one devoted to a single color of paint.

CORK PRINTING ON FELT

Get an assortment of corks and some felt fabric and make some colorful polka-dot art!

Materials
- Tempera paint
- Disposable plastic plates
- Assorted corks
- Felt fabric (available in assorted colors in 12-by-12-inch squares at craft supply stores)
- Newspapers or vinyl tablecloth and wet sponge (to contain the mess)
- Optional: painter's tape (to hold the felt in place while printing)

NO-SEW PRESCHOOLER ARTIST SMOCKS

Here are a few quick, inexpensive ideas for creating preschooler artist smocks:
- Medium or large adult T-shirt
- Mom or Dad's dress shirt or blouse (cut sleeves off as needed and button it up)
- King-sized pillowcase (use pinking shears to cut a giant hole along the top seam for your child's head to slip through, and two large holes along the side seams, one on the left seam and the other on the right seam) at approximately the correct height to serve as armholes.

With adult supervision, personalize or decorate these smocks with fabric markers.

ages 3-5

160

Get Creative Pour a little paint in a plate and show your child how to dip one end of a cork into the paint. Your child dips and prints repeated or different shapes on the felt to create a design with one or more colors of paint.

Polka-Dot Printing on Paper
Follow the instructions for Cork Printing on Felt (above), but this time your child prints on colored construction paper or poster board. (She can even make note cards, greeting cards, invitations, or small color booklets using this easy cork-printing process.)

Okra or Radish Printing
Try the same printing project mentioned above, but instead of the cork, use a fresh vegetable such as a large piece of cut okra or a radish. (Parent uses a kitchen knife to cut the top off the veggies and discard any seeds.) Pour a small amount of paint into your plate-palette. Show your child how to gently dip the cut edge of the veggie into the paint and press it firmly on the paper. Let your child have the pleasure of making freestyle veggie-print designs.

MAKING BLOB CREATURES WITH CLAY

Preschoolers are a little too young to create realistic animals or people with clay, so here's an enjoyable way to mess around with clay and make simple creatures with giant eyes!

Materials
- Nonhardening modeling clay (such as Sargent Art brand) or play dough
- Recycled cookie sheet
- Optional: fork, spoon, and miscellaneous safe kitchen or play-dough tools

Get Creative Challenge your child to squish, pat, or roll a blobby little creature from clay. These friendly little creatures can be any shape or size your child can create! (Work side by side with your child making your own Blob Creatures too.) Your child can roll and press little clay balls for eyes, or use the handle of a spoon to press eyes into the creature.

MAKING COIL ART WITH CLAY

Older preschoolers can learn to make little coils from clay and pinch, pat, and twist them to see what they can create.

Materials
- Crayola Air-Dry Clay or play dough
- Recycled (repurposed) cookie sheet

Setup Start with a chunk of clay about the size of a silver dollar and place it on the cookie sheet. Give a little demo of how to use fingers (and a little pressure) on both hands to begin a back-and-forth rolling motion to create snakelike (coil) shapes.

Get Creative Let your child experiment with making clay coils and creating freestyle artwork from the coils. Some children will pinch several coils together, some will wind them around into a spiral shape, while others just like the sensation of rolling the coils.

Coiled Coasters
Referring to Making Coil Art with Clay (above), turn your clay coils into functional coasters. Work side by side with your child creating one or more coils, then wind the coils into a circular shape to create a coaster. Let the coasters dry for several days. (Optional: once they are completely dry, let your child paint the coasters with tempera paints.)

MY FIRST CLAY PINCH POT

Next time you and your preschooler host a playgroup, let the children have the fun of pinching balls of clay into little artist pots.

Materials
- White Crayola Air-Dry Clay
- Pencil
- Vinyl tablecloth (to contain the mess on the work table)

Setup Parent cuts one small chunk of clay, about the size of your fist, for each child. Work side by side with your child so he or she sees the process of making a pinch pot.

Get Creative Give a little demo of how to work with clay, with your

ages 3-5

child working alongside on her own pinch pot. First, use your hands to roll the clay into a ball. Push your thumb into the middle of the ball and keep pushing downward until you are about a ½ inch from the bottom. Now pinch the clay with the thumbs and fingers of both hands, rotating the clay pot so that you pinch all the way around the pot. Push slightly, with a bit of pressure, to create a flat bottom on your pot. Continue to pinch all around the pot to thin the sides to a thickness of about ½ to ¼ inch thick. Help your child do these same motions with her clay and fingers. When your pinch pots are finished, use the pencil to carve your initials and your child's initials on the undersides of the pots.

If your child wants to keep the finished pot, let it dry for 4 to 5 days; it should be completely dry and white in color. Optional: let your child use tempera paints to add some color to the pot. (Please note: these pots are decorative only and are not safe for using as food or beverage containers.)

Building and Construction Activities

Children ages three to five enjoy building with blocks, boxes, sand and water, and other child-friendly building materials. The youngest preschoolers may simply play spontaneously with blocks or shoe boxes or take up the challenge of creating a really tall tower. Older preschoolers and kindergartners may be more intentional about what they want to build, starting out with a plan to build a garage, house, or castle and then experimenting and brainstorming to make it happen.

A child might place six blocks end to end and decide this looks like a fence to keep animals in the pasture. And then he may add a toy tractor or stuffed animals to expand on this imaginative play. Or perhaps a kindergartner will hastily place a cookie sheet on top of four cardboard blocks and suddenly get the idea to create a garage. This freewheeling approach to construction is what makes building play such a creative process for preschool and kindergarten kids.

Your child may also be thrilled to get a little experience with real woodworking projects that you yourself have under way. Your three-to-five-year-old child certainly isn't old enough to be around power tools yet, but he can use a sand block to help with a little sanding on a wood project, just to get the feel of working with wood, and the pleasure of building or creating with a grown-up too.

ages
3–5

SOLO BLOCK BUILDING

Preschoolers can have hours of entertainment stacking blocks and creating structures on their own. (It's also a splendid idea for a little self-entertainment while parents are busy cooking, working, or doing chores nearby.)

Materials
- Toddler-friendly blocks (see page 167 for ideas)
- Other miscellaneous building materials, such as empty yogurt containers, butter tubs, or plastic cups

Get Creative Let your child experiment with stacking blocks and other assorted materials to see what she can create. (Some preschoolers jump right in stacking blocks to create a structure, while others take a more reserved approach.)

MIXED-BOX TOWERS AND TOWNS

The shapes of these boxes can jump-start the brainstorming and building process for young children. Help your children transform these boxes into a small town.

Materials
- Assorted shoe boxes
- Medium and large cardboard boxes (recycled from the grocery, automotive, or liquor store)
- Empty oatmeal (round) containers; cereal, rice, or pasta boxes
- Optional: construction paper, markers, scissors (parents use), tape (duct tape for big-box construction or invisible tape or clear packaging tape for small connections)

Get Creative Let your child stack and line up the boxes to see what she can create. Once she's had time to explore the materials, get ready for a parent-child building project. Create a little village of tall buildings (large

PARENTS' BEST APPROACH TO ENCOURAGING PRESCHOOL AND KINDERGARTEN BUILDING CREATIVITY *(Ages 3–5)*

- Have an assortment of age-appropriate building materials easily accessible in the play area.
- Encourage collaborative building projects when your child has a friend over to play.
- Make construction play one of your parent-and-child activities and let your child offer ideas about what to build together.
- Have toys, props, and materials available so your child can embellish and expand her building play into pretend play and art creativity too. (Examples might include toy vehicles, animals and people for pretending, and colored paper and tape to make cardboard structures colorful or fancy.)
- Encourage your child to do solo building projects where she directs her own creative construction. Let her work independently, but be ready to provide a little construction help as needed.
- If your child is superexcited about building, consider a daily routine of building projects while you are cooking dinner. Right before you all sit down for your family meal, circle back to see what your child has created. This is a splendid way to show interest and support for your child's imagination and creativity with building.
- Include preschooler- and kindergartner-friendly building projects in your Family Creativity Night and your child's birthday party too.

cardboard boxes) and one-story buildings (shoe boxes) and use markers to draw windows and doors on the buildings. If you want to get fancy, use colored paper and matching colored duct tape to "paint the buildings" and connect them all together so they look like a downtown block of buildings. Turn one shoe box on its side to create a parking garage and bring out the miniature toy cars to drive inside.

COOKIE-SHEET CONSTRUCTION

Gather up some metal cookie sheets and other household props that are just right for freestyle building projects.

Materials
- Metal cookie sheets (cake pans too)
- Empty yogurt containers or heavy-duty plastic cups
- Optional: cloth dinner napkins, head scarves, dish towels, or pillowcases

Get Creative Let your child experiment with using yogurt containers (upside down) and cookie sheets on the floor to see what he can build. He may discover he can drape a cloth napkin or thin dish towel over the top of a propped-up cookie sheet to create a roof and walls for a building. Or he might create a parking garage for toy cars.

CARDBOARD CASTLE

Gather up several shoe boxes and see what you and your child can create together that might make a clever castle, dollhouse, or building for action figures.

Materials
- Four or more shoe boxes
- Clear packaging tape
- Wallpaper and/or colored-paper scraps and markers
- Scissors (for adult use only)

BEST BLOCKS FOR PRESCHOOLERS

Here are some of my favorite preschooler-friendly building blocks (available online and at local toy stores):
- HABA Little Amsterdam Building Blocks
- Melissa & Doug 60-Piece Standard Unit Blocks (natural wood blocks, unpainted)
- Melissa & Doug Wood Block Set (100 or 200 colored pieces)
- Lincoln Logs Shady Pine Homestead Building Play Set (for children 3 to 5 years)
- Lego Duplo Building Set (71 pieces)

Get Creative Place two shoe boxes side by side and tape the top edges together with clear tape so that you have made a little building (without a roof) with two rooms stuck together. Place two more shoe boxes side by side (in the same way) and tape the top edges together as well. Now join the four shoe boxes together with tape to create a square house with four (open) rooms. Get creative with wallpaper scraps or colored paper taped inside each room to decorate the inside of the miniature rooms. Parents use scissors to cut a door and windows on the exterior walls of the building.

FABRIC FORT HOUSE

What a super way for a parent and child to create a clever table fort together, one that can be used again and again for pretend play.

> *When children build with blocks, they're learning about the physical properties of things. They discover if you don't put the larger block on the bottom, your tower's going to tip over.*
>
> **—DR. MARTI ERICKSON,**
> child development expert, author
> of *Infants, Toddlers, and Families*

Materials

- One recycled flat bedsheet (which you are willing to cut up)
- Painter's tape
- Colored duct tape
- Scissors (parents use)
- Washable nontoxic markers
- Colored construction paper
- Clear 2-to-3-inch-wide packaging tape

Get Creative Drape the sheet over the kitchen table. Use painter's tape on the sheet to mark the edge of the tabletop. (This line of tape shows you where the "roof" of the fort begins.) While the fabric is draped over the table, also use small bits of painter's tape (or a marker) to show where you would like to position windows and door on the fabric fort. Place the sheet on the floor and use duct tape to outline one door big enough for your child to fit through. Use scissors to remove the fabric inside the duct-tape doorway, making the door permanently "open." Use duct tape to outline several windows on the sheet, and then use scissors to remove the fabric inside the duct-tape windows, making the windows permanently "open."

Ask your child to draw flowers on construction paper to hang beneath each window of the fort. Cut around the flower shapes, then tape the flowers below each window using clear packaging tape. (Note: the packaging tape will stick well to the duct tape, so be sure to put small pieces of clear packaging tape onto the duct-tape area for best results attaching the flowers beneath the windows.)

BUILDING OUTDOORS WITH TWIGS AND STICKS

Help your preschooler create a little outdoor habitat with twigs, sticks, grass, and cardboard.

Materials
- Small bucket with a handle
- Small sticks, twigs, or grass (gathered from around the lawn)
- 1 shoe box or small cardboard box

Setup Gather up small twigs and leaves from the yard, and toss your ecobuilding supplies into the bucket as you go.

Get Creative Remove the lid from the shoe box, turn it on its side, and begin to layer the top of the box with leaves or small twigs. Break up larger twigs so they can be stacked along the sides and back of the box to make what appears to be a log cabin, with twigs covering the box.

> *I think the children learn from each other when they work together; they share materials, they observe, they help each other, and they get a sense of adventure from each other.*
>
> —**SUSAN STRIKER**, author of *Young at Art*

BUILDING WITH WET SAND

Parents and preschoolers can work together to build tunnels, buildings, and roads in the sand to experience the joys of creating and building together.

Materials
- Play sand in a sandbox
- Sprinkling can with water
- Plastic containers (such as yogurt cups)

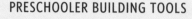

PRESCHOOLER BUILDING TOOLS

There are some good construction toys that are just right for preschoolers' play and pretend. Here are some of my favorite preschooler-friendly toy tools to check out:

- Black & Decker Junior 25 Piece Tool Set
- Learning Resources Pretend & Play Tape Measure
- Green Toys Tool Set (pink or blue tools available)
- Melissa & Doug Take-Along Tool Kit Wooden Toy (24 pieces)

- Small toy sand tools, preschool-safe garden tools, and giant spoons
- Optional: long narrow sheet of cardboard, plastic, or wood (to use for a bridge) and toy cars and trucks

Get Creative Preschoolers love to build in sand alongside a parent or other children. Once they gain a little experience with digging and shaping the wet sand, they will be primed to do interesting solo sand-building projects too. Build a couple of mounds of wet sand and place a narrow sheet of cardboard over the top to create a bridge. Make ramps at both ends of that bridge, using more wet sand to create a road for a miniature car.

SNOW BUILDING

Start a wintertime snow-building tradition in your family.

Materials
- Waterproof gloves for each snow builder
- Small shovel, garden tools, plastic scoops, or containers
- Optional: plastic containers from the kitchen (such as yogurt cups)
- Optional: snow block maker or Snow Castle Kit (3–4 plastic molds to make assorted sizes of snow blocks)

Get Creative Parent and child work together with hands and tools to create a miniature snow fort or igloo. Heap up snowballs or form snow blocks with

ages 3–5

small plastic containers. Then pat the shapes into a building or igloo with hands and tools. Carve out doors and windows and roof and trim.

Build a Serpentine (Curvy) Snow Wall
Instead of snow building with snow blocks, your preschooler may be just as happy to build a miniature serpentine wall that is constructed from wet snow. You can use small plastic tubs to mound the snow into a long curvy shape, then work together with hand tools (and hands) to create the curvy wall.

Music Activities

Children three to five are at a perfect age to get creative with music. They enjoy singing, playing musical games, and creating original songs with parents and friends. They can memorize simple songs quite easily and are thrilled to sing along with other children and parents. They are also super-excited to try out kid-friendly musical instruments, and can often tap along or shake a maraca to the beat of recorded music too.

The musical activities below invite preschoolers and kindergarten-age kids to experiment and see what music they can create. When the focus is on fun and every child is encouraged to participate, musical confidence and appreciation develop quite naturally.

The more fun your child has, the more he or she will want to do musical activities. Along the way your child will come to see that he or she is *musical*! These small steps launch musical creativity in your child's preschool and kindergarten years in a playful, easygoing way. When this spirit of joyfulness is woven into the experience of singing and making music, your child will likely want to get creative with music again and again.

SONG-A-DAY

ages
3-5

Singing a song together gives a little boost of happiness to each day!

Materials
- A few familiar songs that are preschooler-friendly

Get Creative Here's a musical challenge for you and your child: make a commitment to sing one song every day of the week! Blend this routine into your day naturally.

PARENTS' BEST APPROACH TO ENCOURAGING PRESCHOOL AND KINDERGARTEN MUSIC CREATIVITY *(Ages 3-5)*

- Keep the focus on fun. The more enjoyment your child has with music, the greater the connection to music.
- Sing to your child during daily routines and riding in the car together.
- Let your own enthusiasm for music shine through! (You are an influential creative music mentor. If music matters to you, it will likely be enjoyable for your child too.)
- Have age-appropriate music makers available at home. (See the list of preschooler-friendly musical instruments on page 181.)
- Create family traditions that include singing, making music, and musical games.
- Accept your child's way of enjoying music at this age. Some children are reluctant to sing (or play music) at first, but they enjoy listening and observing as others make music.
- Expect preschoolers' music making with instruments to be experimental. They are just exploring and listening to the sounds they create. This is a fine way to lay a foundation for musical creativity.
- Consider participating in a music-appreciation class with your child.
- Go to kid-friendly local music and dance events in your community. Include preschooler- and kindergartner-friendly musical activities in Family Creativity Night and your child's birthday party.

Sing together in the car as you go to and from school. Sing before your child's bedtime. Sing a wake-up song early in the morning. Sing when you prepare food or do kitchen chores together.

TRADITIONAL SONGS FOR PRESCHOOLERS

Sing your favorite tunes to your child and inspire another generation of singers in your family.

Materials

- Traditional songs, folk songs, or current favorites you know

Get Creative Pick a familiar song that is upbeat and enjoyable to sing. It can be a song from your childhood or a current tune you like to sing. You don't need to be a professional singer, just have fun sharing a few songs with your child! Here are some traditional children's songs that are perfect for preschoolers and parents to sing together. Many of these songs are familiar to parents, grandparents, and great-grandparents, reinforcing connections to past generations in a lovely way.

Note: see other classic children's songs in toddler and elementary sections (on pages 89–91 and 278–82). Many of these songs are age-appropriate for preschoolers too.

A-Tisket A-Tasket
A-tisket a-tasket
A green and yellow basket
I wrote a letter to my love
And on the way I dropped it,
I dropped it, I dropped it,
And on the way I dropped it.
A little boy (girl) he picked it up
and put it in his (her) pocket.

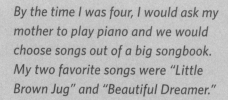

> *By the time I was four, I would ask my mother to play piano and we would choose songs out of a big songbook. My two favorite songs were "Little Brown Jug" and "Beautiful Dreamer."*
>
> —**CATHY FINK,** Grammy Award-winning musician, singer, songwriter

The Farmer in the Dell
The farmer in the dell,
The farmer in the dell,
Hi-ho, the derry-o
The farmer in the dell.
The farmer takes a wife,
The farmer takes a wife,
Hi-ho, the derry-o
The farmer takes a wife.
The wife takes a child,
The wife takes a child,
Hi-ho, the derry-o
The wife takes a child.
The child takes a nurse,

ages
3–5

SINGING EVERY DAY!

Here is a poem I wrote for the children in our family.

Let me know your answer,
Will you sing with me?
Old Susannah wants to hear,
The banjo on your knee.
Can you sing a happy song?
With ears hanging low,

Or wobbling to and fro,
Wherever you may go?
We can sing some silly songs,
To pass the time away,
Loud or soft, fast or slow,
Singing every day!

The child takes a nurse,
Hi-ho, the derry-o
The child takes a nurse.
The nurse takes a cow,
The nurse takes a cow,
Hi-ho, the derry-o
The nurse takes a cow.
The cow takes a dog,
The cow takes a dog,
Hi-ho, the derry-o
The cow takes a dog.
The dog takes a cat,
The dog takes a cat,
Hi-ho, the derry-o
The dog takes a cat.
The cat takes a rat,
The cat takes a rat,
Hi-ho, the derry-o
The cat takes a rat.

The rat takes the cheese,
The rat takes the cheese,
Hi-ho, the derry-o
The rat takes the cheese.
The cheese stands alone,
The cheese stands alone,
Hi-ho, the derry-o
The cheese stands alone.

The More We Get Together
The more we get together,
together,
together,
The more we get together,
the happier we'll be. (repeat)
For your friends are my friends,
And my friends are your friends,
The more we get together,
the happier we'll be.

Mulberry Bush

Here we go round the mulberry bush,
The mulberry bush, the mulberry
*   bush,*
Here we go round the mulberry bush,
So early in the morning.
This is the way we wash our
*   clothes . . .*
So early Monday morning.
This is the way we iron our
*   clothes . . .*
So early Tuesday morning.
This is the way we mend our
*   clothes . . .*
So early Wednesday morning.
This is the way we scrub the floor . . .
So early Thursday morning.
This is the way we sweep the house . . .
So early Friday morning.
This is the way we bake our bread . . .
So early Saturday morning.
This is the way we go to church . . .
So early Sunday morning.

The Muffin Man

Do you know the muffin man,
The muffin man, the muffin man,
Do you know the muffin man,
Who lives on Drury Lane?
Yes, we know the muffin man,
The muffin man, the muffin man,
Yes, we know the muffin man,
Who lives on Drury Lane.

Do Your Ears Hang Low?

Do your ears hang low,
do they waggle to and fro?
Can you tie them in a knot,
can you tie them in a bow?
Can you throw them over your
*   shoulder like a continental soldier?*
Do your ears hang low?
Do your ears stick out,
can you waggle them about?
Can you flap them up and down
as you fly around the town?
Can you shut them up for sure when
*   you hear an awful bore?*
Do your ears stick out?
Do your ears stand high,
do they reach up to the sky?
Do they hang down when they're wet,
do they stand up when they're dry?
Can you signal your neighbor with
*   the minimum of labor?*
Do your ears stand high?

Three Little Monkeys

Three little monkeys
Jumping on the bed,
One fell off and bumped his head.
Mother called the doctor,
And the doctor said,
"No more monkeys jumping on
*   the bed."*
Two little monkeys
Jumping on the bed,

ages
3–5

One fell off and bumped his head.
Mother called the doctor,
And the doctor said,
"No more monkeys jumping on
    the bed."
One little monkey
Jumping on the bed,
One fell off and bumped his head.
Mother called the doctor,
And the doctor said,
"Get those monkeys back to bed."

The Alphabet Song
A-B-C-D-E-F-G
H-I-J-K-L-M-N-O-P
Q-R-S
T-U-V
W-X
Y and Z
Now I've sung my ABC's
Next time won't you sing with me?

B.I.N.G.O.
There was a man who had a dog
And Bingo was his name-O
B.I.N.G.O.
B.I.N.G.O.
B.I.N.G.O.
And Bingo was his name-O.

London Bridge
London Bridge is falling down,
Falling down, falling down,
London Bridge is falling down,
My fair lady.
Build it up with wood and clay,
Wood and clay, wood and clay,
Build it up with wood and clay,
My fair lady.
Wood and clay will wash away,
Wash away, wash away,
Wood and clay will wash away,
My fair lady.
Build it up with silver and gold,
Silver and gold, silver and gold,
Build it up with silver and gold,
My fair lady.
Silver and gold will be stolen away,
Stolen away, stolen away,
Silver and gold will be stolen away,
My fair lady.
We'll set a man to watch all night,
Watch all night, watch all night,
Set a man to watch all night,
My fair lady.

> *Children with special needs can experience the same benefits from music as children without special needs. They may improve their language, their social interactions, their overall cognitive awareness and engagement, and their physical movements.*
>
> **—DR. KRISTI SAYERS MENEAR, PHD,**
> Certified Adapted Physical Educator

SONG BASKET

Here's a charming musical activity for parents and preschoolers or preschool playgroups!

Materials
- Paper
- Markers
- Basket or shoe box

Setup Brainstorm with your child about the songs she already knows and write a different song on each of several scraps of paper. Fold the papers in half and drop them in the basket.

Get Creative Let your child select a song from the Song Basket and the two of you can sing the tune together, or else each of you sings a solo song. Include other family and friends into this musical routine too.

> *I think music-play, prior to formal music lessons is just what the doctor ordered. The goal of these activities is to help the children become musical, that is, to become tune-ful, beat-ful, and artful. Then, once they are musical, if they choose to pursue more formal music study, they will be more successful.*
>
> **—JOHN FEIERABEND,** artist director of the Feierabend Association for Music Education and author of *The First Steps in Music*

HOORAY FOR SILLY PRESCHOOL SONGS!

Homemade silly-songs can be hilariously creative. You can sing in the voice of a big, gruff bear or waddle around quacking a song like a duck named Waldo! There's more going on in this happy scenario than meets the eye. For starters, your child is watching, listening, and soaking up your willingness to be playful and inventive with music. And because your preschooler loves to imitate what you do, this silliness provides an invitation for your child to become musically creative (and sometimes silly) too.

ages 3–5

Picture-Song Basket

In this version of Song Basket, make a list of the songs your child knows and create little icons or quick line drawings to represent each song. (For example, "Mary Had a Little Lamb" could have a simple sketch of a lamb on a scrap of paper.) Fold these pieces of paper and toss them into the basket. Let your child select a song from the basket and "read" it to you and everyone sings.

SONG SAGE

Your older preschool child (four or five years old) becomes the music teacher in this lovely way for parents and children to make music.

Get Creative Once a week, when you are in the car or sharing a quiet moment together, ask your child if he has learned any new songs at school that he can teach you. Listen carefully while your child sings the song once or twice through and you join in to sing along on the next round.

CREATE A SILLY ANIMAL SONG

Pick a familiar song and change it up to create your own Silly Animal Song together.

Materials

- Familiar children's tunes to use as samples (and a dose of imagination)

Get Creative Ask you preschooler to come up with one animal that he would like to sing about! (Pig? Pony? Skunk? Anything goes!) Pick a familiar melody. ("Yankee Doodle Dandy" is a spirited tune that is easy to adapt.) Create one singable line to get started and just keep ad-libbing more lines to create a song. Don't strive for perfection, just take a creative leap and have some fun. (Keep your day job!)

Here is a sample Silly Animal Song I created (sung to the tune of "Yankee Doodle") to encourage you to create a song to delight your preschooler, too.

Danny Donkey

Danny Donkey went to town,
A riding on a tractor,
He drove so fast he lost his hat,
And the goats came chasing after.
Danny Donkey slow it down
Danny Donkey Dandy,
Grab your cap and hold it tight
Or your hat will be goat-candy!

Create a Fill-in-the-Pause Song

Here's an easy way to enjoy inventing songs together, with your child offering up ideas too. You (parent or caregiver) sing the first part of each line of a familiar song, then make a very long pause and ask your child to create something new to sing to fill in the blank. You can give a little demo of how this works with an older child or second adult filling in the long pause with new lyrics. Fill in the blanks to create your own silly verses for a new version of "She'll Be Comin' 'Round the Mountain." (Check out the original lyrics to "She'll Be Comin' 'Round the Mountain" on page 282.) Here are some sample fill-in-the-blank lines to serve as an example:

- She'll be drivin'____(example: "a magic carpet, when she comes")
- She'll be wearin'____(example: "a football helmet, when she comes")
- We'll all have ____(example: "a hot fudge sundae, when she comes")

MUSICAL-ECHO SONGS

This musical activity gives your child a chance to create his own little melody for you to sing or hum along to!

Materials
- Xylophone, glockenspiel, or any other easy musical instrument

Get Creative Give a little demo of how to tap any three notes on the xylophone—1-2-3—and then pause and tap one final note. Let your child tap three or four notes and then a long pause while you sing (echo) those same notes right back singing, "La-la-la la."

EXPERIMENT WITH PRESCHOOLER-FRIENDLY MUSICAL INSTRUMENTS

Purchase a few of these favorite instruments and start a small collection for your child that might grow over the years at holidays and birthdays.

Materials
- Sand blocks
- Tambourine

ages 3–5

UPBEAT AND CREATIVE MUSIC FOR PRESCHOOLERS

Here are three award-winning collections of children's songs that serve as delightful examples of musical creativity:

- *Singable Songs Collection* by Raffi. This collection includes some traditional favorites along with playful and silly original songs that children three to five will enjoy.
- *Grandma Slid Down the Mountain* by Cathy Fink. A collection of fourteen lively and sometimes wacky songs for young children. Available on the artist's website: www.cathymarcy.com.
- *Sunny Day* by Elizabeth Mitchell (produced by Smithsonian Folkways of the Smithsonian Institution). A collection of folk tunes for children that celebrate the wonder of the natural world and the beauty of everyday routines. These songs are geared toward young children and feature Elizabeth Mitchell and her young daughter singing together, and include a children's choir too.

- Musical shakers
- Kid's accordion
- Chimalong (similar to xylophone)
- Lap harp (similar to Autoharp)
- Ukulele
- Harmonica
- Recorder
- Child's (toy) piano

Get Creative Pick just a few instruments to get started. Create a Music Box or designate a cupboard or shelf to hold these instruments so your child has easy access for spontaneous music making. Give a little demo on the basic way to use a new instrument and let your child experiment or create simple tunes. (Check out more preschooler-friendly musical instruments in the toddler section on page 97.)

SING A SONG FROM YOUR HERITAGE

Consider teaching your child a few songs that reflect your heritage, or favorites from past generations in your family. It's an excellent way to keep traditional tunes running through the generations of your family.

I sang the first verse and the chorus of the Irish favorite "Molly Malone" to my children when they were young. (I sang only the kid-friendly parts of the classic tune to keep things upbeat!) It is now twenty years later, and my daughter is a professional musician who sings "Molly Malone" from time to time whenever she performs with a local Irish band. It's a delight for me to see how this favorite parent-and-child song has been recycled by the singers in our family.

I include the words from several verses of "Molly Malone" (below) in case you'd like to share a part of this lovely Irish favorite with your child too.

Molly Malone

In Dublin's fair city where girls are so pretty,
I first set my eyes on sweet Molly Malone.
She wheeled her wheelbarrow
Through streets broad and narrow
Crying, "Cockles and mussels alive, alive-o,
Alive, alive-o, Alive, alive-o,"
Crying, "Cockles and mussels alive, alive-o."
She was a fish monger and sure 'twas no wonder
For so was her father and mother before,
They wheeled their wheelbarrows
Through streets broad and narrow,
Crying, "Cockles and mussels, alive, alive-o,
Alive, alive-o, Alive, alive-o,"
Crying, "Cockles and mussels alive, alive-o."

ages 3-5

HAVE FUN WITH A TOY PIANO

Yes, it's just a little toy piano, but it may spark some interest in music making that may lead to a bigger keyboard in the future.

Materials

- Toy piano (for example, Melissa & Doug Learn-to-Play Piano)
- Optional: children's color-coded piano songbook (available with some toy pianos)

Get Creative The littlest musicians will enjoy exploring their piano's high and low notes and with making loud and soft sounds. More experienced "maestros" can follow a color-coded songbook to learn child-friendly favorites!

HOMEMADE BONGOS

This little set of drums is enjoyable for parents and kids to make together and simple and satisfying for preschoolers to play. (It's easy on the ears too.)

Materials

- Two extra-large sheets of construction paper (12 by 18 inches)
- Markers
- Scissors (for adult use only)

> *Parents—remember, your kid thinks you are a star, and all they care about when you are singing together is that you are singing together!*
>
> —**CATHY FINK**, Grammy Award–winning musician, singer, songwriter

- Two empty cardboard oatmeal or bread crumb containers (with lids)
- Clear packaging tape or invisible tape
- Duct tape

Get Creative Encourage your child to create a colorful design on the two large sheets of construction paper with the markers. Then cut and use this artwork to cover each of the "bongos," using clear tape to hold the paper in place around each of the two oatmeal containers. Put the plastic lids on the two drums and stand the containers upright, placing them side by side (with lids touching). Wrap the duct tape around the midsection of the first drum. Once the tape is nearly all the way around that first drum, lay the two drums on the table (side by side) and continue wrapping duct tape around the second drum. Now your homemade bongos are ready for your child's tapping and can launch his music-making creativity into action.

MUSICAL EGG SHAKERS

These little shakers are easy to make and create a pleasant sound.

Materials
- Six empty plastic Easter eggs
- Six different raw grains and dried beans (one for each egg), such as: rice, macaroni noodles, navy beans, garbanzo beans, pinto beans, and lentils
- Clear packaging tape

Setup Open each plastic egg and put 1 to 2 tablespoons of one type of grain, bean, or dried pasta into each plastic egg. Wrap the midsection of each egg with tape to hold the shakers firmly together.

Get Creative Encourage your child to experiment with shaking the shakers, loud and soft, fast and slow, to create a variety of musical sounds. Your child might also have fun testing each shaker to hear the slightly different sounds created by each type of bean or grain inside!

CLASSICAL MUSIC FOR LITTLE KIDS

Don't be shy about introducing kids to classical music. *First Steps in Classical Music: Keeping the Beat!* compiled by Child Development Music Specialist Dr. John Feierabend, is a child-friendly collection of classical tunes. Each track is short, uplifting, and perfect for rhythm, dance, and active listening. (Each piece included on this CD is approximately 2 minutes long, making this a good way for young children to sample classical music.) This CD is available online at www.amazon.com and other CD sellers.

ages 3–5

WHAT PLEASANT SOUNDS FROM A CHIMALONG

The Chimalong is a musical instrument created by Woodstock Chimes (www.woodstockchimes.com) that is made up of eight precision-tuned aluminum musical pipes. Children use two rubber-tipped mallets to play around with musical sounds or tap out a melody—without driving their parents out of the room (it produces a lovely sound)! A little songbook is included and allows older children to play melodies by color-coded instructions. The Chimalong is available at toy stores and online at various retailers.

TUBE KAZOO

This old-time music maker sounds a bit like a kazoo and is fascinating for kids to try!

Materials
- One or more empty toilet paper rolls (cardboard)
- Waxed paper
- Rubber bands or ponytail ties

Setup Stretch one layer of waxed paper over each end of the cardboard tube and secure it in place with rubber bands.

Get Creative Show your child how to hum over the Tube Kazoo to make a vibrating, musical sound. Here's a tip to help you demonstrate kazoo sounds: Hold the Tube Kazoo upright and place your bottom lip firmly up against the waxed paper near the top side of the kazoo. Open your mouth a bit so that your top lip hovers just over the top (waxed paper) drumhead on the kazoo. Now hum a tune singing "who-who-who" sounds rather than words. (Try humming the song "I've Been Working on the Railroad" with this "who-who" sound.) Experiment with the placement of your mouth and sounds until you get a genuine kazoo sound. Encourage your child to give it a try and see what sounds she can create with a similar humming technique.

CIRCLE SHAKERS

These funky musical shakers take 5 minutes to make and give hours of play-along, musical enjoyment to preschoolers. (Check out five more homemade musical instruments just right for preschoolers on pages 98–99.)

Materials

- Two small paper or plastic disposable plates (appetizer or dessert size)
- Markers or crayons
- Dried beans, such as pinto, navy, split peas, or kidney beans
- Stapler (for adult use only)
- Duct tape (extra wide)

Get Creative Flip each plate upside down and encourage your child to draw (or scribble) on the underside of each. Put one plate (right side up) on the table and sprinkle 3 to 4 heaping tablespoons of dried beans on that plate. Place the second plate on top of the first plate in the upside-down position (creating a flying-saucer shape). Use the stapler to staple the two plates together around the edges. Cover the edge of the shaker with duct tape to cover all the staples and hold the shaker together. Show your child how to hold and use the shakers to make music.

MUSICAL SERENADE

Some preschoolers love to set up a little stage and give a performance at home.

Materials

- Any musical instrument a parent (or grandparent or caregiver) can play

> " *If you have a piano or keyboard, just sitting with your child on your lap and then plunking out a little song with them is a wonderful activity.* "
>
> **—STEPHANIE STEIN CREASE**, author of *Music Lessons*

ages 3–5

Get Creative Give your child the spotlight by encouraging him or her to sing a familiar song all the way through while you provide the musical accompaniment on piano, guitar, or any other instrument. Practice a little together and put on a one-song musical performance for family or friends at your next family get-together.

UP-DOWN MUSICAL SOUNDS

Here's an easy way to introduce your child to the variety of sounds and patterns a musical instrument can make.

Materials
- Xylophone, toy piano, or glockenspiel

Setup Introduce your child to the Up, Up, Up (higher, higher, higher) musical game. Tap a key at a low- or mid-range register and move up the musical scale, tapping each key and singing "Up, up, up" (or "La-la-la") as you go higher.

Get Creative Encourage your child to sing along in his own playful way as you tap out notes. Then, let your child become the music maker, tapping out notes going up, up, up or down, down, down, with you singing along to his melody.

FOLLOW-THE-LEADER DRUMBEATS

Try this music activity with everyone in the family or try it with a group of kindergarten children!

Materials
- Bongos (see page 183 for instructions on how to make them)

Get Creative A parent or older child is the drum leader and he or she picks an easy-to-follow beat. The leader plays their chosen beat slowly and deliberately on the drum, pauses, and then the child (or group of children) echoes that same beat back again (with you playing the beat softly too). Note: if your preschooler is very young, simply tap a slow, consistent rhythm and your child echoes your beat as best he can. If your child is an older preschooler, you can vary your beat and challenge your child to echo the beat, for example, with two slow beats, then three quick beats in a row.

Dance Activities

All children three to five years old can be creative and imaginative with dance. The very best way to think of dance in this stage is quite simply *playful movement to music*!

Children ages three to five are thrilled to try whimsical, interpretive dances with others, and will readily take up the challenge to "dance like a tree blowing in the wind" or "dance like a playful kitten." They enjoy silly follow-the-leader dancing and can sometimes mimic the dance steps of others quite accurately. Or they may choose to resist the "follow" part of the activity and prefer instead to be a leader of their own freestyle dancing. Every child approaches dance in his or her own unique way.

Fun is the magic ingredient in these dance scenarios for children, but a great deal is going on behind the scenes too. Children are developing a comfort and familiarity with dance. They are expanding their coordination and their ability to move to the beat of the music. They are sometimes imagining a creature or animal or theme and putting that idea into their own expressive movements. (This is how they begin to translate imagination into action.) And older kids in this age range may be able to memorize a few dance steps and perform a short choreographed dance with other children.

Much of this creative development with dance happens naturally during the three to five years when children are given opportunities to engage in dance activities. You are an important promoter of dance creativity for your child. And you can set the stage for your child's creativity with your enthusiasm and by setting aside time for your child to have fun with dance activities.

ages 3-5

ZOO ZOMBA

Just imagine how all the animals in the zoo might dance and then do your very best imitation.

Materials
- Recorded music with a danceable beat (appropriate for preschoolers)

Get Creative Explain to the children that Zoo Zomba is a dance activity where each of the dancers pretends to dance like many different animals. Select one grown-up or older sibling to be the dance leader (caller) for the first round or two of dancing.

Before your turn on the music, ask the children if they are familiar with the animals in the zoo. Call out a few of the animals in your dance routine and ask if anyone knows how that animal moves? ("Can anyone show us how an elephant moves?" for example.)

PARENTS' BEST APPROACH TO ENCOURAGING PRESCHOOL AND KINDERGARTEN DANCE CREATIVITY *(Ages 3-5)*

- Have an upbeat collection of danceable music available for your child to turn on whenever she or he is in the mood to dance.
- Create a dance costume box, with a few recycled hats, silk scarves, dance outfits, and props.
- Encourage dance activities whenever your child has playmates or play-groups over to play.
- If your child is reluctant to dance with a group, be respectful and accepting of his preference and let your child warm up to the idea over time. (Some reluctant dancers will nevertheless join in dance activities with one playmate or parent with ease—so give this a try.)
- Create your own entertaining dance traditions at family celebrations, with all generations dancing. (Consider a Musical Birthday March, page 49, during birthday celebrations and outdoor dance activities at family picnics and reunions.)
- Include preschooler-friendly dance activities in your Family Creativity Night.
- If your child shows an interest in dance lessons, pick a class in your community that is age-appropriate with a focus on fun movement and dance activities with others.

Then turn on the music and the dance leader calls out a specific animal—"bear," for example—to begin the dance. The dance leader and all the other dancers give their best interpretation of that animal dancing around the room. (Older kids may be capable of adding some dance steps to their animal interpretations too: twirling, bopping, bending, swaying.) A few moments later the dance leader calls out another animal—"peacock," for example—and leads the children in a peacock dance.

Here are some ideas for Zoo Zomba routines that are preschooler-friendly.

Make up some moves and give it a try!

Elephant Stomp

Imagine you have huge, heavy feet and one giant trunk. Now dance around the room in your very best elephant style.

Peacock Strut

Get some colorful streamers (or scarves) and prance and dance around the room like a proud peacock.

Kangaroo Hippity-Hop

Figure out a way to hop to the music like a graceful kangaroo and use those arms to add more excitement to your style.

Penguin Popper

Create your best impression of a dancing penguin who wiggles and waddles and pops to the music.

Turkey Trot

Create an energetic dance for a happy gobbler, with long legs and a wobbly neck too. Use your imagination to invent other moves (and sounds) that a turkey might make on the turkey disco dance floor!

Wacky-Waddle (Ducks)

Invent a dance step that is just right for those big webbed feet of a dancing duck. Add a wiggle or a waddle or a quack to the music.

Monkey Mash

Some silly monkeys might twist and shout, and others might shimmy and shake. Put on a monkey hat and create your best monkeyshine dance routine.

HAPPY-HOPPIN' DANCE PARTY

Host a preschooler-friendly dance party filled with energetic music and dance activities! Appoint a friendly, easygoing parent to be the dance-party leader. Turn on the music and let the dance party begin with one or two adults leading the activities. Some of the dancing can be copycat (follow the leader), some can include favorite preschool dance activities like: Zoo Zomba, Magic Dancing Beans, or Trees in the Wind, and add some freestyle dancing too.

Ballerina Bear

Turn on the music, grab your tutu, and pretend to be a Bear Ballerina gliding across the stage in a dance performance at the zoo.

MAGIC DANCING BEANS

Preschoolers have their own charming ideas about what magic means, and here's a chance to put those ideas into dance.

Materials
- Recorded music with a good dance beat

Get Creative When the music plays, dance around like a magical dancing bean. How does a magical dancing bean dance? That's up to you! And when the music stops, sit down quickly. When the music starts up again, jump up quick as you can and dance around the room like a magical dancing bean again.

Freeze Dancing

Preschoolers enjoy doing another version of Magic Dancing Beans, in which they dance enthusiastically, then freeze (or stop) when the music stops! Put on some music and let one grown-up or older sibling stop and start the music.

TREES-IN-THE-WIND DANCING

These dancing trees have fingers and arms that wave in the wind and a tree trunk that spins around and around.

Materials
- Recorded instrumental music with a windy, wavy feel to it

Get Creative Challenge the children to pretend to be trees—dancing in a wind, with a soft, medium, or strong wind blowing! You might give a quick little chat about the trunk of the tree (your midsection) and the branches of the tree (your arms) and the leaves of the tree (your hands), to get all the tree parts moving to the music.

> "Activities that foster creativity provide children with special needs an opportunity to express their developmental strengths and individualism while integrating their skills and abilities across multiple domains."
>
> —DR. KRISTI SAYERS MENEAR, PHD, Certified Adapted Physical Educator

ages 3–5

Butterflies Dancing

Challenge the group of preschoolers to dance like butterflies on a beautiful spring or summer day and see what spontaneous, expressive dance moves the children can invent.

Pretend Activities

The preschool and kindergarten years are a fabulous time for make-believe and pretend. Children enjoy costumes, puppet shows, acting out fantasy scenes, pretending to be a truck driver or chef, playing Guess-What-I'm-Doing charade games, and inventing make-believe scenarios for dolls, stuffed animals, and action figures.

Much of this pretend gets under way when children have access to props and toys that engage their imaginations. For example, the youngest children will use a toy cell phone or kitchen set to pretend to be a grown-up chatting or cooking in the same way as their parents. Kindergarten kids are likely to use props and imagination for more elaborate fantasy play; a sword creates a scene for a knight, or a sparkly crown launches "princess pretend."

One of the charming things about make-believe during the three-to-five-year-old stage is that children often talk out their imaginative ideas as they create their scenes. A child playing alone may give a play-by-play account of feeding their baby doll, for example, or filling up their fire truck with gas. Or when a child pretends with others, one child may assume the role of director and the others are actors upon the stage receiving directions of what to do next.

When your child engages in the pretend activities below, imagination and creativity are in high gear. Your job is to provide a few simple toys and props, time, and encouragement for dabbling in pretend creativity. These make-believe experiences will engage your child's imagination and allow your child to experiment with a playful, child-friendly version of acting.

ages
3-5

WORKER PRETEND PLAY

Preschoolers just love to pretend to be the grown-up workers!

- Create a dress-up box with assorted hand-me-down or recycled hats, clothing, accessories, boots, shoes, backpacks, purses, briefcases, and other costumes for pretend play. (See "Create a Dress-Up Box for Preschoolers" in sidebar on page 196.)
- Have safe toys and household props on hand and encourage your child (and playmates) to enjoy freestyle pretend play. (For ideas, see "Household Items to Launch Freestyle Pretend Play for Preschoolers" on page 200.)
- Have a special low cupboard in the kitchen that is filled with safe, nonbreakable kitchen items so your child can pretend to make dinner while you are making the real thing.
- Encourage your child to do pretend activities with playmates and playgroups at your home. (This is a terrific alternative to screen-time activities.)
- Have an assortment of easy-to-use puppets and put on a puppet show with your child as a quick, enjoyable way to enter the world of pretend together.
- Include preschooler-friendly make-believe ideas in your Family Creativity Night.

Materials
- Toys for pretend play
- Assorted safe household props

Get Creative This spontaneous pretend play is one of the very best ways for your child to enjoy acting in a make-believe world. The secret to inspiring this sort of play is just having assorted props, toy tools, toy kitchen set, vehicles and dress-up clothes!

Here are a few of the top preschool worker-pretend ideas, with a list of props to jump-start the play:

Fix-It (Repair Shop)
Help your child set up a fix-it bench and toy tools. An apron, ruler, safety goggles, rags, and a toy wagon can make for some fun extra props. When your work station is set up, ask your child what he wants to fix first. A toy

CREATE A DRESS-UP BOX FOR PRESCHOOLERS

Every creative child needs a box of costumes and cast-offs to launch pretend play and theatrics. Round up clothing and accessories for a dress-up box over several weeks of sorting and scavenging through closets, secondhand stores, or yard sales. Or have an annual Dress-Up Box shopping spree. Start a (low-cost) family tradition of finding interesting dress-up clothes at your local secondhand store or yard sales. Look for adult clothing items that can easily be cut or altered to create costumes: worker shirts and glittery party tops (cut into child-sized pretend party dresses). Find purses, wallets, accessories, and ballerina outfits too. You may find recycled Halloween or holiday costumes, hats, and assorted pretend-play props too. Set a small annual budget for dress-up costumes and make this into an exciting scavenger hunt in the family.

Schedule a family dress-up party at home. Include kids, parents, grandparents, and aunts and uncles too. Have a picnic in the living room or order pizza. Sort through the dress-up collection (above) and let everyone try on items to create silly, mismatched costumes! This is a magnificent way to launch your child's interest in solo dress-up/pretend play. Here are some ideas to get you started:

- One large plastic tub or box with a lid (aka "the costume box")
- Assorted recycled clothing and accessories:
- Hats (see Hats Galore on page 108 for ideas)
- Bow tie
- Briefcase, backpack, wallets
- Capes
- Disguise glasses (with big plastic nose and eyebrows, and so on) or plastic toy glasses
- Gloves (dressy gloves, old leather gloves, mittens, ski gloves)
- Jewelry
- Leotards

→

ages 3-5

- Mesh curtains (for brides, ghosts, gowns)
- Plastic swimming fins and snorkeling gear
- Purses
- Scarves
- Shawls
- Shirts (Hawaiian shirts, sleeveless T-shirts, worker shirts with names embroidered on them)
- Shoes (work boots, snow boots, slippers, sandals)
- Swimming trunks
- Vests

lawn mower? A tricycle? Let your child's imagination launch his own way of fix-it pretend play.

Animal Doctor

Here's a good imaginative play activity for one or two preschoolers who act out scenes helping sick animals. Put together a doctor kit for your little

veterinarian—cotton pads, an Ace bandage (or scarves), and empty spice jars (for pretend medicine) to help round out other traditional toy doctor tools. For solo play your child is the doctor and the stuffed animals are her patients. Two or more kids can ad-lib pretending to be the doctor and pet owners, with playful scenarios full of sound effects and drama from the animals!

Truck Driver

Preschoolers love to imitate what they see real truckers do. They drive a big rig, pretend to pump gas, fix the engine, go into a truck stop, and talk on the phone! Help your child gather up toys and props to get the big-rig-pretend started: a riding toy for the truck (or else a large cardboard box for your child to climb inside), a trucker hat, maps, toy walkie-talkie (or toy cell phone), wallet with pretend money, toolbox, and a toy gas pump.

Firefighter

Many kids ages three to five are enthralled with fire trucks and sirens and they love to pretend to be firefighters too. Just a few props and toys can get this play started: a ride-on toy fire truck (or a giant cardboard box painted red); a small, recycled garden hose (aka the fire hose); a toy firefighter's hat, yellow parka or pretend firefighter clothes and suspenders, rubber boots.

Police Officer

For solo police play, preschoolers love to pretend to be an officer chasing speeders, turning on the siren, and giving out speeding tickets!

When two or more children play, they may go outside to chase the bad guys around the lawn or set up a stakeout. Gather up some props to help your child's imaginative play get started: a ride-on toy for the police car, a hat, a toy badge, and handcuffs are essential; toy cars with plastic people (drivers who get speeding tickets); a walkie-talkie or cell phone; a jacket, boots, and sunglasses round out the costume. And don't forget a small notepad and pencil for writing traffic tickets!

Schoolteacher

When one child plays "school" or "teacher," the stuffed animals are the students and everyone is assigned a name. The teacher gives out assignments, reads stories, and takes the children out to recess or on field trips. Two or more preschoolers will ad-lib spontaneous school scenes; sometimes a teacher gets cross and students go to the principal's office too. The props needed to jump-start the play are: assorted school supplies, a small desk or kitchen table, books, and stuffed animals. Sometimes a simple challenge from a parent helps start the make-believe action: "Could you tell a story to the students [animals] in your pretend classroom?"

ages 3–5

Barbershop or Hair Salon

Freestyle-barbershop-pretend is fun for solo play, or it can be a lively way to play with a friend or a parent, who pretends to need a haircut and a shave! Help your child gather up the props needed for the first round of play: a stool or chair (for the customer), magazines, a towel or folded bedsheet for the barber's cape, and a toy barber kit with combs, brush, toy clippers, and pretend razor. (Be sure to say, "No cutting of hair, only pretend!") For the girl's version of hair-salon-pretend add a toy hair dryer and brush, curlers, barrettes, headbands, plastic tub, and pretend nail accessories for soaking-and-manicure-pretend. Include a large-size doll (or Raggedy Ann) as the customer. To mix a little money-pretend into this business, add a toy cash register, toy money, and empty plastic bottles (for hair products for sale).

SUPERHERO (OR HEROINE)

The props get mixed with your child's imagination to create a satisfying round of saving the day!

Materials
- A superhero cape (see next project)
- Colored tights
- A helmet, headgear, or crown (see page 109 to make an easy crown)
- Magic wand or toy sword (see page 203 to make a magic wand)
- Belt to hold magic wand or toy sword

Get Creative Costumes set the stage for superhero play, so provide a few props and let your child's imagination invent a delightful way of pretending to be a superhero coming to the rescue.

MAKE A QUICK (NO-SEW) SUPERHERO CAPE

Every superhero needs a cape to get his magical powers working!

Materials
- Scissors (for adult use only)
- One recycled adult-sized T-shirt (a dark or bright color is best)
- Two 10-by-10-inch pieces of felt in different colors
- Nontoxic white glue, such as Elmer's

HOUSEHOLD ITEMS TO LAUNCH FREESTYLE PRETEND PLAY
FOR PRESCHOOLERS

Children ages three to five are wonderfully clever at turning ordinary household items into props for imaginative play. A cardboard box might become a rocket ship! Yogurt cups might become dishes for animals at the pet shelter. A plastic kitchen funnel might become a party hat for a teddy bear. These props are already in your home, so gather up a few safe ones and let your child's imagination put them to good use. Here are some favorite household items and toys for freestyle make-believe:

- Assorted kitchen utensils: ladles, scoops, measuring cups and spoons, whisk, rolling pin
- Cardboard boxes and shoe boxes
- Catalogs, magazines, maps, tour books, coupons
- Child-sized life jacket (or water vest)
- Cloth tote bags or book bags
- Colander
- Empty plastic food containers with lids
- Empty plastic spice jars
- Kitchen timer
- Laundry basket
- Muffin tins or plastic ice cube trays (great for sorting pretend coins)
- Office supplies: small calculator, notepad, briefcase, file folders, envelopes, address labels
- Paper lunch bags and paper grocery bags
- Plastic bucket
- Poker chips
- Recycled backpacks
- Recycled bedsheets, tablecloths, towels (for pretend picnics, forts, capes)
- Small cooler with handle
- Small recycled suitcase
- Wooden clothespins

ages 3–5

Get Creative Use scissors to remove the sleeves from the shirt. Make a vertical cut up the front of the shirt, from the bottom hem to 1 inch below the neckline (keep the neck of the shirt intact). Cut a large diamond shape from the first piece of felt to create a superhero logo to glue to the front of the cape. Use scissors to cut the letter of your child's name from the second piece of felt and glue it to the felt diamond. Place a heavy stack of books on top to apply pressure while it dries. When the glue is thoroughly dry, remove the books and the cape is ready for superhero action! Just slip your child's head through the neck of the shirt and let the make-believe begin.

KNIGHTS AND DRAGONS MAKE-BELIEVE

The pretend dragons can be friendly or fierce. It's all up to your child's imagination.

Materials
- Knight's tunic (see next project for directions to make your own)
- Toy sword
- Large belt with buckle (borrowed from mom or dad)
- Toy helmet, crown, or knight's hood
- A village or castle to defend!

Get Creative Some preschoolers may want to create a village to defend (with blocks, forts, and so on); others may battle or chase a dragon (stuffed animal).

MAKE AN EASY NO-SEW KNIGHT'S TUNIC

Parents do the cutting and children do the decorating to create a colorful garment for Knights in Shining Armor pretend play.

Materials
- Scissors (for adult use only)
- One plain recycled adult-sized T-shirt (in a dark or bright color)
- One 12-by-12-inch square of felt fabric
- Glitter-glue pens
- Nontoxic white glue, such as Elmer's

Get Creative Use the scissors to remove both sleeves from the T-shirt. Cut a scalloped edge around the bottom of the shirt. Cut a large crest or shield shape from the felt. Let your child use the glitter-glue pens to decorate or create designs on the felt shield. Let the glue dry thoroughly for an hour or longer. When completely dry, glue the felt shield on the T-shirt. (Press firmly.) Let the glue dry thoroughly. Once dry, your knight's tunic is ready to be used for fantasy play!

MAKE A ROBIN HOOD VEST

Parent and child work together coloring and cutting to create an easy costume for pretend play as Robin Hood!

Materials

- One large paper grocery sack—turned inside out so there is no logo ink on the outside
- Scissors
- Pencil
- Markers
- Colored wrapping paper and/or colored construction paper
- Tape
- Optional: a hat, plastic sword, or a stick horse for Robin Hood to ride

Get Creative Fold and flatten the bag and place the bag on the table so that the opening is at the bottom. Use the scissors to cut a V-shaped neck opening at the top edge (through two layers of paper) that will be large enough to go over your child's head. Next, cut two large half circles at the sides of the bag for the armholes. Use the pencil to sketch a wide belt and giant belt buckle on the paper vest. Cut the wrapping paper and/or construction paper to create a big, colorful paper belt and giant paper buckle, and position them on the paper vest where indicated by your pencil marks. Use the tape to secure the paper belt and buckle to the vest. Let your child use markers or crayons to decorate the paper vest with more designs

CREATE A THEATRICAL HAT BOX FOR PRESCHOOLER PRETEND

A collection of clever hats can provide a spectacular way to jump-start theatrical play! See Hats Galore on page 108 (toddler section) to create your own hat box. Or consider purchasing a few hats for preschool theatrics.

You can easily find hats for clowns, police officers, cowboys, firefighters, nurses, sailors, chefs, sea captains, gladiators, soldiers, train conductors, flamenco dancers, musketeers, Vikings, wizards, kings and queens, knights, and jesters. One of my favorite online resources for hat and music education and theatrical supplies for kids is www.musicmotion.com.

ages 3–5

and colors. Help your child slip the Robin Hood vest over his head and look in the mirror to check out the finished costume. Add a hat or plastic sword or other props to start the pretend.

KING-AND-QUEEN PRETEND PLAY

Every child likes to play the part of a king or a queen—and it all begins with a crown!

Materials
- Crown (see page 109 for directions to make your own)
- Magic wand (see next project for directions to make your own)
- Superhero Cape (page 199 or pillowcase with a big safety pin)

Get Creative This activity is entertaining and amusing for playgroups. Give everyone a simple crown, magic wand, and cape, and you'll be pleasantly surprised to see the spontaneous theatrical scenes the children create together.

MAKE A MAGIC WAND FOR KINGS AND QUEENS

Create a simple wand and let the royal pomp and circumstance begin.

Materials
- Scissors (for adult use only)
- Colored construction paper
- Foam board
- Tape
- Curling ribbon or crepe paper streamers
- Stickers
- Nontoxic markers

Get Creative Parents cut 3-to-4-inch stars from the construction paper, two for each Magic Wand. Decorate each star with stickers and markers. Cut a wand handle from the foam board 20 inches long and 1 inch wide. Tape the stars to the front and back of one end of the foam wand. Create long streamers of curling ribbon or crepe paper and tape to the wand just below the star.

WINGS FOR BIRDS AND BUTTERFLIES

These lightweight wings will help your child's imagination soar.

Materials
- Scissors (for adult use only)
- One large paper grocery bag with paper handles
- One or more rolls of colored streamers
- Tape

Get Creative Use the scissors to cut the bag into one long, flat sheet of paper with two handles (one handle at each end). Next trim the paper slightly so that it resembles the shape of butterfly or bird wings. Cut pieces of the streamers to decorate the wingspan. Help your child use the tape to stick the streamers to the paper wings to resemble feathers. Help your child position the wings across his shoulders and upper back and insert his hands into the paper handles to hold the wings in place as he "flies." For added excitement, teach your child a simple birdcall that he can call out as he soars around.

Paper-Bag Nest for One Giant Bird
Help your child create a giant bird's nest on the lawn for more bird-pretend. Just crumple paper grocery bags or sheets of brown craft paper (or newspaper) into a nest-like mound. Then, when your little bird (and her feathered friends) gets tired of flying, she can take a little rest in her nest!

> " Pretend play is one of the best ways of igniting creativity. "
>
> —**DR. STANLEY GREENSPAN**, former clinical professor of psychiatry and pediatrics at George Washington University Medical School, author of *The Growth of the Mind*

BIG-ADVENTURE CAMP-OUT

Provide a few camping and hiking supplies and enjoy the theatrical adventure that unfolds with your child's active imagination!

ages 3–5

Materials

- Bedsheets and several kitchen chairs (to make the tent) or make a kitchen-table fort (see page 113 for directions)
- Sleeping bags
- Cardboard box (turned upside down) for the pretend camp stove
- Water jug, thermos, canned food, snacks
- Hiking boots, rain jacket, hat
- Cooking utensils and pot
- Plastic plates and cups
- Stuffed animals (for camping pals)
- Battery-powered lantern
- Books
- Newspapers and rubber bands (to make some rolled pretend firewood)

Get Creative Help your child to set up "camp," and let the creative play begin. Children love to pretend to gather firewood, cook a meal, look for animals in the wild, turn on the lantern and read in the dark, and invent some fantastic mountain climbing adventures too.

PIRATE-SHIP ADVENTURE

Ahoy, captain! It's time to take to the high seas in search of treasure!

Materials

- Cardboard pirate ship (see next page for directions to make your own) or a plastic laundry basket for a pretend ship
- Pirate costume, such as a bandanna, loose pants, a scarf for a belt, and an eye patch
- Pirate props, such as a toy knife, a treasure map, or a stuffed parrot
- Pretend money or gold or other treasures

Get Creative Pirate-ship-pretend takes many twists and turns with your preschooler's imagination, and it all begins with a very simple costume and some simple props.

A Pirate's Telescope

Here's the easiest pretend-play prop in the world: Save your empty cardboard paper-towel or toilet-paper tubes and let your child turn them into "pirate telescopes" for peering across the sea during pretend-pirate playtime. You can cover your telescope with colored construction paper and tape, decorate it with original artwork, or leave it plain.

MAKE A GIANT PIRATE SHIP

Start with one or more big appliance boxes and create a clever ship for your little pirate and the neighborhood buccaneers!

Materials
- One or more big cardboard appliance boxes
- Duct tape
- Scissors
- Tempera paints
- Paintbrush
- Small bucket of water

Get Creative Plan the overall shape of your ship, then piece together the cardboard boxes or several sections of cardboard panels and secure them together with the duct tape. You can use the scissors to cut out big round holes on each side of the ship and create some cardboard cannons too! Since this project takes a hefty dose of adult planning and trial and error, this is primarily a project for parents, grandparents, or caregivers to do as a surprise. Bring your pre-schooler into the creativity toward the end to help with decorations or painting.

RODEO AND COWBOY (OR COWGIRL) PRETEND

Round up a couple preschoolers in your child's playgroup and let the rodeo begin!

Materials
- Toy horse stick
- Cowboy costume, such as a hat, vest, blue jeans, bandanna, and boots

Get Creative Provide a simple costume and a horse to ride (aka a horse stick) and take this freestyle pretend play outdoors to see what happens next. Kids might create a little corral on the lawn or make the patio the barn! They may find some hay (grass) for the horses, and create rodeo acts for stuffed animals and horses too.

PRETEND HIGHWAY

Use giant sheets of paper on the floor to help your child create a big highway for preschooler make-believe.

Materials
- Butcher paper
- Invisible tape

ages 3–5

- Markers
- Blocks
- Plastic people, buildings, trees, and other toy props to create a little town
- Miniature cars and trucks

Setup Cut two long sheets of butcher paper and place them side by side on a wooden, vinyl, or tile floor and use a little invisible tape to hold the paper in place. With the markers draw a winding road across the entire large span of paper.

Get Creative Encourage your child to build a town (with blocks and at least two people) and create his own highway pretend play with cars and trucks.

You (dear parent) are a silent actor and your child is the audience making guesses about what you are doing in this game of parent-and-child theatrics.

Get Creative Give a brief explanation about how to play this acting-out game: "I'm going to act out some of the things that I do each day. See if you can guess what I am doing!"

Parents mimic any of these actions (without props) and your child tries to guess what it is:
- Sweeping the floor
- Talking on phone
- Making dinner
- Driving a car
- Running
- Mowing the lawn
- Digging a hole
- Planting plants in the garden
- Watering the flowers (with a hose or a watering can)
- Reading a book
- Raking leaves
- Washing the car

For added fun encourage your child to act out more everyday actions, and you become the guesser!

ZOO CHARADES

This is an acting game and guessing game rolled into one happy preschooler pretend activity.

Materials
- Paper and pencil
- Clip art or sketches of zoo animals
- Paper bag

Setup Create a list of about ten to twenty different zoo animals your child is familiar with. Draw a quick sketch (or print some clip art) of each animal, creating ten to twenty small pieces of paper with a different animal on each scrap of paper. Fold the papers in half and toss them in the paper bag.

Get Creative Each person takes one paper from the bag and takes a turn acting out the actions (and sounds) of that animal while the others guess.

ages 3–5

NURSERY RHYME THEATRICS

Preschoolers can try a little bit of puppetry with you providing words for the theatrics!

Materials
- Finger-Puppet Stage (see page 119 for directions to make your own)
- One or two finger puppets
- Favorite nursery rhymes, such as "Higglety, Pigglety, Pop," "Jack and Jill," "Three Blind Mice," "Teddy Bear, Teddy Bear," "Hickory, Dickory, Dock," and so on

Setup Position the Finger-Puppet Stage on the kitchen table. Put a chair nearby for your preschool puppeteer. Give a quick little demo of how to slide the finger puppet onto your finger and make it march (or dance) upon the stage!

Get Creative Let your child select a familiar nursery rhyme for you to read. Read the rhyme slowly the first time or two, then quicken the pace of the reading and invite your child puppeteer to match the marching or dancing of her puppets to the rhythm of your poem or nursery rhyme.

CREATE FINGER-LEG PUPPETS

Help your child create a little home-made cardboard finger puppet for the Nursery Rhyme Theatrics. Here's how to make Finger-Leg Puppets:

Materials
- Scissors (for adult use only)
- Card stock or poster board
- Markers or crayons
- Invisible tape

Setup Cut a rectangle about 7 by 5 inches from the card stock or poster board.

Get Creative Encourage your preschooler to draw a person or animal (or monster) character on the card stock. (The character might be as simple as a circle or an oval with eyes or a smile.) When the drawing is finished, parents use the scissors to cut around the basic outline of the character to create the card stock puppet. Next, parents use the scissors to cut two holes about ¾ inch in diameter toward the bottom of the paper puppet. (These holes should be about ⅜ inch apart.) Show your child how to slip two fingers through the holes from the back of the puppet and bend fingers (like bending knees) to make the puppets dance or walk upon the stage.

PAPER-BAG PUPPETS

Once preschoolers see how to make their first paper-bag puppet, they can make these easy hand puppets on their own!

Materials

- Paper lunch bags
- Markers or crayons
- Preschooler scissors
- Optional: construction paper, small pom-poms, felt or fabric scraps, buttons, glue, tape

Get Creative Give a short demo of how to place your hand inside a flattened lunch bag, putting four fingers into the end of the bag and your thumb in the underflap of the bag. Now move or pinch your fingers and thumb together repeatedly to make the underside of the bag flap open like a mouth. Then, work side by side with your child, with each artist drawing a large animal or person's face on his bag. Encourage your child to use markers to create colorful eyes, eyebrows, nose, and mouth on the bag puppet. Cut pieces of colored paper or fabric scraps to create ears, nose, or hair, and tape these and other decorations on your puppets. Then help your child slip his or her hand inside and pinch or move fingers and thumb together to make the puppet "talk."

ANIMAL PUPPETS-ON-A-STICK

Start with a painter's stir-stick, attach a drawing of a favorite animal, create a little costume, and voilà! Your puppet-on-a-stick is born!

Materials

- Markers or crayons
- Card stock
- Nontoxic white glue, such as Elmer's
- Fabric scraps
- Yarn
- Colored construction paper
- Glitter glue
- Preschool scissors
- Duct tape

- Painter's wooden stir-stick (available at hardware or paint stores)

Get Creative Work side by side with your preschooler, with each of you drawing an animal on a sheet of card stock. Glue fabric scraps, yarn, and colored paper onto the animal to make the puppet colorful and creative. Use glitter glue to draw added features and add sparkle. When the animal is finished, carefully use scissors to cut around the outline of the animal. Tape the painter's wooden stir-stick to the back side of the paper animal to create a puppet. To put on a puppet show, use the top of the kitchen as the stage, turn on some music, and make the puppets dance!

STORYBOOK PUPPET SHOW

This is an easy and joyful way for parents and preschoolers to share puppets and engage in some make-believe.

Materials
- An assortment of animal puppets (you can find a dozen velour animal hand puppets for under $20 on www.amazon.com)
- A favorite children's book with an animal character, such as *Curious George* or *Bark, George*

Setup Pick an animal puppet that matches up with the children's story. Position yourself at the kitchen table with the book and puppet and your child sitting on the opposite side of the table.

Get Creative Read the story and pause as needed to let your puppet act out some of the action in the story. Invent a silly voice for the character too. (Parents might embellish the action by

WHERE TO BUY MARIONETTES

You may find a few marionettes for sale at your local toy shop. There are also many marionettes (people and animals) available online quite inexpensively. One retailer to check out is www.sunnytoys.com.

adding a few new extra lines to some of the pages of the story.) Once your child gets the idea of acting out the story, let him or her become the puppeteer while you read the story, briefly pausing along the way for puppet dancing and actions!

CARDBOARD-BOX PUPPET STAGE

Here's an easy way to make a puppet stage to inspire hours of creative productions!

Materials
- Scissors (for adult use only)
- Large or medium cardboard box
- Colored construction paper
- Tape
- Markers
- Assorted miniature props

Get Creative Use the scissors to remove the four flaps from the bottom of the box. Tuck the four remaining top flaps inside the box to create sturdy side walls to the stage. Turn the box on its side so that you have created an open window. Use the construction paper and tape to line the inside of the box, creating "painted" walls and a floor. Use the scissors to cut three or more strips of narrow construction paper of equal size. Then cut a scalloped edge along the bottom of each strip. Next, tape the strips together to create a "curtain" that will run across the top of the box and along the sides. Attach the curtain to the stage (box) using tape. Add simple miniature props to the stage.

To put on a short play, set the box on the kitchen table, and your child puppeteer can crouch or kneel behind the stage to put on a little puppet show for you!

HANG A LITTLE PUPPET THEATER IN YOUR DOORWAY

The Doorway Puppet Theater by HearthSong is a store-bought puppet stage made of cloth that fits securely into any doorway by means of a spring-loaded rod that adjusts to any height. (For ages 3 and up; winner of a Parents' Choice Award.) Available from www.hearthsong.com.

ages 3–5

MARIONETTE PUPPETRY FOR PRESCHOOLERS

Older preschoolers and kindergarten kids can have fun working a simple marionette to put on a spontaneous puppet routine!

Materials
- One easy-to-use marionette (designed especially for kids)

Get Creative Older preschoolers will enjoy naming their puppet and learning to make their marionette dance and move. Eventually your child may put on a simple puppet show by introducing herself in the voice of the puppet and dancing and talking a few lines about herself (the puppet character)!

Two-Friends Puppet Show
If you have two marionettes, one for you and one for your child, you can let your child start a little skit or conversation for her puppet while you play along spontaneously with the second puppet as the first puppet's best friend.

Creativity with Words

Children three to five years old are at a spectacular age for creativity with words and language. They are enthralled when a parent or caregiver spontaneously invents a tall tale about a loveable animal or a madcap-adventure story, and they will happily add their own imaginative ideas about what might happen next. They are thrilled with the idea of making a homemade book. They will take turns with other kids inventing hilarious stories from Tall-Tale Beginnings (page 216), ideas such as "Let's tell a story about the fastest dog in the world!" When children see that words and language can be used in such a clever way, and that they too can make imaginative books with original stories and illustrations, a giant light goes on in their young minds about the amazing creativity that can happen with words.

Your job is to include playful, imaginative storytelling and creative word activities in your child's routine and encourage your child to be creative with language too. Each time your child joins in to create an animal character or add ideas for a story or book, he gets more and more comfortable with the creative process. This is a snapshot of how word creativity develops in the preschool and kindergarten stage. And it all begins with a fun, open attitude from parents and caregivers and a willingness to be playful with words.

CREATE SIX-QUESTION STORIES (TOGETHER)

Here's an easy and entertaining way for parents, grandparents, or caregivers and preschoolers to invent imaginative stories together.

ages
3–5

Materials
- Pencil and paper

Get Creative Explain to your child that you'd like to make up a fun story together about an animal, person, or creature. Then ask your child the six questions (below) to get ideas to start the tall tale. (Jot quick notes to remember if necessary.)

- What animal or person should our story be about? (Child says, "An alligator!")
- What is his/her name? (Child says, "Andy!")
- Where does he live? (Child says, "In a house.")
- What color is the house? (Child says, "Pink!")
- What does the ____(alligator) like to do for fun? (Child says, "Play baseball!")
- What is the ____'s (alligator's) favorite food? (Child says, "Pizza!")

When all the answers are given by your child, start your story. Announce the character and start inventing silly or amusing details and actions, working each answer into the story. Keep these stories short enough to hold your preschooler's attention (perhaps 3–6 minutes max).

Here's a sample of the very beginning of my story about Andy the Alligator:

There once was a little alligator named Andy. He lived in a big pink house in the swamp. Andy had a sign in his front yard that said, BASEBALL IS THE BEST SPORT IN THE WORLD! Andy's best friend, Ralph, lived next door in a little blue house. He was an alligator too. . . .

Continue with an imaginative, captivating story.

TALL-TALE BEGINNINGS

Make a list of your own ideas to invent clever stories for your child (or use the themes listed below) and let the tall tales begin!

Materials
- Paper and pencil
- Scissors

Setup Brainstorm a list of possible preschooler-friendly story ideas that you could invent. Write your best ideas on a list.

Get Creative Pick three of your favorite story ideas and ask your child, "Which story sounds like the most fun to hear?" Then mention three quick ideas. Start your tall tale with one good line and just keep inventing more imaginative action (and characters) to entertain your child. (Keep it moving along quickly, and make the story only 3–5 minutes long.)

Here are some sample Tall-Tale Beginnings your three- to five-year-old may enjoy:
- The biggest pumpkin in the world . . .
- The fastest dog in the world . . .
- The slowest turtle in the world . . .
- The cat who never stopped singing . . .
- The doughnut that rolled around the world . . .
- The four-year-old mayor who ran the town . . .
- The puppy who learned to read . . .
- The cat who sailed across the sea in a sailboat . . .

You get the idea. Get your imagination in gear and come up with your own clever, silly, or sensational Tall-Tale Beginnings and start weaving your tall tales!

Tall-Tale Beginnings for Two

Here's a little twist on the Tall-Tale Beginnings idea. Tell an amusing story and partway through, pause at a critical point and ask your child, "What do you think might happen next?" and weave his or her imaginative ideas into the story or just let your child continue telling the story from there. (There are no right or wrong answers, just imaginative, playful ideas for creating a story.)

STORY-TIME GUESSING GAME

Here's a delightful guessing game to play with your child while you are riding in the car or having quiet time together!

Materials
- A familiar (favorite) children's book or story

Get Creative Pick a character in one of your child's favorite picture books and play a little word-guessing game with your preschooler. For example, you might say, "This animal likes to wear red shoes." "This person works outside in his garden." "This animal is a monkey who sometimes gets in trouble." Then ask your child, "Can you guess who it is (from one of the books we read)?"

MOTHER NATURE STORY BASKET

Find magazine photos with nature scenes and toss them in a basket for a special ad-lib story time for you and your child!

Materials
- Magazines with a variety of nature and outdoor photos, such as plants, streams, lakes, ocean, fish, animals, insects, trails, trees, mountains, meadows, farmland, and so on

Setup Tear out nature photos and put them in a file folder marked "Nature Photos for Stories."

Get Creative Select three photos from your "Nature Photos for Stories" file and toss them in a small basket. Let your child select a photo that she likes and you create a story about something in that photo that catches your eye. (Kids kindergarten-age or older might enjoy becoming the storyteller too.)

BABY-TIME STORIES

Preschoolers and kindergartners love to hear lighthearted stories about their early weeks and months of life.

Materials
- Your imagination
- Optional: a favorite baby photo of your child

Setup Find a quiet time to snuggle up together for a homemade story.

Get Creative Tell your child a few of the happy details about the first days or weeks or months after he or she was born or adopted into your family. What lullabies did you sing? What books did you read together? Who came to visit? What favorite activities did your child like? What places did you visit together? What playmates came by? What toys were favorites?

FARMER BROWN STORIES

Invent spontaneous tales about a happy farmer and his barnyard animals to delight your preschooler (and dabble in creativity with words).

Get Creative Create silly or outrageous stories about the everyday events in the life of Farmer Brown and his animals. (Give Farmer Brown a distinctive personality: Make him old or young, happy or forgetful, musical or mechanical, experienced or inexperienced. Let his idiosyncrasies or personality help guide the action and antics in your stories.)

Amazing Animals on Farmer Brown's Farm
Create a fantasy world where the animals do the most amazing things when Farmer Brown is fast asleep. Perhaps there is a nightly concert of music or a barnyard dance. Maybe the animals wear costumes and put on a play. Imagine and create tall tales about the surprising and clever things those farm animals can do. Tell about their fearless leader or the shenanigans that happen each evening. Add more chapters as ideas pop into your imagination.

ages
3–5

PET-ADVENTURE STORIES

Invent a lovable or mischievous pet, and let your child offer ideas to help set the stage for some amazing pet-adventure stories.

Get Creative Ask your child to select a pet that you know for a series of animal-adventure stories. (Perhaps your family dog or grandma's cat!) Ask your child if there is someplace surprising or silly that this pet might travel to. Then use your best imagination to create a story with the pet character and place that your child mentioned. (If the place mentioned doesn't give you much to work with, then make that place just a short stopover on the way to a second amazing place in the plotline of the story!)

> *Imagination is one of the most fun things you can engage in with your child. You have an opportunity to do a tremendous amount for your child just by those few minutes of shared make-believe or storytelling.*
>
> **—DR. JEROME SINGER**,
> professor of psychology and child study,
> coauthor of *The House of Make-Believe*

TWO-FRIENDS STORIES

Create magical stories about the everyday adventures of two best friends, who happen to be animals!

Materials
- Pencil and paper

Get Creative Ask your child to come up with two animals who might be friends in a homemade story. Anything goes in this imaginative world—the animals do not have to truly be compatible! Begin your story by selecting one place the friends are going, and embellish with details to make the story entertaining. Some stories might include a bit of mischief, surprise, or problems, and end with a solution or happy ending.

WRITE A POEM OR RHYME ABOUT YOUR CHILD!

Create a simple poem about something endearing about your child or favorite activities you like to do together. To get started, brainstorm about your child's personality, interests, favorite activities, or your routines together. Write a beginning line of a poem and just keep going. Get comfortable writing ideas (or the next line of the poem) and crossing off any words that just aren't quite right. Make it silly or make it tender. It can be a poem with rhymes or no rhymes. Anything goes! This is a terrific way to show your child that anyone can invent a little poem about someone they know.

"MY FAMILY!" BOOK

Let your older preschooler discover the joy of creating a book about something near and dear to his heart: his family!

Materials
- Homemade board book (see Create Your Own Board Books for Your Toddler, page 128)
- Rubber stamp set with all the letters of the alphabet
- Nontoxic ink pad or markers
- Nontoxic glue (or invisible tape)
- Photos of each member of the family

Get Creative Help your child use the rubber stamps (or else hand print) to create the name of one family member at the top of each page in the book. Next, your child glues or tapes a photo to match up with the names on each page.

"MY SHAPES!" BOOK

Parents and preschoolers can create their own shapes book to read aloud. (It's a lovely keepsake too.)

Materials
- Scissors (for adult use only)
- Colored construction paper
- Nontoxic white glue, such as Elmer's
- Homemade board book (see Create Your Own Board Books

ages 3–5

for Your Toddler, page 128)
- Markers or crayons

Setup Parent cuts multiples of the following shapes from colored construction paper: circles, squares, rectangles, triangles.

Get Creative Help your child sort all the circles into one pile, the squares into another, the rectangles into a third, and the triangles into a fourth. Then let your child glue the matching shapes onto one page of the book in any pattern he or she likes. (Use one page for each shape.) When all the gluing is done, you use the marker to write the word for the shape across the top or bottom of the page.

"MY ALPHABET!" BOOK

Here's a creative book-making project to get your child excited about letters of the alphabet!

Materials
- Colored construction paper
- Rubber stamp set with all the letters of the alphabet
- Nontoxic inkpad and/or markers and crayons

- Photos of a few favorite objects of people to use as illustrations on some of the pages of the alphabet book
- Scissors (for adult use only)
- Nontoxic white glue, such as Elmer's
- Homemade board book (see Create Your Own Board Books for Your Toddler, page 128)

Get Creative Help your child print (or stamp) the letters of the alphabet, writing one big letter on each piece of paper. Help your child match the illustrations or photos with the appropriate letters, and glue them on each page. When the letters and illustrations are finished, your child can create a book cover with the letters "A-B-C" printed on it.

Alphabet Poster
Help your child create a big poster with every letter of the alphabet! (Best for children five years old.)

Invite your child to use a marker to write one big letter of the alphabet (from A to Z) on colored 3-by-5-inch file cards. Use glue or tape to place the letters on a piece of poster board in the order of the alphabet. When the gluing is done, your child may want to finish off the poster by adding glitter-glue designs or decorations to make the poster sparkle.

THE VEGETABLE GARDEN BOOK

This colorful book of photos and words will help your child celebrate the bounty of the garden.

Materials
- Homemade board book (see Create Your Own Board Books for Your Toddler, page 128)
- Preschooler-safe scissors
- Nontoxic glue or invisible tape
- Photos from a garden or seed catalog
- Rubber stamp set with all the letters of the alphabet
- Nontoxic ink pad or markers

Get Creative Your child will be entertained cutting and gluing vegetable photos on the book pages and working with you to stamp or print the names of each vegetable beneath each photo. Once all the pages of the book are finished, decorate the cover by adding more photos and a title.

Beautiful-Flower Book
Follow the same directions listed above for The Vegetable Garden Book, but use photos of flowers found in seed or garden catalogs to create a colorful book with words and pictures of flowers.

COLORFUL-CATS BOOK

A handmade book that celebrates the colors of the rainbow!

Materials
- Homemade board book (see Create Your Own Board Books for Your Toddler, page 128)
- Black marker
- Computer printer or copy machine
- Colored markers or crayons in a rainbow of colors
- Rubber stamp set with all the letters of the alphabet
- Nontoxic ink pad or markers

Get Creative Encourage your child to draw a cat on one piece of paper using the black marker. (Anything goes. Let your child make his own original cat drawing.) Once the drawing is finished, create seven copies of your child's black-and-white cat drawing using card stock loaded into a copy machine or computer printer.

Next, let your child color each drawing a different color so that there is a yellow cat, a red cat, a blue cat, a green cat, an orange cat, and a purple cat! When all the drawings are colored, use the rubber stamps and nontoxic ink to stamp the words for each color on the pages. (Or help your older child print the letters for *Red*, *Blue*, and so on.) Have your child create a multicolored cat on one last piece of paper and use this for the front cover of the book.

Colorful-Butterflies Book

If your child is fascinated with butterflies, encourage him to create a Colorful-Butterflies Book similar to the Colorful-Cats Book above. (Show your child a photo of a butterfly if he needs a little visual reminder of what a butterfly looks like.) Follow all the other steps in the Colorful-Cats Book (above).

"MY FAMILY!" POSTER

Preschoolers enjoy making giant, colorful posters with letters, words, and pictures—and this one is all about family!

Materials
- Colored poster board
- Photos of family members (or photos of your child with other family members)
- Glue (or tape)
- Markers
- Rubber stamp set with all the letters of the alphabet
- Nontoxic ink pad or markers

Get Creative Your child selects favorite photos of family members to arrange and glue on the big poster board. You can work together to think of funny captions to put under some (or all) of the photos or help your older preschooler stamp or print names under the photos.

"My Friends!" Poster

If your child has favorite playmates and you have some photos of them playing, help your child create a "My Friends!" poster similar to the "My Family!" poster above. Encourage your

223

child to use markers, glitter glue, and crayons to decorate the poster or make it more colorful.

MAKE A STAR-BRIGHT POSTER

Your child can create the artwork for a colorful poster and help a bit with stamping words on the poster too.

Materials
- One black marker
- Words for the "Star Bright" poem (see below)
- One sheet of light-blue poster board
- Glitter-glue pens in an assortment of colors (such as Crayola)
- Optional: nontoxic ink pad and rubber alphabet stamps
- Optional: yellow construction paper, glue, and scissors (to create a moon)

Get Creative Parents write the words for the "Start Bright" poem in one area of the poster board using a marker (leaving lots of room for your child's star drawings and design). Encourage your child to create his own rendition of stars on the poster using the assorted glitter-glue pens.

Let the glitter glue dry thoroughly before touching or hanging the finished poster.

Optional: older preschoolers might like to help print the word *star* in the title of the poem (or throughout the poem) by using a nontoxic ink pad and medium-sized rubber stamps for the letters S-T-A-R.

Star Bright
Star light, star bright,
First star I see tonight,
I wish I may, I wish I might,
Have the wish I wish tonight!

ages 3–5

GRADE-SCHOOL CREATIVITY

Ages 6–12

Children six to twelve years old are at a superb age for creative projects. They have the physical capabilities for manipulating tools, materials, and instruments to create in art, music, building, dance, and theatrics. They also have an extensive command of language, so many opportunities exist for creative writing and imaginative storytelling too. Children this age notice habits, peculiarities, funny expressions, and routines of the people in their world, and this heightened awareness often gets worked into their creative writing and storytelling projects. Children six to twelve understand basic safety issues, can follow instructions, and can be excellent problem solvers too. This is a terrific time for doing both independent projects and collaborative projects with others, such as friends, siblings, parents, grandparents, and caregivers.

Your job as a parent is to encourage your child to try all sorts of creative projects that seem appealing, and to keep much of the focus on fun. When you present a positive and pressure-free attitude about doing creative activities, your child will likely approach projects in this same upbeat, can-do way. And as your child incorporates imagination, brainstorming, experimentation, and problem solving into these activities, creative skills, habits, and passion will develop quite naturally.

Art Activities

Art creativity is in full bloom during the ages of six to twelve. Children will enjoy drawing, painting, printmaking, collage, nature crafts, papier-mâché, mixed-media projects, photography, and working with clay.

Some kids will enjoy ongoing art projects that span several days. Others like the immediate satisfaction of finishing their artwork in one sitting. Some children of this age may prefer familiar art activities and materials (such as paint and paper) and to do these same activities again and again for quite some time. Others will want the thrill of trying something new each time they do art.

Children six to twelve are very clever at creating their own variations of activities and experimenting with techniques. One child may decide to make an entire painting with small colorful dots instead of brushstrokes. Another child may start out doing a big painting on poster board and decide to add scraps of colored paper or fabric to incorporate elements of collage. Your job is to provide art materials and a bit of encouragement and support, keeping an open mind about the types of projects your child wants to tackle. When your child does art activities on an ongoing basis, he or she will be knee-deep in experimentation, with creativity and imagination expanding and growing with each new project.

ARTIST SKETCHBOOK IDEAS

Every artist needs one or more sketchbooks to capture clever ideas and for practicing drawing too!

Materials
- Assorted drawing pencils or pens
- Journal or notebook

ages 6-12

PARENTS' BEST APPROACH TO ENCOURAGING
GRADE-SCHOOL ART CREATIVITY *(ages 6–12)*

- Keep the focus on fun and maintain a positive, accepting attitude about your child's artwork, with your child in charge of what to make and how to make it.
- Set aside a space in your home where art projects can be done and a little mess can be tolerated.
- Stock up on inexpensive art materials that can be used in a variety of ways. Consider a few artist-grade art materials for your child to experiment with and to use for special projects. (See pages 232–233 for suggestions.)
- Encourage your child to invent her own variations to some of the art activities and to use art materials and tools in new and interesting ways. (For example, perhaps a wad of burlap fabric can be dipped in tempera paint and used instead of a brush to create an abstract painting on poster board. Let your child test out her own ideas as long as she keeps safety of materials in mind.)
- Encourage your child to do art projects with friends who come over as an alternative to screen-time activities.
- Display your child's artwork throughout your home (and frame some of the favorites too).
- Do some parent-and-child art activities and include art creativity in Family Creativity Night and at your child's birthday party too.
- Consider signing your child up for art classes in your community if he expresses an interest and your family budget will allow it.

Get Creative Encourage your child to create a sketchbook for drawing something he or she is especially fascinated with. Ideas might include animals, people, superheroes, trees, insects, reptiles, fashion, or any category of interest that excites your child. Here are some possible themes or ideas to consider for an Artist Sketchbook. Your child picks one of interest and starts drawing.

The Happiest Pet on the Block

Encourage your child to draw his favorite family pets or animals in the zoo and add costumes or silly hats and articles of clothing. Let him mix his imagination with his sense of humor and see what he can create in his Happiest-Pet sketchbook.

Zoo Sketchbook

Challenge your child to create her own book of zoo animals—from A to Z, checking out a zoo animal book at the library or Googling photos of animals online for reference.

Amazing-Vehicles Sketchbook

Invite your child to create a book of real or imaginary vehicles, with wheels or wings or sails that move across the land or sea or sky, and to use his imagination to create whimsical decorations and designs.

Surf's-Up Sketchbook

Show your child how she can make drawings about stand-up paddle boards, kayaks, surfing, windsurfing, parasailing, kite-boarding, boogie boards, or any other water-sport equipment.

She can add some people or animals or creatures from her imagination and draw them riding the waves.

Nature Notebook

Challenge your child to draw anything in nature that is fascinating: trees, insects, flowers, gardens, farm crops, animals, rivers, lakes, oceans, mountains. Make it real or supernatural!

Good-Friends Sketchbook

Encourage your child to draw real or imaginary friends playing (or doing) something fun together. Invent silly outfits, magical adventures, or fantastical scenes.

My-Fashion-Invention Notebook

In this activity your child becomes a superstar designer of hats, shoes,

> *I loved designing clothes and drawing them. My Barbie doll had some chic outfits with handbags to match that I made. I also created fashion catalogs; one was called "Bonbonniere" because I was going through a French craze when I was in grade school. Loved fleur-de-lis and drew them all over the place!*
>
> **—MELANIE HALL,** artist and award-winning illustrator of over twenty-five children's books, including *Winter Song: A Poem by William Shakespeare*

ages 6–12

cowboy boots, clothing, jewelry, and backpacks for kids or grown-ups.

Out-in-the-World Sketchbook
Your child sketches some of the characters and things she sees out in the world: riding the bus, taking the train, sitting in the backseat of the car, going through carpool lanes, traveling on vacation.

GIANT GUARD-DOG (OR ANIMAL) MURAL

Your child imagines a fierce or friendly guard dog, draws him on a giant piece of butcher paper, and hangs it on the bedroom door as the ultimate "Keep Out!" sign.

Materials
- Roll of butcher paper
- Invisible tape
- Colorful markers and colored pencils
- Optional: glitter-glue pens

Get Creative Cut a giant piece of butcher paper about 8 feet long. Place this paper on the patio or basement floor and use a little tape to hold it flat to the floor. Now invite your child to use markers and colored pencils to sketch a giant furry friend. Your child can invent distinctive features to make this guard dog fierce or friendly!

Giant Tree Mural
Your child imagines that his room is a treehouse and he creates a giant tree to adorn the entrance to his bedroom. He sketches it, colors it, and then hangs it up on the door with invisible tape.

COMIC-STRIP DRAWINGS

Challenge your child to invent her own comic-strip character!

Materials
- Drawing paper
- Fine-line markers and colored pencils

Get Creative Get a giant piece of paper and help your child draw three or four squares to serve as the frames for the comic strip. Then your child draws a character doing something different in each of the squares, and adds words in conversation bubbles that match up with these characters or action. If your child invents a character he likes a lot, he may decide to create a comic book filled with original comic strips.

SPLURGE ON ARTIST-GRADE DRAWING SUPPLIES
FOR CHILDREN AGES 8 AND UP

If your child loves to draw (and your family budget will allow it), consider purchasing a few artist-grade drawing supplies for him or her to try when doing special projects. These high-quality materials make a fine birthday or holiday present. You might consider getting one pad of special paper and one set of drawing pens, drawing pencils, or nontoxic pastels, for example. You'll find a wide assortment of professional-quality drawing supplies and drawing paper at your local art supply store or online. (Two examples of online retailers include www.artistcraftsman.com and www.dickblick.com.) Here are some terrific artist-grade drawing supplies for children ages 8 and up to experiment with:

Pencils
- General's Drawing Pencil Set (this set includes charcoal pencils, graphite pencils, sketch-and-wash pencils, layout pencils, white charcoal pencils, and others)
- White China Markers—terrific for drawing on black or brown paper for contrast drawing
- A set of colored pencils (there are many brands to choose from)
- A set of watercolor pencils (for example, Mondeluz Aquarelles Watercolor Pencils)

Erasers
- Kneaded eraser
- Mars plastic eraser (for example, Staedtler brand)
- Gum erasers

Drawing Pens
- A set of 6 black drawing pens with various-sized tips (Sakura Pigma Microns brand, for example)

$\longrightarrow$

ages
6–12

- A set of colored drawing pens (for example, there are twenty pens in a set by Staedtler)
- A set of dual-tip colored pens—with a fine tip on one end and a brush tip on the other (for example, Tombow brand)

Pastels
- A set of nontoxic artist pastels—these are chalk-like pastels (for example, Sargent Art brand)
- A set of water-soluble oil pastels (for example, Portfolio Series brand)

(Note: Be sure to select nontoxic chalk pastels for children, as well as oil pastels that are safe for kids to work with. Other types of chalk pastels may result in irritating dust particles.)

Drawing Paper for Special Projects
- Bristol Smooth pad (best for pens and markers)
- Bristol Vellum pad (best for pencils)
- Multimedia (or mixed-media) paper (good for assorted drawing projects)
- Paris Bleedproof Paper for Pens—super-smooth finish (for example, Borden & Riley brand)

COMIC-STRIP CREATIVITY FOR TWO

Here's an entertaining drawing project for parent and child or two or more friends.

Materials
- Ruler
- Pencils and erasers
- Drawing paper

Setup Each person uses a ruler, a pencil, and paper to create four rectangles or frames to use for creating a comic strip.

Get Creative Each artist draws four different comic scenes. (They draw people or animals doing some sort of actions in each of the four frames so that the drawing is basically telling a story without words.) When both artists are finished drawing, they trade papers,

233

and create conversation bubbles with imaginative or humorous words to finish the other person's comic strip.

Sometimes a little brainstorming will help your child discover exciting things to draw.

Materials
- Paper
- Pencils or drawing pens
- Eraser

Get Creative If your child is stumped on what to draw, a good place to start is to just pick something that he or she is fascinated with and draw it. Here are some ideas to consider:

- **Vehicles:** Ships, boats, cars, planes, skateboards, scooters, bicycles, surf or paddle boards, helicopters, unicycles, tanks, trucks, bulldozers, tractors, trains, subways, buses, gondolas
- **Places:** Neighborhoods, cities, farms, forests, mountains, beaches, fantasy places, magical cities of the past or future, buildings and dwellings of every kind (houses, huts, teepees, cliff dwellings, apartment buildings, tents, yurts, underground homes, igloos, tree houses, birdhouses, doghouses, and so on)
- **People:** Characters in favorite books, friends, family, fantasy characters, cartoon characters, leaders of real or imagined worlds (tribes, clans, nations), babies, children, elders
- **Animals:** Pets; wild-kingdom animals; zoo animals; mythical, imaginary, silly animals; animal characters in costumes (from your imagination)
- **Flying Creatures:** All sorts of birds, ducks, butterflies, dragonflies, fireflies, fairies
- **Doodles and Abstract Designs:** Make designs without any real objects, just fill the paper with shapes, doodles, and colors and see what interesting drawings you can create.

ages
6–12

- **Double-Doodle Drawings:** Create a doodle with a friend (or parent), with one artist drawing a line (or shape) for a few seconds, then stopping, and the second artist placing her pencil where the first artist stopped and creating more of the drawing. The fun of double-doodling is that you really ad-lib what you are drawing together as you go. (No talking, please, to add to the suspense!)

WEARABLE ART

Start with a shirt, skirt, shorts, or pants from the thrift store and create colorful drawings to wear!

Materials
- Cardboard
- Recycled cotton clothing
- Nontoxic fabric markers (for example, Crayola Fabric Markers)
- Optional: paper, pencil, eraser, or colored pencils

Get Creative Help your child slip the piece of cardboard between the front and back sections of the shirt (so the markers do not bleed through). Invite your child to create a freestyle drawing on the clothing using fabric markers,

or sketch a design or idea with paper and pencil first, then draw on the clothing with the fabric markers (using pencil-and-paper drawing as a guide).

Artful Fabric Shoes

Your child sketches out a small design on a pair of new or recycled canvas shoes using fabric markers. She may wish to add some bright or creative shoelaces to finish off her shoe-design creativity.

CREATE A FUN-THINGS-WE-DO-TOGETHER SWEATSHIRT

Here's an idea that turns your child's drawing into a fashion statement! Kids use puff paints to draw a colorful drawing on a shirt about something special they enjoy doing with the person this homemade gift is for (such as basketball, fishing, reading, or baking cookies).

Materials

- Paper and pencil
- 1 adult-sized sweatshirt or hoodie
- Fabric puff paint
- 1 piece of cardboard

Get Creative Help your child slip the piece of cardboard between the front and back sections of the shirt (so the markers do not bleed through). Your child sketches out a drawing on practice paper first, then draws a similar drawing on the sweatshirt using the fabric puff paints. (Follow the manufacturer's directions for preparing the fabric and use of the puff paint.)

My kids made two of these sweatshirts for me many years ago for Mother's Day. My daughter (age four at the time) drew a pink-and-green stick figure (person) with a baseball and bat (because we loved to go to Cincinnati Reds games together). My son (age six at the time) drew a bright, multicolored drawing of a basketball player shooting hoops because we loved to play H-O-R-S-E together on the weekends.

ages 6–12

LETTER ART

Your child draws a big letter on a piece of paper to see what sort of imaginative character, animal, or object she can turn that letter into!

Materials

- Paper
- Drawing pencil
- Colored pencils (or markers)
- Eraser

Get Creative Challenge your child to make a clever (or silly) drawing with one, two, or three of the initials from her name. The letters might be turned sideways, backward, or upside down! Your child may make one of the letters giant and the others small, or turn one letter into a person (perhaps a police officer?), or an animal (perhaps an elephant?), or a wild and wacky monster with two heads. To add more creativity she may decide to put a hat on its head and draw some boots on its feet—you get the idea. Just encourage your child to turn on the imagination and see what she can draw!

Mystery-Loop Drawing

Invite your child to draw a page full of loops, circles, and curves without looking. (He closes his eyes or puts on a blindfold.) After he thinks he has filled up the page, he opens his eyes and creates a colorful design by filling in some of the shapes he made with colored pencils or markers.

FAMILY-TREE DRAWING

This is a terrific drawing idea to capture the characters in your family tree!

Materials
- A roll of white butcher paper
- Invisible tape
- Drawing pens or pencils
- Colored pencils (or markers)

Get Creative Help your child tape big sheets of paper to the floor to create a super-huge drawing surface. Then your child draws a giant tree on long sheets of butcher paper. Next, she draws the faces of all the people in your family on the tree! Your child may draw cartoon drawings or realistic drawings—whatever she likes.

Adventure-Drawing Challenge
Challenge your child to think of a family member, person, animal, or magical creature, then invent a big adventure for your being and draw it!

CRAZY-CREATURE FLIP BOOK

This is a good project for parents, grandparents, or caregivers to do with a child, with each person making his or her own Crazy-Creature Flip Book!

Materials
- 6 or more pieces of card stock for each artist (8½ by 11 inches)
- Pencil
- Eraser
- Markers
- Scissors
- Stapler
- Ruler

Setup Each artist selects one piece of card stock and folds it into three equal pieces—just as you'd fold a letter to place it inside an envelope. Help your child fold three other pieces of paper in exactly the same way (envelope-style), making creases where you fold. Now open the pieces of paper so that they are each flat.

Get Creative Next, ask your child to think of four animals she'd like to draw and you do the same. Now you both draw the first animal on a sheet of paper, with the head and neck of that animal in the top section of the paper, above the crease. Next, draw the midsection and arms of the animal in the middle section of the paper. Then, draw the feet and legs (and tail) of the animal in the bottom section of the paper. Each of you repeats this same drawing process three more times on the other pieces of paper, drawing three other animals, following the one-third, one-third, one-third rule for where to draw the head and neck, midsection and arms, legs and feet. When four pages are filled with animal drawings, each artist stacks his drawings in a pile. Place a blank sheet of card stock on the top and bottom of this stack for the front and back book covers. Next, staple these papers together along the left side to create a booklet. Design the cover of the books using markers and crayons. Fold each of the pages to the left and make a crease about 1 inch from the left edge of the paper, using the ruler as a guide. Next you will be cutting the inside pages you created— but you will NOT be cutting the front and back covers of your book. (These covers need to be in whole pieces to help hold your booklet together.) Use the scissors to cut a line through all four of the pages with animal drawings—right where the folds of the paper are, cutting from the right edge of the paper toward the left, stapled edge. Stop cutting about 1 or 2 inches *before* you reach the left edge. Flip the top, middle, and bottom pages of the book to create mismatched (crazy) animals!

Crazy-Costumes Flip Book

Work with your child to create another flip book (similar to the one above) by drawing a person or animal in four different costumes. For example, draw a person wearing a clown costume, then draw that same person wearing a cowboy costume, then a king's costume, then a pirate's costume. (Draw each person following the one-third, one-third, one-third rule described above, with head and neck in the top third, then midsection and arms in the middle section of the paper, then feet and legs in the bottom third of the paper.) When the drawings are finished, create a little flip book by following the directions above. When finished, flip the pages of the book to reveal wacky combinations of costumes.

ages 6-12

SNOWFLAKE COLLAGE

Cut small snowflakes from colored paper and arrange them on a black mat board or construction paper to create an artful collage.

Materials
- Scissors
- Copy paper in assorted colors
- Nontoxic white glue, such as Elmer's
- 11-by-14-inch black mat board or large sheet of black construction paper

Get Creative Help your child cut the colored paper into squares approximately 2 by 2 inches. Fold each piece of paper in half, then fold it in half again to create a square. Now your child folds it into a triangle and cuts tiny triangle shapes along each edge of the paper triangle. When she opens the paper, a colored snowflake is born! Encourage your child to create more

A DRAWING TIP

Here's a way that might help your child draw animals, objects, and people. Let's say your child wants to draw a bear. He or she starts by looking at a photo of a bear and studying the photo briefly to look for shapes in that animal's head and body. Ask your child if he sees an oval where the belly is. Does he see a triangle, square, or rectangle shape in another part of the animal's body or face? Encourage your child to look carefully and then quickly sketch some of the shapes he sees to get the drawing started. Then he uses a pencil to add more details, or uses an eraser to blend those shapes into a finished animal drawing.

colored snowflakes and create a collage by gluing the snowflakes on the black mat board, overlapping the snowflakes, or arranging them on the mat board in a colorful design. Let your child frame her favorite Snowflake Collage in a black shadow box or deep frame and give it as a gift!

Circle Snowflake Collage

Help your child follow the same project idea above, but start by cutting colorful paper circles (instead of squares), then fold, cut, and paste them on the mat board as in the above description.

Puzzle-Pieces Snowflake Collage

Invite your child to create colorful paper snowflakes using the directions for Snowflake Collage (above), but instead cut each snowflake into puzzle-like pieces (two, three, or four pieces each) and glue the pieces on the mat board in an interesting design.

Accordion Snowflake Collage

Your child can follow the directions to create a Snowflake Collage (above), but this time he folds small paper squares like an accordion, with about eight small vertical folds. He then cuts small triangles on each side of the folds, and opens the accordion snowflakes and glues them onto the mat board in an artful design.

Recycled-Materials Snowflake Collage

Your child cuts small circles, triangles, and squares from the Sunday comics in your local newspaper. She follows the directions in Snowflake Collage or Accordion Snowflake Collage (above) to make paper snowflakes. Finally, she arranges all the shapes on black or colored mat board and glues them in place.

Curlicue-Circle Collage

Help your child fold a colored piece of construction paper in half lengthwise and then cut four or five half circles along that folded edge. While each half circle is still folded, ask your child to use scissors to cut small curved slits all around the center of the folded paper circle. (It's best to experiment with the curvy shapes to see what your child likes: some might look like half of a valentine's heart, some might look like an apostrophe or the curvy part of a question mark.) Then your child unfolds the paper to reveal a design. Finally your child uses glue to paste these shapes on a black or colored mat board or construction paper to create a colorful collage.

ages
6-12

Encourage your child to toss some of his or her least favorite drawings or prints or paintings into a "recycled art box" (cardboard or plastic box with a lid) and cut these rejects into small shapes to use in future collage projects.

Triangle Collage

Your child starts with a black-or-white mat board, some glue, and brightly colored paper (assorted colors). He first cuts small to medium triangles from the paper and experiments to create an artful collage or design. Encourage your child to experiment with overlapping some of the triangles to create a pattern, or arranging the triangles so that their points are touching.

HODGEPODGE PAPER COLLAGE

Scraps of paper can be torn, rolled, and crumbled to create a very distinctive collage!

Materials
- 11-by-14-inch mat board or large sheet of construction paper (white, black, or bold color)
- Assorted paper scraps made out of construction paper, linen paper, tissue paper, rice paper, gift wrap paper, and so forth
- Scissors
- Nontoxic white glue, such as Elmer's

Get Creative To get started, your child experiments with tearing, folding, crumpling, and rolling small scraps of paper for a collage. (Ask your child to try crumpling paper, then smoothing it out flat to see if he likes that look too.) When he is satisfied with the textures and shapes of the papers, he can create a collage by gluing the paper scraps to the mat board. He might decide to fill the entire mat board with paper shapes or else leave some empty spaces.

Color-Mosaic Collage

Your child uses the materials listed above, but this time she creates a mosaic-style collage with small shapes of colored paper and glue. To begin, she'll use scissors to cut small rectangles, squares, or triangles from each sheet of colored paper and arrange them in piles according to color. Next, she'll squirt or brush a generous amount of glue on the mat board to create a line, shape, or design. Then that sticky area will be filled with one color of paper mosaics. Encourage your child to repeat this process with glue and other colors of paper to create a finished design.

Fancy-Footwork (or Handprint) Collage
Challenge your child to create colorful footprints (tracing his or her feet on paper) and arranging them on a giant piece of colored poster board or mat board. Your child may decide to overlap the footprints, or punch holes or cutouts in the shapes to create a clever design. Anything goes!

MOTHER NATURE COLLAGE

Have a nature scavenger hunt in your backyard or park with your child and gather interesting materials for a Mother Nature Collage.

Materials
- Natural materials, such as tree bark, stones, seashells, leaves,

husks, pods, and tiny tree branches (shake out the bugs before you bring these objects inside)

Get Creative Work with your child to gather natural materials outside. Then these treasures are arranged on a sheet of mat board in a design that your child thinks is interesting. (You and your child can each make a separate collage or work together on one.) Glue all the materials in place on the mat board with white glue. Let the glue dry completely before moving the collage.

MOUNTAIN COLLAGE

Cut long scraps of magazine photos and create a mountain design on mat board for a colorful collage.

- Color photos from magazines or newspapers
- 11-by-14-inch mat board (any color)
- Glue stick

Setup Help your child gather a large collection of magazine photos with interesting and vibrant colors. Invite her to select various shades of green photos or pick red, orange, yellow, and brown to create an autumnal mountain collage. Or she may take a completely different approach and make an abstract or rainbow-colored mountain-collage design.

Get Creative Let your child cut strips of the colored magazine photos into curvy, mountainlike shapes. When all the strips are cut she can arrange them on the table so she can make choices about the first shapes and colors she needs to glue on the mat board to start her collage. Then she'll continue to glue colorful strips on the mat board to create a finished Mountain Collage.

Mixed-Material Mountain Collage
Help your child follow the basic idea above, but this time he can add more texture, color, and pizazz to his collage by using some of the following materials to outline or accentuate parts of the mountains: glitter glue (create wavy lines of color with the glue); twine, string, or yarn (use glue to attach it to the top or bottom of the mountain range or any other areas below); colored paper or fabric scraps; and scissors to create individual trees and glue them in the foreground of his collage.

FIND INEXPENSIVE MAT BOARD FOR COLLAGE AND OTHER ART PROJECTS

Mat board is a terrific material to use as the base for collage and other projects, but whole sheets can be expensive. You can lower the cost tremendously by finding "value packs" of mat board (scraps) at your local art or craft store. The mat board scraps are typically about 11 by 14 inches, and the cost where I live is only $6 for a pack of twenty-five to thirty pieces. (You might also see if your local frame shop has scraps to offer for free or low cost.)

SPIRAL PAPER MOBILES

Create a colorful mobile (or paper sculpture) and hang it up and watch the colors twist and turn in a most amazing way.

Materials
- Four large sheets of colored construction paper (12 by 18 inches) or poster board (various colors)
- Scissors
- Fishing line, string, or ribbon
- Hole punch
- Invisible tape

Get Creative Work with your child to create this giant mobile together. Start out by placing two of the sheets of construction paper together. Use the scissors to make them both approximately

---

WHAT'S INSIDE THE COLLAGE BOX FOR ELEMENTARY-AGE KIDS?

Collage offers a marvelous way to experiment with colors, shapes, and interesting designs that include a variety of materials. There are no rules to collage making, so your child uses her own ideas to cut shapes from assorted papers and materials to see what she can create. Help your child round up some clever supplies before she begins so she can mix and match as she goes. Here are some suggestions to get started:

- Paper, including colored construction paper, textured drawing or writing paper, watercolor paper (painted), wallpaper, poster board, wrapping paper, paper bags, corrugated cardboard, recycled maps, magazines, cereal and pasta boxes, tissue paper, foil, glossy folders, cellophane, doilies
- Assorted fabric, such as lace and ribbon scraps
- Natural objects, such as leaves, grass, stones, bark, twigs, moss, shells
- Glitter glue
- Nontoxic white glue, such as Elmer's
- Markers
- Scissors
- Mat board (or foam board) for collage base or background

12 by 12 inches. Next, use the scissors to round the corners on both sheets. Now cut a really chunky or fat spiral from each sheet of paper, with only four loops and the width of each circular loop quite fat—about 3 inches wide. Leave a center circle in the spiral that is about 2 inches across. Repeat this same spiral-cutting process with the remaining two pieces of colored paper. Now place all four sheets of paper in a stack. Use the hole punch to cut a hole through the center point of all four papers, and thread the fishing line or string through them all, then tie a knot. Lift the string up in the air and let the multicolored spirals dangle. Parents or grown-ups can hang the mobile from the ceiling by using invisible tape. Or hang it on a tree limb on a sunny day to create an outdoor sculpture!

Sunny-Day Paper Tree Sculptures

You and your child can create a dozen colorful spiral mobiles (described above) in various sizes: medium, large, and extra-large. Attach string or twine to each of the paper mobiles and work with a grown-up to hang them on the low branches of a tree to create a colorful sculpture that dances in the wind. (This is a great way to decorate your yard for a birthday party or family picnic too.)

Your child makes a giant doodle with a blindfold over his eyes, then turns the drawing into an abstract painting!

Materials

- Long scarf (to use as a blindfold)
- Fine-tip marker (black or any color)
- 1 small to medium-sized canvas board
- Paintbrush
- Children's acrylic paints (professional-grade acrylics can be expensive, but a set of six or eight children's or student-grade acrylics are available at a reasonable price online or at your local art supply store)
- Small bucket of water

Get Creative Tie a blindfold loosely around your child's eyes. Then invite her to draw a giant doodly, loopy drawing over the entire canvas board without lifting her pen (and without looking). Then she removes the blindfold and paint the shapes (or loops) various colors to create an abstract painting.

Doodle Animal Art

Your child puts on the blindfold and tries to draw an animal with his eyes closed, then turns it into a colorful abstract animal painting; or while blindfolded your child does a big, random doodle of any kind on the paper or canvas board using a pencil or fine-tip marker, then removes the blindfold to see what sort of wild or wacky animal he can paint using his doodles.

MAGICAL MYSTERY LANDSCAPES

Imagine mountains with polka dots, meadows with stripes, a forest with zigzags, and create a colorful magical painting!

Materials
- Pencil and kneaded eraser
- Heavy drawing paper
- Colored pencils

Get Creative Your child uses the regular pencil to sketch a landscape scene: mountains, a farm, a forest, hills and valleys—whatever she likes! Then she colors the sky and other areas of her outdoor scene with dots, zigzags, wavy lines, and stripes to create a magical mystery landscape.

MASKING-TAPE PAINTINGS

Make really colorful, unique geometric paintings on canvas boards or tiny boxes!

Materials
- Masking tape
- Tempera paints or children's acrylic paints
- 3 small (2 inch) foam paint rollers
- 3 or more small disposable plastic plates

- One 5-by-7-inch white canvas panel
- Old vinyl tablecloth or newspapers (to contain the mess)

Setup Pour separate colors of paint onto each of the three small plates so your child has at least three colors to work with. Cut ten to twelve pieces of masking tape, each about 6 to 9 inches long, and loosely attach one end of each piece to the kitchen counter.

Get Creative Help your child place one or more pieces of tape around the white canvas panel, in any direction she likes. The tape can be positioned diagonally (corner to corner), vertically (top to bottom), or horizontally (side to side). Let your child dip a roller in the lightest-colored paint (yellow, for example) and roll it all over the canvas panel, including on top of the masking tape.

Let this paint dry thoroughly. Next, your child adds more strips of tape to the canvas in any direction she likes. Then the next layer of paint (orange, for example) is added. Let the paint dry. Your child continues with as many layers of tape and paint as she wishes, starting with the lightest shades and going to the darkest shades. When she

> *My seven-year-old son, Sam, is extremely creative. He told me once, "When I'm working on a sculpture or drawing, I tell myself this is going to be a masterpiece! And if I goof up, I just start over!"*
>
> —Sally from Ohio

is done and the paint has completely dried, gently peel the tape off, one strip at a time.

Tape-Painting on Burlap
Encourage your child to try the same painting process (above), but instead of using a canvas board, he applies the tape and paint to a piece of white or cream-colored burlap that he has first held in place on top of a piece of cardboard.

Tape-Painting on a Jewelry Box
Your child can make a creative and original jewelry box using this same Masking-Tape Painting process (above), but instead of painting on a canvas board, she paints on the lid of a small cardboard gift box (for example, a 6-by-7-inch white cardboard jewelry gift box with removable lid, available at paper-supply stores for a very modest cost). Tape and paint are applied to the lid of this white, shiny gift box just as

you would the canvas described above. Gently remove the tape when the paint has dried.

SPLATTER PAINTINGS

Your child can create distinctive splatter paintings outdoors using painter's tape and paints!

Materials
- Scissors
- Painter's tape
- Canvas board
- Disposable plastic cups
- Nontoxic washable tempera paints
- Large paintbrush (for each artist)
- Small bucket of water
- Optional: safety goggles or old sunglasses to protect your eyes from the paint
- Vinyl tablecloth or newspapers (to contain the mess)

Setup Pour separate colors of paint into each cup so your child has assorted colors to work with.

Get Creative Your child cuts strips of tape and places them on the canvas board in any pattern or shape he likes. The areas he puts the tape on will not be splattered with paint, so he can get creative with stripes, boxes, or any shapes he likes using the tape. After the tape is applied, he dips the brush in the paint and drizzles or splatters it on the canvas board. He continues with more paint colors. (A mess-free way to do a splatter painting is to soak the brush with paint, hold it a few inches above and parallel to the paper, and tap the handle-end of the brush right above the bristles to help the paint splatter onto the paper below.) Once the paint dries thoroughly, the tape is removed to reveal the finished design.

DRIP-DROP INSPIRATION PAINTINGS

Here's a painting challenge that can help your child create colorful freestyle paintings and drawings.

Materials
- Watercolor paints
- Small pointed paintbrush
- Drawing paper or card stock
- Small bucket of water

Get Creative Your child dips the brush in water and then into one watercolor paint. Next she drips little drops of concentrated watercolor paint from

ages
6–12

a small, pointed paintbrush onto parts of the paper. (It's best to hold the brush a few inches above the paper and tap the brush just above the bristles to drip the paint.) When the paint is dry, your child stands back and looks at the dots on the paper. She uses her imagination to decide what she might turn those dots into. Perhaps a page of monarch butterflies with colorful dots and black circles drawn around each dot, or colorful snowflakes falling on a winter scene. The color drops on the paper are the inspiration for your child to paint and draw something colorful and creative!

BLOBBY ABSTRACT PAINTINGS

Your child gets creative with blobs of paint and keeps going until he has a design he is happy with!

Materials
- Scissors
- Large sheet of cardboard
- Washable tempera paints in assorted colors and squeezable bottles
- Canvas board or large sheet of poster board or heavy paper

Get Creative Help your child use the scissors to cut about ten or twelve squares from the cardboard (about 3 by 3 inches each). These cardboard squares become the "blotters" to make the colored "blobs." Next, squeeze big blobs of paint in various spots on the poster board. (Encourage your child to experiment with putting a few blobs of one color right next to a blob of another color.) Next, your child places the cardboard squares on top of all the blobs of paint and applies pressure to squish the paint flat on the paper. He carefully removes the cardboard squares to reveal his blobby painting. He might also save the cardboard blotters full of color and create a cool collage with them (see below).

Blob-Square Poster Painting
Your child can create a second work of art by using the colored cardboard squares (blotters) used above (in

the Blobby Abstract Paintings) to create a giant collage on poster board. Optional: add words, slogans, or a poem to make a unique artful poster-painting.

Here's a satisfying, freestyle way for your child to create abstract art on burlap fabric outdoors!

Materials
- 3 or more colors of fabric paint (or tempera)
- 3 or more small squeeze bottles (available at craft stores)
- Vinyl tablecloth
- A 12-by-12-inch (or larger) piece of burlap fabric of any color
- Painter's tape

Setup Put one color of paint in each squirt bottle.

Get Creative Go outside and lay the tablecloth on a hard surface (concrete patio or sidewalk). Tape the burlap to the tablecloth to contain this messy project. Challenge your child to create a colorful, quick, loopy design on the burlap with the first color of paint. Next, she creates another quick design

with the second and third colors of fabric paint. Let the paint dry completely before moving the painting. Help your child hang her burlap painting up to admire or she can cut it up and use it for future craft or art projects.

Painted-Burlap Collage
Invite your child to create several burlap paintings (see the various burlap projects above) on two or more different colors of burlap. After the paint has dried, he cuts small pieces of the painted burlap and glues them on a mat board or hardboard panel to create a colorful, artful collage with lots of texture and with the scattered threads making an interesting design.

PLEXIGLAS PAINT-AND-PRINT

It's a painting and printing project rolled into one satisfying art activity! (See Cookie-Sheet Printing-Paintings on page 155 for more painting/printing projects.)

Materials
- 1 large sheet of Plexiglas (available at art-and-craft supply stores) or recycled metal cookie sheet

ages 6–12

MAKE TWO PORTFOLIO BOXES FOR SAVING YOUR ARTWORK

If your child makes a lot of artwork, then he may want to create two boxes (portfolios) to keep his work in. One box can be labeled "Keep Forever." (You know what's inside this one: all your child's favorite artwork. Trust me—it's really fun for your child to look at his work many years from now, so encourage him to keep his best stuff!)

The second box can be labeled "Recycle This Artwork." In this box, your child puts any artwork he created that he thinks is ho-hum (according to his own review—this is the work he is not that excited about). But this rejected work can be cut up and used to create other artwork or other fun things. He might consider using these scraps for future collages, handmade stationery, book covers, or other fun and fascinating things he can imagine.

- Large sheets of heavy drawing paper
- Tempera paints
- Paintbrush
- Newspaper or vinyl tablecloth (to contain the mess)

Get Creative Invite your child to create a painting or design on the Plexiglas surface (or the underside of an old metal cookie sheet) using the paints and brush. When she is satisfied with her painting, she quickly places a sheet of paper on top of the Plexiglas painting and uses her hands to firmly press the paper onto the Plexiglas. Then she carefully peels one corner of paper toward the center and slowly removes the paper from the Plexiglas. Then she places the print, paint side up, on the table to dry thoroughly. (This is a fun project for parent and child and a terrific solo art project after your child understands the basic printing process.)

POTATO-PRINT SCARF

Kids are excited to make this beautiful scarf by printing shapes cut from a potato! (This project needs a little help from a grown-up.)

Materials

- XXL men's cotton T-shirt
- Cardboard or aluminum foil
- Kitchen knife (for adult use only)
- 2 or 3 large (raw) potatoes
- 2 to 3 colors of fabric paint
- 2 disposable plastic plates

Setup Help your child cut a wide swath from the midsection of the T-shirt to use as the printable area for the scarf. In other words, you are removing the neck and sleeves and the bottom few inches of the shirt, but keeping the midsection to create an infinity scarf (looped scarf with no ends).

Place cardboard or foil between the two layers of the cut-out section of T-shirt before the printing begins. (This cardboard absorbs extra paint so it does not bleed to the back side of the scarf.) Use a kitchen knife to cut the potato in half. Then use the knife to score a 1- or 1½-inch-square shape in the center of each half of the potato. Next, place the knife on each of the four sides of this square and remove ¼ inch of thickness all around so that the square becomes raised from the rest of the potato. (When finished cutting, the square will look just like a rubber stamp with a raised, square shape in the middle.) Create a second square potato stamp using the other half of the potato.

Pour one of the colors of fabric paint onto each of the two plastic plates.

Get Creative Encourage your child to dip one potato in each of the two fabric paints and begin printing all across the front surface of the scarf. Next, your child dips the second potato in the other color of paint and adds more prints to the scarf. Let the paint dry thoroughly. When dry, flip the scarf over and let your child print more square shapes on the backside of the scarf too. (Follow the manufacturer's directions for setting the dye and washing the finished scarf.)

Tomato-Can Scarf

Follow the same basic instructions in the Potato-Print Scarf (above), but this time your child uses a small (6 ounce) tomato paste can, and uses burlap as the printing object instead of a potato! (See page 159 for instructions on making your burlap circle prints.)

Potato-Print T-shirt

Follow the same basic directions for the Potato-Print Scarf (page 251), but this time help your child create a T-shirt with multicolored squares (or diamonds) printed on it. Create a freestyle print design, or sketch out a design on paper and use painter's tape to help guide your printing.

Kitchen-Masher Printing

Follow the same basic directions for the Potato-Print Scarf (page 251), but this time help your child use a recycled potato masher (kitchen gadget) as the print object instead of a potato. (A potato masher has a curvy metal shape on one end and a wooden or plastic handle on the other end. Your child dips the curvy metal end of the masher into the fabric paint and begins printing on the T-shirt or other fabric.)

Masher-Print Apron

Start with a plain white cotton apron and fabric paints. (Plain cotton aprons are available at art and craft stores.)

Follow the directions in the Kitchen-Masher Printing activity (above), but this time help your child create a colorful, curvy abstract design on an apron. These aprons are good handmade gifts for parents and grandparents.

Triangle-Sponge Printing

Work with your child to do a printing project similar to the Potato-Print T-shirt (page 251), but this time cut a new kitchen sponge into three triangles of various sizes and use these shapes as the printing objects (instead of the potato). Let your child decide upon a basic design before he starts, or he might just create a spontaneous design with several colors of fabric paint.

CELERY PRINTS ON PAPER

Your child can create a clever print design with one or many colors of paint, and a stalk of celery and paper! Who knew celery could be so artistic!

Materials
- Several long stalks of celery
- Knife (for adult use only)
- Children's acrylic or tempera paint
- Disposable plastic plate
- Heavy drawing paper or construction paper

Recycle an old potato masher tool and let your child create colorful abstract prints on paper and fabric!

Materials

- Three or more colors of fabric paint
- Several sheets of heavyweight drawing paper
- A white or cream-colored piece of burlap fabric
- One recycled (wavy) potato masher
- Disposable plastic plates (for paint trays)
- Washable tempera paints in squeezable bottles (four or more colors of paint)
- Painter's tape
- Vinyl tablecloth (to contain the mess)

Get Creative Use knife to trim the stalk of celery (let your child decide if she wants to use the wide or narrow part of the stalk for printing). Pour a little paint in the plate, let your child dip the cut end of the celery in the paint, and experiment with printing on a practice sheet of paper. Now she can create a celery print design of her own on the paper using one or more colors of paint. Encourage experimenting with different colors of paper and paint until she finds a color combination and design that she is satisfied with. Let the paint dry thoroughly and hang the finished print on the wall to enjoy the artwork. (Or turn these designs into greeting cards or wrapping paper.)

Setup Put the tablecloth on the work table. Pour one color of paint on each of the plastic plates. Place one sheet of drawing paper on the table. Help your child cut a piece of burlap approximately the same size as your drawing paper. Use tape to fasten the burlap to the drawing paper and the tablecloth.

ages 6–12

Get Creative Your child dips the masher in one paint color and presses firmly on the burlap. He repeats with at least two more colors to create a curvy design all over the burlap. Next he can squirt a few blobs of a final color of tempera paint on the burlap painting. He places a sheet of drawing paper on top of the burlap painting and uses his hands to apply firm pressure (rubbing) all over the paper. Then he carefully peels the top paper off the burlap painting to reveal an abstract print on the paper and burlap. Let the paint dry thoroughly. Your child may wish to display his colorful print and painting on the wall or cut it up for his next artful collage.

ARTSY SPONGE-PRINTING

Kids enjoy using compressed sponge material (Sponge 'Ums) to create their own customized shapes for printing!

Materials

- Sponge 'Ums (compressed sheets of sponge material, available at teacher-supply or craft stores)
- Scissors
- Newspaper
- Fine-tip felt marker
- Tempera paints
- Disposable plastic plates
- Poster board, watercolor paper, or newsprint

Get Creative Your child uses a marker to draw any shape or object on the sponge material. (Perhaps she will draw a circle, half-moon, giant lips, butterfly, or any other shape that strikes her fancy!) She uses the scissors to cut the sponge shape from the Sponge 'Ums, and wets the sponge and wrings out the excess water. Then she dips the sponge in the paint and uses it to print on the paper.

HODGEPODGE PRINTING

Look around your home for safe, interesting objects that are just right for your child's creative printing!

Materials

- Assorted household items to use for printing, such as large (but thin) buttons, plastic or metal lids (various sizes and textures), cork tiles (thin sheets of cork for bulletin boards, cut into any shapes you wish), bubble wrap, corrugated cardboard (tear outer paper off to see the ridges), textured fabric scraps (such as corduroy)
- Children's acrylic, tempera, or fabric paint
- Nontoxic ink pad
- Disposable plastic plates
- Heavy paper

Get Creative Encourage your child to experiment with dipping objects into acrylic paint, tempera paint, the ink pad, or fabric paint to print on paper, cardboard, poster board, or fabric.

CLAY-CRITTER CHALLENGE

Your child makes a list of his favorite animals and starts creating a collection of clay critters!

Materials

- White air-dry modeling clay (for example, Crayola Air-Dry Clay)
- Vinyl tablecloth or old cookie sheet (to contain the mess)
- Assorted clay tools or small kitchen tools to create details
- Optional: tempera paints and paintbrush

Get Creative Challenge your child to think of ten animals, insects, or creatures that are fascinating or familiar. (Here's my list: alligator, dragonfly, catfish, porcupine, penguin, skunk, dolphin, ladybug, egret, and octopus.) She writes down the name of each of the critters on a small piece of paper, folds it in half, and tosses them all in the paper bag. Then, when your child is in the mood for creating critters with clay, she selects one of the papers and tries to make the animal or creature listed. (Your child may like to look at animal photos to see details and shapes of the animals before creating the critters.)

ages
6–12

Your child may need to use little dabs of water to help smooth out the clay as she goes if it seems dry. She can also use clay tools (or kitchen utensils, such as a fork, butter knife, spoon, or craft sticks) to add details. Keep the focus on the fun of creating with no worry about making

HOMEMADE SALT-DOUGH CLAY

This clay requires a little cooking and stirring (so it's a project that involves an adult), but once it cools, it's an easy, soft clay for creative projects for children six to twelve.

Ingredients
- ½ cup cornstarch
- ¾ cup water
- 1 cup salt
- Assorted food coloring
- Paper plate

Directions Mix the cornstarch, water, and salt in a small pan. Place the pan on the stove over low heat and stir constantly so it does not stick to the bottom of the pan. Continue to cook and stir until the mixture thickens and clumps and becomes difficult to stir. (The mixture in the center of the pan will thicken first, so stir that to the side and keep heating and stirring until every bit of the liquid has turned into thick clumps.) Remove from the heat and place the lump of dough on a paper plate, letting it cool to room temperature. Knead the dough until the texture becomes smooth. Divide into smaller lumps and knead a different color of food coloring into each lump to create different colors of clay. (Use a little liquid dish soap and the scouring side of a kitchen sponge to easily remove food coloring from your hands.) Once it cools your child can get creative with this colorful clay.

SIGN UP FOR A POTTERY CLASS!

If your child loves working in clay, it might be time to sign her up for a pottery class! Some classes for kids teach how to make hand-built clay creations. Some classes will teach how to use a real potter's wheel to create bowls, cups, and pots too. (Thrilling!) Students also learn to glaze (paint) their pottery with colorful pottery glazes (special pottery coating) and the teacher will fire their work in a kiln (clay oven) to turn the piece into a permanent work of art. Check for classes at your local arts organizations, or ask the staff at a nearby art supply store if they know about private pottery studios in your town.

a perfect animal! If your child wants to save her creatures, let them dry completely (for several days) and then she can use tempera paints to paint them.

Clay-Coil Creativity

Challenge your child to make something creative using clay coils. He starts by pinching off a ball of clay and gently rolling the ball back and forth with three or four fingers. Then he applies a bit of pressure as he rolls and watches the ball begin to turn into a snakelike coil. He can make more coils and wind them, one by one, into a spiral to create small, decorative bowls or pots. You can offer a bit of help to show how to pinch, twist, and shape these coils together to make imaginative creatures or objects. (Use a paper clip to add a little detail or texture as you go.) Encourage your child to experiment to see what he can create with clay coils.

PAPIER-MÂCHÉ MASKS

Your child can make imaginative animal masks or theatrical masks from newspapers and homemade paste and add the finishing touches with paint once they dry! (Safety note: parents must supervise all balloon play for children under eight years old to prevent choking on deflated balloons or balloon pieces.)

Materials

- Newsprint paper (or recycled newspapers)
- Papier-mâché goop (see recipe on page 260)
- Scissors
- Large balloon (to make two masks)
- Large plastic bowl or giant ice-cream tub
- Cookie sheet
- Safety pin
- Duct tape
- Washable nontoxic tempera paint
- Single-hole punch
- Yarn, ribbon, feathers, fabric, or other bits of embellishments
- Vinyl tablecloth (to contain the mess)

Setup Cover your kitchen table with the tablecloth. Make the goop (page 260) and let it cool. Help your child tear or cut newsprint into 1-by-6-inch strips. Tear a lot of paper strips before you begin the messy part of the project. Place the cookie sheet on the table and place the bowl or margarine tub on top. Blow up a balloon and knot the end. Place the knotted end of the inflated balloon inside the plastic bowl and secure to the bowl using duct tape.

Get Creative Give a short demo of how to dip a newsprint strip into the bowl of goop, making sure it is completely covered in goop. Pull the strip out, holding it over the goop bowl, and smooth off any excess goop by sliding your index and middle fingers

> In first grade we made a life-sized papier-mâché Santa Claus. I finished painting it all by myself while everyone else listened to Miss Willis reading a story. I loved dipping a big broad brush in jars of tempera paint and the smell of the paint and the drips! I was in heaven!
>
> —**MELANIE HALL,** artist and award-winning illustrator of over twenty-five children's books, including *Winter Song: A Poem* by William Shakespeare

259

down the length of the paper strip. Then place this strip around the balloon. Repeat this process, with you and your child placing wet strips of paper on the entire balloon, with about four layers of goopy paper strips covering it. Allow three to four days for it to dry completely. (Note: drying times will vary depending upon your climate and humidity.) When the strips are dry, pop the balloon with a safety pin.

Then help your child with the next two-step cutting process. First, insert the scissors at the bottom of the oval and cut the balloon-shaped paper creation in half lengthwise to create two masks. Second, use the scissors to cut out eyes and a mouth opening (or if the mask is purely decorative, just draw the eyes, nose, and lips). Encourage your child to use the paints to turn the mask into a creative and colorful animal or character face. Your

PAPIER-MÂCHÉ GOOP

Be sure to clean up any spilled goop while it's still damp. (Once it dries, it is more difficult to remove from floors and other surfaces.)

Ingredients
- 2 cups cold water
- ½ cup flour
- 2 cups boiling water
- 4 tablespoons sugar

Directions This goop-making process is for adults only, because it involves cooking and hot liquid. To begin, stir the cold water and flour together in a large bowl until all the lumps are dissolved. Pour 2 cups of tap water into a pan and boil it on the stove. Add the water-and-flour mixture to the boiling water, stirring to combine, and bring this goopy mixture to a boil again. Now remove from the heat and add the sugar. Let the goop cool completely.

ages 6–12

child can decorate with yarn, feathers, fabric, and the like. Help your child punch holes on each side of the masks (by the ears) and tie ribbons through the holes, knotting them off on the inside of the masks. Tie the ribbons in a bow to hang this artwork on the wall, or tie the ribbons around your head to wear the masks.

CREATIVE PHOTOGRAPHY CHALLENGE

Children six to twelve love to get creative with a camera! See what imaginative photo collections your child can make, or turn photos into a collage or other artwork too. This project is best for kids ages ten and up.

Materials
- Camera

Get Creative Challenge your child to find some colorful or interesting objects or places to capture in photographs. He can select a category or theme of photo scenes that he would like to capture or study and make his own collection of photos. Here are six photography themes to look for in the neighborhood or community to help your child get started:

Colors

Encourage your child to pick a color (or combination of colors) and take photos of interesting objects in that color. Then your child creates something with these color photos—perhaps an album, possibly a collage, or these photos (or pieces of the photos) can be used in some other interesting art project.

Nature

Challenge your child to look for color, texture, shapes, and beauty in all the things outdoors. Plants, animals, water, sand, mud, puddles, insects—the list goes on and on. Let your child find some artful natural objects or beings and capture them on camera.

Places

Your child starts by noticing colors, shapes, buildings, sidewalks, mountains, farms, schools, playgrounds, auto repair shops, stores, banks, and so on, and then he looks to see what clever close-up or distant photos he can take.

Friendship

Your child takes photos of friends doing something worthy of a good photo. These friends can be people or animals, spending time together. The idea is to capture their actions or facial expressions with photography.

Babies

Human babies and animal babies are wonderful to photograph because they sleep, play, and move about in ways quite different from grown-ups. Invite your child to take candid photos while a baby in the family or animal baby in the yard or barn is just doing what babies do.

Humorous Photos

Challenge your child to take humorous photos of your family pet or people doing silly things, or of family members having a good laugh. (Your child photographer could make a whole collection of laughs and smiles!) Or she might pick an object, such as a teddy bear or stuffed animal, and create silly situations for that teddy bear to be in and then take photos.

Building and Construction Activities

Children six to twelve can be very ingenious and creative builders. Building with blocks, boxes, and other miscellaneous household items presents a fun and fluid form of creativity that involves the pleasure of seeing a three-dimensional structure emerge quickly. As kids build, one good idea quickly gives rise to another. Your child may build an apartment building with a bunch of recycled shoe boxes and then suddenly get the idea to make shrubs and trees to complete her creation. And when the paper trees won't stand up properly, she may adapt her plan with pieces of cardboard that make those trees stand tall.

One of the most important things you can do to encourage this style of freewheeling construction creativity is to dispel the idea that building with blocks and boxes is just for preschoolers. To get this point across, gather up some blocks, boxes, and assorted household items and make a time for parent-and-child building activities together. To achieve this goal, join in a few construction activities with your child whenever time permits. There are projects below that are just right for parents, grandparents, and caregivers to tackle along with their six-to-twelve-year-old child. Grown-ups can also share a little expertise about how to use techniques for simple building projects in a very playful, nonpressured way.

DOWNTOWN CITYSCAPE

Start with an assortment of shoe boxes and empty cereal or pasta boxes and your child creates a big city or downtown blocks with shops and houses.

Materials
- Scissors
- Colored poster board
- Colored construction paper
- Assorted shoe boxes with lids (try boot boxes too, which are larger)
- Cereal and pasta boxes, and round cardboard oatmeal containers
- Markers
- Colored duct tape
- Optional: one medium-sized cardboard storage box (aka the big city parking garage)
- Invisible tape

Get Creative Help your child cut the poster board or construction paper to create a road or grassy area for the city and place it on the floor. Next, work together with your child to create enough buildings to make a downtown, with both tall buildings (large cardboard boxes) and one-story buildings (shoe boxes), and let your child use the markers to draw windows and doors on the buildings. If your child wants to get fancy, use colored paper and matching colored duct tape to "paint the buildings" and connect them all together so they look like a downtown block of buildings. He can also turn one larger cardboard box into a big parking garage and bring out the miniature toy cars to drive inside.

Cover the boxes with colored paper and use tape to hold it in place. Use markers and scissors to create windows and doors in the boxes. Help your child arrange the buildings into a small town. He may also want to make signs for the shops and tape them in place. Once your child builds a Downtown Cityscape with you, he may be able to create more buildings on his own to expand the construction.

TREES FROM PAPER BAGS

Your child can make easy paper trees to go along with the cardboard buildings or paper roads that she creates.

Materials
- A green marker
- Brown paper lunch bags
- Scissors
- Tape

Get Creative Work with your child to create the first tree together so she understands the process. Use a green marker to color the top 3 inches of a paper bag. When you've colored all around the top, use the scissors to cut fringe into the open (green) end of the bag. Stand the bag up and twist tightly in the middle section of the bag to make the tree trunk. (Note: the

> *The key is to challenge children to create their own ideas. Sure, give them facts and give them knowledge, but challenge them to do something new and innovative.*
>
> **—DR. STANLEY GREENSPAN,**
> former clinical professor of psychiatry and pediatrics and author of *The Growth of the Mind*

ages
6–12

bottom section of the bag, below the twisty part, will be the "roots" of the tree that will allow the tree to stand upright.) Use the tape to secure the trees to the road or sidewalk made of poster board or construction paper.

SHOE BOX DOLLHOUSE

Challenge your child to see what clever apartment building she can make with shoe boxes of various sizes (and a lot of tape).

Materials
- 4 or more cardboard shoe boxes
- Heavy-duty stapler and staples
- Colored construction paper
- Roll of wide clear packaging tape
- Scissors
- Optional: Colored paper, scraps of wallpaper, tape, markers, or other decorative materials

Get Creative Work with your child to create this dollhouse. First, remove the lids from the shoe boxes. Lay two shoe

265

boxes on the table, side by side and with the opening up (and bottom of the box down). Staple two shoe boxes together to create two (open) rooms in the dollhouse. Lay two more shoe boxes side by side in the same way and staple them together. Now place all four shoe boxes back to back and use the tape to hold the four shoe boxes together to create dollhouse. Use colored paper, scraps of wallpaper, tape, markers, and other materials to decorate the inside of each of the four rooms. (Use scissors to cut colored paper to fit inside the rooms of the dollhouse.)

Extra-Large Dollhouse

You can work with your child to add more shoe boxes to your building to create an even bigger house. Each time you stack another box on top, staple or tape it to the others. You can also stack the boxes in a different way to create a courtyard or lawn in the center

and a four-sided building created around that grassy area. Encourage your child to brainstorm and offer ideas to help design and build this Extra-Large Dollhouse.

MINIATURE CARDBOARD FURNITURE

After making a Shoe Box Dollhouse (above), you and your child can use the shoe box lids, along with scissors, tape, markers, and colored paper to create small furniture to go inside the apartments.

Materials
- Shoe box lids, cardboard, or heavy card stock
- Scissors
- Tape
- Colored construction paper
- Markers

Get Creative Create miniature beds, tables, couches, stoves, refrigerators, and even stairs and rugs using thin cardboard (from the shoe boxes) or heavy card stock. Help your child draw shapes, then cut and tape the pieces together. Work together to add colored paper or decorate with markers to make the furniture colorful.

Here's a quick way to build a parking garage with one ramp going up to the top deck and a side ramp going down!

Materials

- 1 large shoe box with a lid
- Roll of 2-inch-wide clear packaging tape or duct tape
- Scissors
- 1 large sheet of cardboard (12 by 12 inches)

Get Creative Work with your child to make a cardboard parking garage. First, remove the lid and turn the

DO A WOODWORKING PROJECT WITH YOUR CHILD

If you have basic carpentry skills and a few woodworking tools, perhaps it's time to tackle a woodworking project with your child. It's a fabulous experience for your child to see that he or she too can learn skills and create something useful or decorative with wood and tools. You can be a terrific role model, mentor, and teacher, with your child eventually coming to believe that with a little practice he or she too can make useful and creative things with wood and even other materials. Here are some possible projects: small wooden treasure box (or jewelry box), birdhouse, small (child-sized) wooden carpenter's tool carrier (with dowel rod for handle), window boxes or planter boxes, small wooden box for puppet stage, toy box, small table, doll furniture, and so on. (Be sure to have safety goggles available for everyone.)

Jobs that your child can do: measuring, hammering, sanding (by hand only, not with an electric sander), attaching hinges or small hardware.

shoe box upside down on the floor. Place the lid (facing up) on top of the overturned shoe box to create the top deck of the parking garage. (Note: the upward-facing lid creates a sort of railing or ledge all around the parking garage.) Let your child use pieces of tape to hold the lid to the shoe box. Now use the scissors to cut out a 4-inch section of "railing" from one end of the shoe box. (This is where you will attach the up-ramp so cars can enter the top floor of the garage.) Also use the scissors to cut a 4-inch section from another area of the lid to create your down-ramp so cars can drive down and out of the parking garage. Now you or your child can cut two 4-inch-wide pieces of cardboard for the ramps. Let your child

tape the ramps in place, then he can drive his miniature cars up into the parking garage.

SHOE BOX CONSTRUCTION CHALLENGE

Your child turns on her imagination to see what she can create with one or more shoe boxes!

Materials
- Shoe boxes or other empty boxes, such as cereal, pasta, or rice boxes
- Tape
- Scissors
- Miscellaneous household or recycled materials
- Optional: markers or construction paper

THE GLOBAL CARDBOARD CHALLENGE

Every year in October kids all around the world use huge sheets of cardboard to see what they can create. It's called the Global Cardboard Challenge, and it is organized by the Imagination Foundation. Check out their website, http://imagination.is/our-projects/cardboard-challenge, to see some more cool ideas (and a video) of what kids have made from cardboard boxes. Ask your school or neighborhood to organize your own event next October so you can be part of the global challenge to create something imaginative with cardboard!

ages 6–12

Get Creative Challenge your child to see what she can create with shoe boxes, tape, and other stuff she finds around the house. Here are a few challenges your child might try to build: boat, doghouse, zoo-animal cages, fire truck, go-cart, sled, train, wagon.

GIANT CARDBOARD PLAYHOUSE

This is a fine and challenging creative project to do with your child over a weekend!

HERE'S A BOOK WITH CONSTRUCTION KNOW-HOW

Building Big by David Macaulay is a book for kids with interesting information about how things are constructed. This author shows how bridges, tunnels, skyscrapers, domes, and dams are designed and built. This book also shows how imagination, common sense, and problem solving mix together to design and construct buildings. This book can give kids lots of ideas for creative construction projects and designs. Find his book at your local library or bookstore!

Materials

- Scissors
- Two giant cardboard boxes from huge appliances (check appliance, furniture, and building supply stores for large recycled boxes)
- 2- or 3-inch-wide packaging tape or duct tape
- Marker
- 2 or more shoe boxes
- Tempera paint and brushes (or roller)
- Optional: invisible tape and wallpaper or a roll of butcher paper or colored construction paper
- Optional: photos, drawings, or artwork (for decoration)
- Carpenter's knife (Adult use only. Remove knife from work area immediately after using it to avoid accidents.)

Get Creative Use scissors to cut the end flaps off one end of each of the big boxes. Lay the boxes on the floor, with the open ends of each box joined together. Use duct tape to tape these boxes together. Draw a door on the playhouse with a marker and use the knife to cut it on two sides only so that it is still attached along the left edge. Bend it carefully. Now you can open and close the door to enter the playhouse. Let your child draw windows, and tape the shoe boxes under the windows to create flower boxes. Take the cardboard playhouse outside or in the basement and use the paint and roller or brushes to paint the exterior of the playhouse. If your child wants to get fancy on the inside, tape wallpaper or colored paper to one or more of the walls. Let your child hang photos and drawings as artwork to decorate.

ages 6–12

CITY SKYSCRAPER

Create your best version of a skyscraper with cardboard, paint, and tape!

Materials
- Assorted-size cardboard boxes (check with grocery stores and liquor stores)
- Scissors
- Invisible tape or rubber cement
- Tempera paint and brush or small roller
- Colored markers
- Colored construction paper
- 2-inch-wide clear packaging tape or colored duct tape

Get Creative First help your child get some ideas about what skyscrapers look like. Check out some photos of skyscrapers (such as the Empire State Building) in magazines or in books at your local library so you have some good examples of tall buildings to create.

Work with your child to stack the boxes, with the largest ones on the bottom, to create a tall, skyscraper-like building. Use the scissors to cut scraps of cardboard from one of the extra boxes, and fold and tape these to create some small architectural details on the building. Paint all the boxes and let the paint dry. Add windows by using markers or paint, or by taping small squares of construction paper to the boxes. Use the wide packaging tape to tape all the boxes together to make your skyscraper more stable and permanent. Once your child sees the basic process, she may enjoy working independently on her own clever skyscrapers in the future.

BUILD A TWO-STORY BARN (WITH A HAYLOFT)

Here's a fun and easy way to create a two-story barn with a hayloft from cardboard boxes!

271

Materials

- Scissors
- Two medium-sized cardboard boxes
- 2-inch-wide clear packaging tape
- Optional: tempera paint and brush
- Yellow or white Easter grass or yellow construction paper

Get Creative Help your child cut the flaps (or lid) off the top of one of the boxes. Then turn the box on its side with the opening facing you. Next, slide one of the cardboard flaps that you removed into the midpoint of the box to create a hayloft running from side to side. Use tape to hold it tightly in place against the inside of the box.

Help your child cut the second box into sheets of cardboard to create a roof for the barn, and use tape to attach the roof. To add color, your child can paint the roof and the outside of the barn. When finished, he might fill the hayloft with yellow or white Easter grass or cut his own "hay" from yellow construction paper.

BUILD AN INDOOR FORT

Here are the basics for making a fort, but the excitement happens when your child adds his own creativity to make the fort unique.

Materials

- Kitchen or dining room chairs
- Small table or card table
- Blankets, bedsheets, tablecloths
- Large pillows
- Cushions or heavy books
- Large rubber bands or elastic hair bands

Get Creative Encourage your child to arrange chairs or small furniture together to create the basic structure of a fort. He can drape blankets, sheets, or tablecloths over the top of the furniture to begin making the fort. Then use heavy books or cushions to hold the sheets or blankets in place. (Or if he is using tall chairs with wooden backs with spindles, he might use rubber bands to hold the sheets and blankets in place.) Half the fun of building a fort is discovering ways to make it bigger and better as your child gets creative.

MAKE A MINIATURE ECO-HOUSE

Gather up some twigs, grass, and nature materials outdoors, grab a shoe box—and see what kind of habitat you can create together. (Note: be sure to shake out the bugs and critters or they will hitchhike right into your house!)

Materials
- One shoe box with a lid
- Assorted natural materials: twigs, grass clippings, leaves, shells, acorns, hay
- Optional: sturdy sticks or twigs

Get Creative Remove the lid from the shoe box and turn the box on its side, with the opening facing outward. Gather small twigs, grass clippings, dirt, or other natural materials with your child to cover the dwelling. Work together to place natural materials on top of the house to make a natural roof. Heap grass, hay, leaves, or dirt around the ends of the house to create two exterior walls made of natural materials. (If you'd like to create a patio, use the shoe box lid for the roof of the patio, with a few sturdy twigs as pillars or supports to hold the roof up in the air.) Once your child makes an Eco-House with you, she can get creative on her own, with more outdoor Eco-House building projects in the future.

Miniature Teepee
Challenge your child to gather twigs or sticks in the backyard or park to make a miniature teepee. He can use twine or string to weave and tie around the

end of the sticks to help hold the top of the teepee shape in place, or use a hair tie or rubber band to secure the ends together. (Provide a little bit of construction help as needed to get the project going.) Add fabric scraps or ribbon to mix color with natural building supplies for an alternate, decorative look if your child likes! Encourage your child to experiment and let his imagination find its way into the finished teepee construction.

SNOW-SCULPTURE DESIGNER

Now your child will be ready with some clever ideas about what to build after the next big snowstorm!

Materials
- Snow
- Sketchbook
- Optional: containers for scooping snow

Get Creative Give your child a little sketchbook labeled "Snow Sculptures and Buildings" to write down all her best ideas for small-, medium-, and large-scale things she would like to create with snow. (Half the fun is designing and drawing these creations in a snow sketchbook!) Then, after the next big snowfall, challenge your child to pick one of her snow sculptures or designs and try to build it with a friend or parent.

SUPER INVENTIONS SKETCHBOOK

Your child can brainstorm about something real or imaginary that he would like to invent in the future and put his best ideas in an inventions book!

Materials
- Sketchbook
- Pencil
- Eraser

Get Creative Ask your child to imagine something fabulous she would like to invent or design. Perhaps she'll design a spaceship with amazing gadgets or a futuristic houseboat that can travel the world at lightning speed. She can sketch out her design with paper and pencil. Here are a few design challenges (below) to get you started.

Try to design one or more of the following:
- your future dream house
- the vehicle of the future
- a house that travels with you

(on water, land, or in the air)
- a better refrigerator
- a rocket ship or space shuttle
- a pirate's ship
- a better doghouse
- a new type of skateboard
- a futuristic lawn mower
- a skyscraper of the future
- a city in outer space

Next-Best-Inventions Notebook
Challenge your child to start a notebook with lists and descriptions of any real or silly inventions he would like to see next. (No drawings in this notebook, just words and descriptions about your child's ideas.) He can just jot notes in his "Next-Best-Inventions Notebook" whenever a good idea pops into his mind.

Gather up boxes and materials so your child can become a creative inventor of robots! The robot can be colorful and whimsical or ever so serious!

Materials
- Assorted-size cardboard boxes (small, medium, and large)
- Various kinds of tape (duct tape, clear packaging tape, invisible tape)
- Scissors (for use by adults or older kids)
- Optional: empty toilet paper rolls (cardboard tubes), plastic water bottles, disposable cups, lids from water bottles, egg cartons, markers, glue, pipe cleaners

Get Creative Parents and kids work together to create cardboard robots with a variety of materials, such as those suggested above. (Older kids may prefer to design and create their own robots.) It's a challenging project, requiring trial and error to see what looks best and how it holds together. Try to keep it positive and enjoyable and be ready to help with the minor frustrations in the building or creative process.

DESIGN THE INSIDE OF A CASTLE

Your child imagines a clever design for the inside rooms in a castle, with inventions and features to protect the lady and lord from invaders!

Materials
- Sketch paper (or writing paper)
- Pencil and eraser
- Colored pencils
- Optional: castle books with design details, such as *Castle* by David Macaulay (ages 10 and up) or *Castle: How It Works* by David Macaulay (ages 7 and up)

Get Creative On the sketch paper, your child uses the various pencils to draw the rooms of the castle as squares or rectangles. She imagines some clever and creative inventions and gadgets that she might draw (or describe in words) to make an imaginary castle even better or to keep it safe from invaders.

ages 6–12

Music Activities

The six-to-twelve-year-old age group offers a large window of opportunity for musical creativity. Children love to experiment with child-friendly musical instruments, and many are enthusiastic about inventing original songs. They are still young enough to enjoy singing some classic children's songs with parents, siblings, and grandparents, and they like to play musical games too.

Some of the older children in this age range may get excited about a particular musical instrument and decide to try music lessons. Others may take a more playful approach and cobble together an impromptu band with several friends, singing and playing musical instruments in the living room or garage. All of these musical experiences are a terrific way to provide a solid foundation for musical creativity.

Your job as a parent is to offer a home environment that is supportive of your child's interest in music. Sing together, listen to music, and provide access to a few inexpensive musical instruments to experiment with. Encourage your child to be playful and creative and invent her own songs too. These are the small steps that set the stage for musical creativity to grow and expand throughout this period of your child's life.

TRADITIONAL SONGS FOR MUSICAL CREATIVITY

Select a repertoire of songs to sing in your family, and your child can use these melodies to create her own original songs too!

Materials
- Traditional songs, folk songs, or current favorites you know

Get Creative Learn the songs together, or parent and child take turns teaching each other familiar songs they know to create a collection of songs to sing on the go (in the car) or at home. Here are the words to ten excellent traditional children's songs that are enjoyable to sing together. What's more, once your child knows these melodies he can easily invent new verses or borrow these melodies as an easy way to begin to write his own songs.

PARENTS' BEST APPROACH TO ENCOURAGING
GRADE-SCHOOL MUSIC CREATIVITY *(ages 6–12)*

- Have a collection of recorded children's music on hand that is playful and fun for your child to listen to at home and in the car.
- Sing familiar songs together on a regular basis just for the fun of it. (Let your child have the pleasure of selecting favorite tunes to sing.)
- Have a few child-friendly musical instruments at home for your child to try. (See Best Musical Instruments, page 293.)
- Encourage your child to do fun music activities with his friends as an alternative to screen-time activities.
- Do some of the songwriting activities below with your child. (This is a terrific way to encourage your child to get comfortable and excited about creating her own songs during childhood.)
- If you can play a musical instrument, ask your child to sing a favorite song as you play along.
- Go to child-friendly music events in your community.
- If your child seems interested in music lessons, look for a teacher who offers an age-appropriate, positive approach to teaching music skills.
- Include singing and musical games during Family Creativity Night and in your child's birthday party activities.

This Old Man

This old man,
He plays one,
He plays knick-knack on my thumb
With a knick-knack paddywhack
Give a dog a bone,
This old man goes rolling home.
This old man,

He plays two,
He plays knick-knack on my shoe
With a knick-knack paddywhack
Give a dog a bone,
This old man goes rolling home.
This old man,
He plays three,
He plays knick-knack on my knee

ages 6–12

With a knick-knack paddywhack
Give a dog a bone,
This old man goes rolling home.
This old man,
He plays four,
He plays knick-knack on my door
With a knick-knack paddywhack
Give a dog a bone,
This old man goes rolling home.
This old man,
He plays five,
He plays knick-knack on my hive
With a knick-knack paddywhack
Give a dog a bone,
This old man goes rolling home.
This old man,
He plays six,
He plays knick-knack on my sticks
With a knick-knack paddywhack
Give a dog a bone,
This old man goes rolling home.
This old man,
He plays seven,
He plays knick-knack up to Devon
With a knick-knack
    paddywhack
Give a dog a bone,
This old man goes rolling
    home.
This old man,
He plays eight,
He plays knick-knack on
    my gate

With a knick-knack paddywhack
Give a dog a bone,
This old man goes rolling home.
This old man,
He plays nine,
He plays knick-knack on my spine
With a knick-knack paddywhack
Give a dog a bone,
This old man goes rolling home.
This old man,
He plays ten,
He plays knick-knack now and then
With a knick-knack paddywhack
Give a dog a bone,
This old man goes rolling home.

Yankee Doodle

Yankee Doodle went to town,
a-riding on a pony,
Stuck a feather in his cap
and called it macaroni.
Yankee Doodle keep it up,
Yankee Doodle dandy,

> I always loved to sing. Long before karaoke came around, I would sing along with my favorite recordings of Broadway shows; playing all the characters and creating the dances.
>
> —**CATHY FINK,** Grammy Award–winning musician, singer, songwriter

Mind the music and the step
and with the girls be handy.

The Ants Go Marching

The ants go marching one by one,
Hurrah, hurrah.
The ants go marching one by one,
Hurrah, hurrah.
The ants go marching one by one,
The little one stops to suck his thumb,
And they all go marching down
Into ground to get out of the rain,
Boom! Boom! Boom!
(Next verses:)
Two by two . . . tie his shoe
Three by three . . . climb a tree
Four by four . . . shut the door
Five by five . . . take a dive
Six by six . . . pick up sticks
Seven by seven . . . pray to heaven
Eight by eight . . . shut the gate
Nine by nine . . . check the time
Ten by ten . . . say "THE END!"

Pop Goes the Weasel

'Round and 'round the cobbler's bench
The monkey chased the weasel,
The monkey thought 'twas all in fun
Pop! goes the weasel.
A penny for a spool of thread
A penny for a needle,
That's the way the money goes,
Pop! goes the weasel.

Up and down the London road,
In and out of the Eagle,
That's the way the money goes,
Pop! goes the weasel.
I've no time to plead and pine,
I've no time to wheedle,
Kiss me quick and then I'm gone
Pop! goes the weasel.

Frère Jacques (English version)

Are you sleeping, are you sleeping,
Brother John? Brother John?
Morning bells are ringing. Morning
    bells are ringing.
Ding, dang, dong. Ding, dang, dong.
(or French version)
Frère Jacques, Frère Jacques
Dormez-vous? Dormez-vous?
Sonnez les matines! Sonnez les matines!
Ding, dang, dong. Ding, dang, dong.

Row, Row, Row Your Boat

Row, row, row your boat
Gently down the stream
Merrily, merrily, merrily, merrily
Life is but a dream.

I've Been Working on the Railroad

I've been working on the railroad
All the livelong day,
I've been working on the railroad
Just to pass the time away.
Can't you hear the whistle blowing?

Rise up so early in the morn.
Don't you hear the captain shouting,
"Dinah, blow your horn."
Dinah, won't you blow,
Dinah, won't you blow,
Dinah, won't you blow your horn?
Dinah, won't you blow,
Dinah, won't you blow,
Dinah, won't you blow your horn?
Someone's in the kitchen with Dinah
Someone's in the kitchen I know
Someone's in the kitchen with Dinah
Strumming on the old banjo, and
    singing
"Fee-fi, fiddle-e-i-o,
Fee-fi-fiddle-e-i-o,
Fee-fi-fiddle-e-i-o,"
Strumming on the old banjo.

If You're Happy and You Know It!

If you're happy and you know it,
Clap your hands.
If you're happy and you know it,
Clap your hands.
If you're happy and you know it,
Then your face will surely show it.
If you're happy and you know it,
Clap your hands.
If you're happy and you know it,
Stomp your feet.
If you're happy and you know it,
Stomp your feet.
If you're happy and you know it,
Then your face will surely show it.
If you're happy and you know it,
Stomp your feet.
If you're happy and you know it,
Shout, "Amen!"
If you're happy and you know it,
Shout, "Amen!"
If you're happy and you know it,
Then your face will surely show it.
If you're happy and you know it,
Shout "Amen!"
If you're happy and you know it,
Do all three.
(clap, clap, tap, tap, "Amen!")
If you're happy and you know it,
Do all three.
(clap, clap, tap, tap, "Amen!")
If you're happy and you know it,
Then your face will surely show it
If you're happy and you know it,
Do all three.
(clap, clap, tap, tap, "Amen!")

The Bear Went Over the Mountain

The bear went over the mountain,
The bear went over the mountain,
The bear went over the mountain,
To see what he could see.
To see what he could see,
To see what he could see,
The bear went over the mountain,
To see what he could see.
The other side of the mountain,

The other side of the mountain,
The other side of the mountain,
Was all that he could see.
Was all that he could see,
Was all the he could see,
The other side of the mountain,
Was all that he could see.

She'll Be Comin' 'Round the Mountain
She'll be comin' 'round the mountain
when she comes,
She'll be comin' 'round the mountain
when she comes,
She'll be comin' 'round the mountain,
She'll be comin' 'round the mountain,
She'll be comin' 'round the mountain
when she comes.
She'll be drivin' six white horses
when she comes,
She'll be drivin' six white horses
when she comes,
She'll be drivin' six white horses,
She'll be drivin' six white horses,
She'll be drivin' six white horses

when she comes.
And we'll all go out to see her
when she comes,
And we'll all go out to see her
when she comes,
Yes, we'll all go out to see her,
Yes, we'll all go out to see her,
Yes, we'll all go out to see her
when she comes.

HALF-AND-HALF SONGS

Try this idea for kids and parents or for two friends working together to create new verses for old traditional songs!

Get Creative Your child picks a song from the list of traditional songs above. (Or check out Sing Traditional Children's Tunes on page 87 for more songs.) He sings a few lines of the song and then creates new verses. (It's extra-fun when two singers take turns, with each person calling out a quick

ages 6–12

idea for a new verse, then both people singing it together.)

Here are four of my favorite traditional songs that are perfect for creating Half-and-Half Songs:

- "She'll Be Comin' 'Round the Mountain" (below)
- "Old MacDonald Had a Farm" (see page 105)
- "Three Little Monkeys" (see page 176)
- "Mulberry Bush" (see page 176)

Here is a sample Half-and-Half Song: Use "She'll be Comin' 'Round the Mountain" as your base song. To start, both singers sing the traditional verse one time through (see page 282 for lyrics). At the end of the traditional verse of the song, the first singer quickly calls out an idea for a new verse, for example, "cooking spaghetti and meatballs," and both singers start singing:

She'll be cookin' spaghetti and meatballs
when she comes,
She'll be cookin' spaghetti and meatballs
when she comes,
She'll be cookin' spaghetti and meatballs,
She'll be cookin' spaghetti and meatballs,
She'll be cookin' spaghetti and meatballs
when she comes.

At the end of that verse the second singer quickly calls out an idea for a verse, for example, "bringing her little doggie," and both singers start singing:

She'll be bringin' her little doggie
when she comes . . .

Keep singing!

SONG STARTERS

Your child uses a familiar melody from a song he knows to start a clever new song.

Materials
- Pencil and paper
- A familiar melody (use a favorite pop song or start with one of the traditional songs listed on pages 278–82)

Get Creative Parent and child can try this activity together as a way to jump-start this fun songwriting activity. Pick a song you know and use the melody, but create all new words. Make it silly or make it serious. Use the pencil and paper to jot down your ideas, or just start singing and see what you can create. Sing your homemade song to your child and challenge your child to use

one of the song starters below to create a song too!

Here's a sample song I created using the "Wheels on the Bus" melody:

Dogs on the Bus

> *The dogs on the bus*
> *Ate pork and beans,*
> *Pork and beans,*
> *Pork and beans.*
> *The dogs on the bus*
> *Ate pork and beans all day long.*
> *The driver on the bus*
> *Said, "That's enough,*
> *"That's enough,*
> *"That's enough."*
> *The driver on the bus*
> *Said, "That's enough,*
> *"Now open the windows, please!"*

(Now add a few more silly verses of your own to this song!)

GROW-GROW-GROW YOUR SONG

Here's a fun and easy way to create new songs and verses with each person taking a turn adding to the song.

Materials
- The "Row, Row, Row Your Boat" song
- Optional: pencil and paper

Get Creative Work with your child to invent songs using the old "Row, Row, Row Your Boat" tune, with all new words. Use the pencil and paper to jot down your ideas, or just take turns singing and seeing what you can create. Here is a quick example to get you started:

Ride Your Bike . . .
> *Ride, ride, ride your bike,*
> *Quickly down the hill,*
> *Merrily, merrily, merrily, merrily,*
> *Don't you take a spill.*

Now encourage your child to turn up his imagination to see what he can create and sing on his own!

ANIMAL-ANTICS SONGWRITING GAME

Animals do humorous things all day long—so add that silliness to a homemade song, with parent and child or two or more friends creating songs together.

Materials
- Pencil and paper
- Paper bag
- Words for the song "The Bear Went Over the Mountain" (see page 281)

Setup Each person thinks of an animal and a place of any kind (for example,

> One way to start making up songs is to replace the words of old familiar songs with your own words. Here's a silly example. Sing this to the melody of "The Alphabet Song"
>
> *I love peanuts, I love jam,*
> *I love turkey, I love ham,*
> *I love sun and skies so blue,*
> *I love me and I love you.*
> *Now I sang this song for free,*
> *Won't you sing this song with me?*
>
> **—CATHY FINK,**
> Grammy Award–winning musician, singer, songwriter

weasel + laundry) and writes the words on a piece of paper. Write as many word combinations with animal + place as you can think of on separate papers. Fold the papers in half so you can't see the writing and toss them in a paper bag.

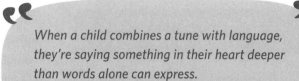

> *When a child combines a tune with language, they're saying something in their heart deeper than words alone can express.*
>
> **—JOHN FEIERABEND,** artist director of the Feierabend Association for Music Education and author of *The First Steps in Music*

Get Creative Take turns pulling a paper from the bag and inventing new verses to the tune of "The Bear Went Over the Mountain" or any other familiar song. For added fun, after you sing the new verse one time through, then the whole group joins in singing it too. Here's a sample of the song created from the words *weasel + laundry*:

The weasel went to the laundry,
The weasel went to the laundry,
The weasel went to the laundry,
So he could wash his clothes.
So he could wash his clothes,
So he could wash his clothes.
The weasel went to the laundry,
So he could wash his clothes.

Create a "What Happened Next" Verse
Add more verses to the Animal-Antics songs you create (above) about other events that happened next.

For example for verse two, of the "weasel" song, the next line might be "But he forgot the soap! But he forgot the soap!"

Create a "Who Else Was There" Verse
Add another verse to your homemade Animal-Antics songs (above) about a surprising or silly person or creature who was also there—for example, in the weasel song: "A fish jumped in the sink! A fish jumped in the sink!"

Animal-Antics Circle Songs
Get a bigger group of friends or family members together and sit in a circle on the floor for a rip-roaring time of everyone taking turns inventing new silly verses for an Animal-Antics song. Everyone can think of silly ideas that pop into their mind, or give everyone a few minutes to write notes with ideas if they prefer to plan ahead with their song ideas.

ages 6-12

CREATE A "SOMETHING" SONG

One favorite word can be the inspiration for a brand-new song!

Get Creative Invite your child to look at the "Something" List (below). Ask her to pick a word on that list and write down three other things that the word reminds her of. For example, next to the word *little* she might write *bird, dancer, shoe*. After the word *yellow* she might write *bus, flower, sunshine*. After she's written twenty or thirty words on the paper, your child picks her favorite words on the list and writes a song. She can sing it to a familiar tune or make up her own melody! Encourage her to keep going until she finds just the words and melody she likes.

The "Something" List
Your child can use this list for creating his own homemade songs. To get some ideas, he writes down the first three words that pop into his mind for each of the following words:

- Little
- Big
- Fluffy
- Shiny
- Hot
- Cold
- Red
- Green
- Happy
- Sad
- Fast
- Slow
- Blue
- Yellow
- Wide
- Narrow
- Round
- Square
- Book
- Friend
- Beach
- Mountain
- Bug
- Bird
- Sweet
- Sour
- Spicy
- Heavy
- Light
- Zoo
- Farm
- Orange
- Purple
- Favorite
- Family
- Surprise
- Container
- White
- Black
- Messy
- Neat
- Hello

CREATE A SILLY-FOOD SONG

Comedian and actor Adam Sandler sings a song about "Sloppy Joe and the Lunch Ladies." Now it's your child's turn to write a silly-food song too!

Materials
- Pencil and paper

Get Creative Try this musical activity with your child to jump-start some songwriting creativity! You each write down some foods that are either silly to say (or sing) or really tasty. Now, you each just start writing a song to see what you can create. Or put two

A SILLY-FOOD-SONGS ALBUM

Check out this wonderful album with wacky food songs from Cathy Fink and Marcy Marxer: *Bon Appetit! Musical Food Fun*. I highly recommend this album; it's entertaining to listen to and a great inspiration about imagination and writing songs. It is available on their website: www.cathymarcy.com (It's no surprise that the duo has won a Grammy Award for their children's music.)

imaginations to work and brainstorm with your child and create a silly-food song together. Once you each create some words for your song, borrow a tune and sing it. Edit as you go. Create songs with confidence! (See the list of Melodies You Can Borrow to Create Your Own Songs, pages 278–82.)

CREATE A BAND-NAME JOURNAL

There are some incredible, awful, hilarious, weird, and fabulous names for real bands! Now it's your child's chance to stretch his imagination to come up with clever names for a band.

Materials
- Notebook or journal
- Pencil

Get Creative Encourage your child to keep a notebook for any clever names for bands or musical groups that pop into his mind. (One of my favorite names for a musical group is The Weepies! I like their music too!) Your child might keep this notebook forever and enjoy reading it many years from now.

ages 6–12

Here's another way to invent creative names for musical groups and have a few laughs during family time. At dinner tonight, ask everyone in the family, "What would you name your very own rock band?" and see what answers they come up with.

My family kept this conversation going at the dinner table when my kids were teenagers. We invented some increasingly weird, silly, and dopey names the more we brainstormed together. (Keep a list!) My family still teases me about my all-time-favorite rock-band name (which everyone else said was the "WORST BAND NAME EVER!"): Yellow Corn. I still like that name! And if I ever create my own rock band . . . that's the name of the band.

UPBEAT AND CREATIVE MUSIC FOR KIDS

Here are three entertaining collections of children's songs that serve as lively examples of musical creativity for kids:

- *Pocket Full of Stardust* by Cathy Fink and Marcy Marxer—These two-time Grammy Award winners present exuberant and playful songs for children with a repertoire of traditional and contemporary folk, old-time country, and swing music. Their splendid harmonies are backed by acoustic and electric guitar, five-string banjo, mandolin, cello, banjo, ukulele, percussion, and many other instruments.

- *You Are My Little Bird* by Elizabeth Mitchell—Elizabeth Mitchell, a Smithsonian Folkways recording artist, has been recording and performing music for children since 1998. (Check out other terrific children's releases from Elizabeth Mitchell.)

- *A Child's Celebration of the Silliest Songs* by various artists (produced by Music for Little People)—This collection of children's tunes includes a mix of old-time songs with funny lyrics and familiar tunes from Raffi. A sampling: "Beans and Cornbread" by Taj Mahal and Linda Tillery, "Shake My Sillies Out" by Raffi, and Little Richard doing "On Top of Spaghetti."

KEEP A SONGWRITER'S NOTEBOOK

(Save the notebooks for future reading and songwriting.)

Professional musicians often carry around a little notebook and jot down good song ideas, and kids can do this too.

Materials
- Notebook or journal
- Pencil

Get Creative Encourage your child to write down phrases, ideas, titles, or whole songs when inspiration strikes.

A SONG ABOUT MOST ANYTHING!

Here's a poem I wrote about the joyful freedom we have to write a song about anything that pops into our imagination!

Did you know that you can sing
A song about most anything?
Monkeys marching to and fro,
Yankee Doodle on the go,
Meatballs rolling down the hill,
Old Susannah, crying still,
Hills and valleys, birds and bears,
A silly song about underwear.
Do it with joy and make it your own.
Sing to tickle your funny bone.

ages 6–12

- It's a good way of remembering any new songs your child is currently working on.
- Kids can make copies of the CD and give them to friends and family as a creative, homemade gift.
- These recordings are a great way to preserve your child's musical creativity and are really entertaining to listen to in the future.

Record songs on a computer or smart phone or get a small audio-recording device that is easy to use.

EXPERIMENT WITH MUSICAL INSTRUMENTS

Pick an instrument and let your child give it a try!

Materials
- Any of the Best Musical Instruments for Kids Ages 6 to 12 (see page 293)

Get Creative Encourage your child to test out the sound and the basic way to play the instrument with freestyle music-making and creating melodies. If one particular instrument seems exciting, your child might request some lessons.

> *Some of the pivotal music memories I have are sitting at the piano with my mother singing folk songs to me. Those were experiences that led me into music.*
>
> **—STEPHANIE STEIN CREASE**, author of *Music Lessons*

PERCUSSION PLAY-ALONGS

Gather a group of friends or family members and create a play-along band!

ages 6–12

Materials

- Recorded music
- An assortment of percussion instruments (see page 293 for ideas)

Get Creative Your child invites a few friends or family members to make some music using an assortment of percussion instruments. Your child can even make Breadcrumb Musical Shakers (page 294). Turn on some recorded music and everyone tries to play along.

BEST MUSICAL INSTRUMENTS FOR KIDS AGES 6 TO 12

- Piano
- Electric keyboard
- Ukulele
- Harmonica
- Kazoo
- Glockenspiel
- Panpipes
- Lollipop drums
- Guitar (best for older elementary-age children)
- Kid's accordion
- Chimalong (similar to xylophone)
- Lap harp
- Recorder
- Bongos (two small drums joined together, each with a different sound)
- Triangle (metal instrument you play with a metal stick)
- Castanets (a wooden percussion instrument that makes a click-clack sound)
- Cabasa (a rattle covered in beads, an instrument originally from Brazil)
- Bread Crumb Musical Shakers (see directions for making this instrument on page 294)
- Kids' djembes (a drum from Africa that you play with your hands)
- Tambourine (small instrument with metal jingles that you tap and shake)
- Wooden clackers (shake them to make a click-clack sound)
- Rhythm sticks (wooden sticks you tap together)
- Conga shakers (small wooden or plastic shakers)

BREAD CRUMB MUSICAL SHAKERS

Here's a super-easy way for your child to make a very respectable musical shaker.

Materials
- About ½ cup of dried rice
- One empty bread crumb container (cardboard tube with lid) from the grocery store
- 2-to-3-inch-wide clear packaging tape
- Optional: colored construction paper and markers to decorate the instrument

Get Creative Your child adds the dried rice to the empty bread crumb container. Then she replaces the container's plastic lid and uses the clear packaging tape to secure the lid permanently. This shaker is used as a percussion instrument to add rhythm to any songs your child sings, creates, or records. It is a good-sounding shaker!

Coffee Shakers
Your child can also use the same container and instructions listed above, but fill it with about ½ cup of whole coffee beans. This shaker creates a

> "It takes skills to "compose" a song, but any child who can make up a melody is composing.
>
> —CATHY FINK,
> Grammy Award–winning
> musician, singer, songwriter

WHERE TO FIND SOME OF THE INSTRUMENTS

Check out the following retailers to find some to the instruments listed on page 293:
- Groth Music www.grothmusic.com
- Musician's Friend: www.musiciansfriend.com/pages/kids
- Music in Motion: www.musicmotion.com
- Woodstock Chimes: www.woodstockchimes.com

ages 6-12

different percussion sound from the rice shaker.

CREATE A MELODY ON A KEYBOARD

Tap on the keyboard and experiment to see what tunes your child can create on the piano.

Materials
- Piano (toy piano, full-sized piano, or electronic keyboard)
- Optional: small recording device

Get Creative Try this activity once or twice with your child to get this musical creativity started. Sit down at the keyboard and tap out a series of six, eight, or twelve notes. Experiment with different notes (make some fast and some slow) until you get a short, catchy melody that sounds good to you. Repeat the melody two or three times, or create a second catchy series of notes and add it all together to make a short song. If you create a portion of a song you like, record it on a small audio-recording device (or computer or phone) so you can remember it or add to it later. Now let your child create her own clever melody following this same process.

Create a Melody on Your Recorder

Your child can easily create his own melodies using a recorder too. Once he has a melody he likes, he invents some words to go along.

Create a Melody on a Glockenspiel or Xylophone

Your child can have fun using a glockenspiel or xylophone to create a tune too. She uses the mallet to tap out the notes; trying different combinations of notes—some fast, some slow—until she gets a short section of eight to twelve notes that sound good to her ears. (Try this activity with your child to get things started.) Encourage your child to record the finished song on a small audio recorder so she can remember the song and add to it on another day. (She might add words too, or make it just an "instrumental song.")

> " Age six and up is the time when many children begin to learn to play a musical instrument. I always say to parents, don't be worried if the first instrument doesn't go so well. Playing an instrument is a little like falling in love. If it doesn't work out the first time, we don't say, "Oh, love is not for you, dear!" We say, "Oh well, try again." So this is what we want to do with our children. "
>
> —**BONNIE SIMON**, executive producer and creative director of the Stories in Music collection of albums for children

Get a group together, and let the wild rumpus begin!

Materials

- One small handheld drum for each person (use real drums, such as bongos, or create your own drums with plastic ice-cream tubs or a large bowl turned upside down)

> " It is creative to learn to play music with others; you are learning to listen, engage, take turns, and create something together. "
>
> —**CATHY FINK,** Grammy Award–winning musician, singer, songwriter

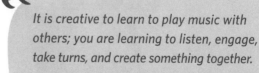

TWO KID-FRIENDLY WIND INSTRUMENTS

Here are two fairly easy instruments kids will enjoy experimenting with:

A Recorder

This is a type of wind instrument (or flute) that is easy to play and inexpensive too. Recorders are made of plastic or wood. To make music, you blow air through the mouthpiece. To change the sound coming from the recorder, you use your fingers to cover or uncover the holes.

- To play low notes, cover a lot of the holes with your fingers
- To play high notes, place fingers over only a few holes
- Practice breathing deeply and evenly to play lots of notes

Panpipes

This is an ancient musical instrument that comprises five or more pipes (or hollow tubes) of various lengths. Some panpipes are made of bamboo, some are made of plastic, and they are often wrapped together by twine. Panpipes can be a bit tricky to play in the beginning. But once your child gets the hang of it, he can make interesting sounds and good-sounding songs. To start, your child holds the instrument under his mouth and blows over the top of the pipes. He keeps aiming his breath and blowing until he hits the right spot—just slightly over the top of the bamboo pipes. (It's helpful for you to try this instrument with your child to give some easygoing, quick tips about how to play.) Encourage your child to experiment with long, slow breathing, and short, fast breathing, and aim at each individual pipe (tube) to create musical sounds.

A SON'S PERSISTENCE ABOUT A SET OF DRUMS

When my son was about twelve years old, he wanted to get a set of drums. I was a single parent at the time, and I was reluctant. For one thing, I thought it would make our home noisy and stressful, with constant arguments about keeping the noise down during much-needed quiet times in the family. Second, I wasn't sure how much lasting interest my son would have for learning this musical instrument. But my son persisted and he did indeed get a set of drums, took lessons, and learned to play. He enjoyed practicing regularly and he also had fun playing with his best friends, who had band practice in our living room over many happy weekends. I saved the note that my son wrote to me to convince me to say yes to a set of drums. Here is that note, which he titled "Why You Should Let Me Get Drums, Mom!":

1. *A good alternative to expensive summer camps that I don't like anyways.*
2. *I have shown interest in the drums for one month and especially in the last ten days.*
3. *I have not only agreed to pay fully for a drum set, but I have shown dedication by researching and riding ten miles on my bike to different music and pawn shops.*
4. *I will agree not to play late at night and we can set a time that I can play.*
5. *I will agree to take lessons in the summer.*

ages
6–12

When engaging kids in music lessons, make sure they are playing an instrument that is a good size for them, and set up easily to play. Make sure it has a pleasant-enough sound to want to hear it over and over again. The same holds true for other creative activities—if the tools of those activities are not a good fit, the activity will be less fun.

—**CATHY FINK,** Grammy Award–winning musician, singer, songwriter

Get Creative Try this activity with your child and his friends or the entire family. You play the role of drum leader and tap a specific beat and play it through two or three times. Then you call out, "All join in," and all the other drummers join in, tapping the same beat. After 4 or 5 minutes another drum leader (your child or another in the group) calls out, "I have a beat," and everyone stops drumming to listen as the new leader taps his or her beat two or three times through so everyone can hear the beat. Then, the new leader calls out, "All join in," and all the drummers tap out the exact same beat as the lead drummer for 4 or 5 minutes. (Repeat this drum routine so that everyone gets a chance to be the leader.)

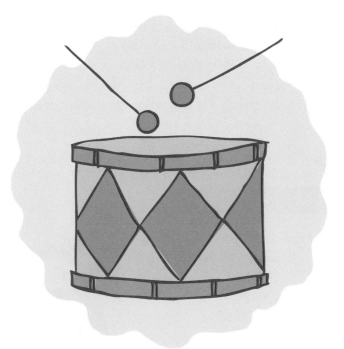

Dance Activities

Every child six to twelve years old can have fun with dance and develop his or her own way of being creative. Dance is not just for the super-coordinated child, it is for every child and every ability. Dance can be playful, dance can be graceful. Kids this age can be challenged to do interpretive dance—where a theme is suggested (for example, a robot, a sneaky cat, or a scarecrow) and each child combines imagination with movement in their own expressive way.

Some children are naturally drawn to dancing, while others are a bit reluctant to join in group dance activities. Children who are hesitant may join in the fun with playful dance activities such as Monster Shuffle, Dance Starters, or Copycat Dancing. Children who are super-excited about dance may gather up a few friends and do Kid Choreography, creating their own dance recitals and putting on performances in the backyard or living room.

The main idea is for every child to have opportunities to dance, and the dance activities below offer a good start toward achieving this goal. The focus here is on fun, with each child expanding and developing their own creativity with dance as they go.

ages 6–12

COPYCAT DANCING

This is a perfect dance activity for Family Creativity Night or a birthday party!

Materials
- Recorded music with a good dance rhythm and beat

Get Creative Turn on the music and select one person to be the dance leader. The leader creates dance

- Make dance a fun, playful, expressive part of family life. (Include dance activities from this book in your Family Creativity Night and in your child's birthday party too.)
- Help your child create a collection of dance tunes that she or he can play anytime for solo freestyle dance or dance activities with friends and siblings.
- Gather up scarves, accessories, clothing, hats, and props that make colorful and theatrical dance costumes for your child.
- If your child has the creative gumption to make up his own dance routine, encourage him to put on a performance at home, with everyone in the family showing support.
- Encourage your child to do creative dance activities with friends and siblings as an alternative to screen time.
- Take your child to creative-dance events and performances in your community to let her see what other sorts of dance creativity can look like.
- If your child expresses an interest in dance classes or lessons and your family budget will allow it, say yes and help him find an appropriate class that is a good fit for his age and interests.

moves and everyone copies what the leader is doing. Encourage the children to have fun and invent silly or interesting movements to go along with the music. The children may add some moves they already know (the twist, the stomp) or invent their own. Let everyone in the dance group take turns being the leader!

MEMORY-LANE DANCING

Parents (or grandparents) become the dance teachers, with kids learning dance steps from them—the previous generation of enthusiastic kid dancers.

Materials
- Recorded music with a good dance beat

Get Creative Parents (or grandparents) do their very best version of favorite dance steps from their past. The moves might be from childhood, the teenage years, or adult years. Here are a few Memory-Lane dance moves to get things started. (Note: if you need a refresher on how to do any of these retro dances, check out YouTube online, and with just a little searching you'll find one or more video renditions of each dance.

> *Creative movement or creative-dance time is a wonderful inclusive activity for all children. In this environment, there is no wrong way to move. It is important to let the child with special needs exhibit independent movement to the greatest extent possible and to limit the movement that someone else takes him or her through.*
>
> **—DR. KRISTI SAYERS MENEAR, PHD,**
> Certified Adapted Physical Educator

The Carlton Dance
This dance was from the television show *The Fresh Prince of Bel-Air*, and a lot of parents seem to recall it.

The Sprain
This silly dance routine is from the television show *Saved by the Bell* and it's easy to imitate. To get it started, one parent does his best imitation of it—hopping and turning on one foot—and the children improvise their own rendition.

The Twist
Here's a classic dance that grandparents and parents will know, and it's entertaining for children to invent their own variations.

The Monkey
This is a classic dance move from the sixties that grandparents and parents may remember. The silliness and happiness of a dance like the Monkey is a great equalizer between kids and grown-ups.

MONSTER SHUFFLE

Here's an amusing dance activity for friends and playmates, as every child invents their own way to dance like a friendly monster!

Materials
- Recorded music
- A dance leader (parent or older sibling)

Get Creative Ask the group of kids to invent their own creative ways that a big (but friendly) monster might dance when the music gets started. You can also jump-start the first round of dancing by giving a demo of your best Monster Shuffle moves—for example, dance like Frankenstein with your arms out straight in front of you, or dance like a mummy as you move slowly around the dance floor.

DANCE STARTERS

Your child gathers a group of friends, calls out a theme or idea, and everyone invents their own expressive or silly ways to move to the music!

Materials
- Recorded music with a good rhythm and beat for dancing
- Pencil and paper

Get Creative Select someone to be the first dance leader to get the action going. Turn on some upbeat dance music. The leader picks a Dance Starter idea (see below) and calls out that idea (for example, "a wiggle worm"), and everyone does his or her own version of a dance about that idea. Some dancers might be graceful and smooth, others might be silly. Half the fun is for the children to dance in their own expressive or fun way, one that mixes the beat of the music and the ideas they are imagining. Let everyone take a turn being the dance leader and calling out Dance Starter ideas (each child makes up other imaginative Dance Starter themes of their own as ideas pop into their mind). Here are some dance ideas to get you started.

Dance like:
- A ballerina
- A turtle
- A fish
- A creepy, crawly bug
- A seagull
- A happy frog
- A wiggle worm
- Big Foot
- A robot
- A waterfall
- The sunshine
- The wind blowing through the trees
- A noisy washing machine
- A tree blowing in the wind
- A bumblebee
- A space alien
- Frankenstein
- An octopus
- A surfer
- A skier
- A snowboarder
- A marching band
- A hula dancer
- A tap dancer
- A rock-and-roll dancer
- A sneaky cat
- A mouse
- A tin man
- A scarecrow
- A chicken

ages 6–12

Create a Dance-Starter Performance
Encourage your child to create an entire dance routine with one of the themes or dance ideas above for a solo dance or dance performance at home with a friend. For example, let's say your child likes the "sneaky cat" idea. Then he just imagines some sneaky situations and actions a cat might do. (These can be real-life scenes or imaginary scenes for an extraordinary cat!) Your child puts a few of these catlike movements together (and repeats the movements a number of times), adding a few other dance moves or steps to make his routine flow with the music.

LETTERS-IN-THE-SKY DANCING

Challenge your child and her friends to invent big, graceful movements to write imaginary letters in the sky!

Materials
- Recorded music that sounds energetic

Get Creative Turn on the music and the children begin to use arms, hands, and movements to pretend to write beautiful letters in the air. (Your child may bend down low or stretch up high, or she may write letters with arms and tapping feet too.) It's especially fun to dance outdoors and cover a lot of ground, or do Letters-in-the-Sky Dancing inside in a large, open room! This is a fun dance activity for a group, but it's also an enjoyable solo dance activity for a child who loves to dance.

DOG-AND-CAT DANCE TROUPE

Your child gathers friends (or family) together and they invent dance routines featuring their best versions of dancing dogs or cats moving to music!

Materials
- Recorded music
- Easy animal costumes—for example, dog or cat ears (see page 106 for how to make these), plain black or brown adult-sized T-shirts, black or brown tights, animal tails (see page 109 for how to make these)
- Children's theatrical makeup (for nose and whiskers)

Get Creative The dancers put on costumes (or animal ears) and create dance moves that mimic the actions and movements of an imaginary dog or cat who loves to dance. Challenge the dancers to use the actions and behaviors of real dogs or cats for inspiration.

> *I built forts, invented dance routines with friends, buried hidden treasures, and drew my own maps to find them. An experimental atmosphere, without pressure to get things "right," was the key to cultivating creativity in my childhood.*
>
> —Kate from New York

Put on a Dog-and-Cat Dance Recital
For more fun, encourage your child to gather some friends together, bring out some dog and cat costumes, and create a performance outdoors in the backyard, with seats for an audience (friends, family, or neighbors). Have someone in the crowd record this original, creative Dog-and-Cat Dance Recital with a video recorder!

ages
6–12

KID CHOREOGRAPHY

Yes, with creativity and a little practice your child can create her very own dance routines with friends and family.

Materials
- Recorded music with a good danceable beat

Get Creative Your child starts by mixing and matching three or four easy dance moves (for feet and hands and whole bodies too) to create a lively dance routine. Encourage your child to match the music, and make it fun. Once the basic dance steps are created they can be repeated several times to make a full-length dance routine. Your child can teach the steps and moves to the other dancers (family or friends) so that everyone dances the routine together. This can be a fun group activity (or even a solo dance activity for a child who loves to create dance routines independently). Here are a few kid-friendly moves your child might consider:
- Tapping feet
- Stomping
- Marching
- Shuffling right or left
- Legs kicking forward
- Hopping
- Twisting
- Arms swaying side to side
- Hands up in the air
- Hands waving overhead
- Clapping
- Shoulders up and down

DANCE PROPS AND COSTUMES

Don't forget the costumes! Create easy dance costumes to embellish your child's dance routines: fancy scarves, long or short skirts, leotards, dress-up clothes, and hats. Ankle bells or foot rattles (made from stretchy fabric and bells, available from Amazon and other retailers) offer a clever way to add a little jingle to your child's dance fun. For group dances, color-coordinate recycled outfits (parents' T-shirts or dress shirts) with tights or pants.

NEIGHBORHOOD DANCE PARTY

Have a dance party at home with all the kids dancing in one big group just for the fun of it!

Materials
- Recorded music with a dance-able beat

Setup Work with your child to select the dance activities she'd like to include in her party before the dancers arrive. Consider some time for freestyle dancing and also dance activities for the entire group to do together.

Here's a basic plan to mix these styles of dance into the party:

(1) Dance Starters; then (2) Copycat Dancing; next (3) freestyle dancing (everyone dances in the big group together in any way they like); (4) take a break for water or snack; then (5) Letters-in-the-Sky Dancing; and finally (6) Zoo Zomba or Magic Dancing Beans.

Get Creative When all the kids arrive, make a quick announcement welcoming all the dancers and mentioning that this will be a big group dance! (This is a signal that everyone is included in one big, happy group. Encourage enjoyment and respect for all.) It's wise to end the dance party before everyone gets too tired. So, 60 minutes of dancing is just about right!

ages 6–12

Theatrical Activities

Pretend and theatrical activities offer superb possibilities for creativity for children ages six to twelve. There are puppet shows and plays to create, skits to act out, characters and silly voices to invent, costumes to wear, and entertaining acting games to play with family and friends.

Some children might get especially excited about doing theatrics as a solo activity: perhaps inventing puppet characters and putting on a puppet show for their parents. It's easy for children this age to work hand puppets themselves, and older kids can even work two at the same time, creating conversations and actions for the two puppet characters. Children can create interesting or quirky characters, make up a small skit, or write a short comedy act for their puppet, memorizing jokes from a kid-friendly joke book!

For many kids, it is the delight of acting or pretend with others that is most appealing. Two kids might put their heads (and imaginations) together to create a skit or short improv routine and act it out—with each actor responding to the actions and words of the other. Some children six to twelve may be excited about acting in a community or school play and the challenge of learning lines, wearing makeup and costumes, and acting upon the stage. Others might take a more playful approach and be equally excited about doing theatrical activities at their Family Creativity Night.

Parents can be terrific creativity mentors, who keep the focus on fun and encourage time and opportunities at home for their child to dabble in a variety of activities to encourage creativity with theatrics and pretend.

WORKER-BEE ACTING CLUB

This is a fast-paced acting-and-guessing game for a group of kids or the family with no acting experience necessary!

Materials
- Paper and pencils
- List of Worker Bee activities (see next page)

Get Creative The first actor picks six actions from the list (below) and writes them on a piece of paper. He quickly and silently acts out the first chore on the list while the others try to guess what he is doing. If no one guesses correctly, after about a minute the actor calls out, "New action," and the actor acts out the second activity on the list. Each actor takes a turn acting out six actions, with the others guessing.

Worker-Bee Scenes to Act Out

- Artist painting
- Baking a birthday cake
- Bricklayer building a wall
- Building a campfire
- Building a sand castle
- Carpenter building something
- Cooking eggs
- Cutting down a tree
- Feeding a baby in a high chair
- Fisherman pulling in his nets
- Folding laundry
- Hanging a picture on the wall
- Having a picnic
- Ice-skating
- Making pancakes
- Mechanic fixing a car
- Peeling and chopping an onion

- Performing in a rock band
- Planting a garden
- Playing baseball
- Playing basketball
- Playing football
- Playing Frisbee
- Playing tennis
- Reading a sad letter
- Setting up a tent
- Skiing
- Surfing
- Sweeping the floor
- Waiter serving restaurant-goers
- Walking a dog
- Washing a car
- Washing the dishes
- Washing a window
- Working out in a gym

WORD-WISDOM CHARADES

Everyone gets a cheat sheet to help with the acting and the guessing of this theatrical game for two or more actors!

Materials
- List of wise sayings (see next page)
- Printer or copy machine (to make copies for all the players)

Setup If you have a big group, divide into two teams.

Get Creative Give each player a copy of the wise-sayings list below. (In order to begin guessing, this list is essential for each person to have in his or her possession while playing.) One person is selected to be the first actor for the game. She picks a slogan from this list and tries to act out the important (boldface) words without saying a word. The others try to guess the correct slogan by watching the acting and glancing at all the phrases listed on the list. Everyone takes turns acting and guessing.

TWO TIPS FOR CHARADES

In the game of Charades, one person acts out a word or phrase using lots of body movements and hand gestures but without saying any words or sounds. The others in the group watch the actor carefully and try to guess the word or phrase he is acting out. Here are a few tips for Charades:

If a word you need to act out is too difficult, then pick a word that sounds similar and act that word out instead. In this case, give the "sounds like" signal to the other players by tugging on your ear. Usually someone will shout out, "Sounds like," when you tug your ear, and then you shake your head yes to show that is what you are now doing!

When someone is guessing a word and getting close to guessing the word, you can make a circling motion with your hands (or a motion that looks like a "Come here" gesture) to signal, "Keep going, you are getting close!"

30 Wise Sayings for Word-Wisdom Charades (*pick one and act it out!*):

- A **picture** is worth a thousand words.
- An **apple** a day keeps the **doctor** away.
- **Birds** of a **feather** flock together!
- Curiosity **killed** the **cat**!
- Don't count your **chickens** before they **hatch**!
- Don't make a **mountain** out of a **molehill**!
- Don't put all your **eggs** in one **basket**!
- Have a **nice day**!
- He who **laughs** last **laughs** best.
- I don't **give** a **hoot**!
- I went on a **wild-goose chase**!
- I'm as **busy** as a **bee**!
- I'm as **free** as a **bird**!
- I'm as **happy** as a **clam**!
- I'm **happy** as a **pig** in **mud**!
- I've been **working like** a **dog**!
- It's none of your **beeswax**!
- Make hay while the **sun shines**!
- More **fun** than a **barrel** of **monkeys**!
- No **news** is good **news**.
- Remember to **stop** and **smell** the **roses** along the way.
- The early **bird** gets the **worm**.
- The squeaky **wheel** gets the **oil**.
- Well, I'll be a **monkey's uncle**!
- What goes **up** must come **down**!
- When the **cat's** away, the **mice** will **play**!
- You can **lead** a **horse** to **water**, but you can't make him **drink**!
- You can't teach an **old dog** new **tricks**!
- You'll catch more **flies** with **honey** than with **vinegar**!
- You're **barking up** the wrong **tree**!

Song-Title Charades

Here's another charades game that is fun for the family or several children, but this time players act out song titles. Use the titles of the Traditional Songs for Musical Creativity (page 277) or Traditional Songs for Preschoolers (page 173), or pick other songs that everyone is familiar with. Take turns acting out the important words in the title while everyone else guesses.

BIG-TROUBLE SKIT

This activity has children (and parents) acting out some short skits of everyday trouble without saying a word. This activity is best for kids ages ten and up.

Materials

- A large room (for walking and moving about)
- Optional: a chair

Get Creative This activity requires two or more children, or a family group. Start by thinking of some problems that might happen in real life that everyone knows about. Each actor uses lots of facial expressions and body language while they act. Encourage your child to exaggerate and embellish his action too. Here are a few samples of real-life Big-Trouble skits to try out. Challenge all the actors to make up more Big-Trouble skits and act them out with friends or family!

Pretend:

- You are eating an ice-cream cone, and the scoop of ice cream drops on the ground. (Invent a second action scene too, such as scooping it out of the dirt and putting it back on the cone, or a dog grabbing it and running away.)

- Your pants get a giant rip when you sit down at your desk!
- You get a flat tire on your car and try to fix it, but the spare tire rolls away!

HAVE FUN WITH IMPROV

Improvisation (or improv) is a fun way to act out a scene without a script, with the actors making things up as they go along.

Materials
- Miscellaneous props that match up with the scenes you are acting out

Get Creative Parents and children (or two or more friends) brainstorm about what scenes they can act out together. Some scenes might be silly and others might be serious. Once the basic scene is decided upon, one actor starts acting, talking, and moving about as needed, and then the other actor joins in with words, actions, and acting too.

Here is a sample improv scene that shows two actors (perhaps a parent and child) getting creative with theatrics. It's called "Cooking-School Theatrics," and the basic idea is that there is a cooking school (with students sitting in the classroom watching) and there is one chef, and also an assistant chef who just arrived from another country and speaks another language. As a result, all kinds of things start to get mixed up, and the actors invent the wackiness as they go.

Props Used
- Two chef hats
- One small basket filled with kitchen utensils: bowl, large mixing spoon, eggbeater, spatula, turkey baster
- One laundry basket filled with household items (to be used as humorous props): a boot, alarm clock, fly swatter, bicycle horn, roll of toilet paper, pair of tweezers, toothbrush, and so on
- Cookbook

Setup Ed and Luigi standing at the kitchen counter (they have the baskets of kitchen gadgets and gag items nearby). EDWARD (head baker): "Welcome to our pastry class. My name is Edward and I am the boss at Rainbow Bakery. This is my new assistant, Luigi, who just arrived from Italy today. We are going to make many delicious pastries today and are very glad you have joined us."

(*Edward looks at his cookbook and silently reads the recipe.*)
ED: "Please get me six eggs."
LUIGI (assistant baker): "Zee eggs!"
(*He hands Edward the imaginary eggs.*)
(*Edward pretends to crack the eggs and mix them in the bowl.*)

Get Creative Next, act out the actions of Ed as he reads aloud a few lines from the cookbook and begins asking Luigi for ingredients and cooking utensils. Sometimes Luigi might offer silly objects from a hidden basket (toilet paper, tweezers, a wig, a shoe) and other times Luigi may offer (or pretend to offer) the correct items. Each and every time Luigi offers an object, he may say, with a strong accent, "Zee spoon" or "Zee milk," even if he is offering a shoe! The scene keeps going this way, with the two actors ad-libbing and eventually finding a good way to end the scene.

THE MISHAP AT THE BARBER SHOP

Children can have loads of fun creating their own clever improv (theatrics) scene, with parent and child or two children working together to act out something that goes wrong at the barber shop!

Materials

- One bar stool or chair
- Assorted barber supplies: comb, brush, water spray bottle, styling gel
- A twin bedsheet (for the cape that's draped around the customer)

Get Creative The two (or more) children (or parent and child) brainstorm for a minute about what the mishap might be that is happening at the barber shop. (Examples: A dog comes in for a shave. An elephant stomps inside the shop for a quick trim. Or the barber accidentally makes a bald spot on the customer's head, using pretend electric clippers.) Figure out together what the trouble might be, and then one actor starts acting and talking and the other actor joins in.

The Mishap at the Beauty Shop

Two or more children (or parent and child) work together to come up with a funny story about something unexpected (or disastrous) that happens at the beauty shop. Perhaps the purple dye got mixed up with the yellow hair dye on the day the beauty contestant came for a hairdo! Put your imaginations together to create a story idea, then one actor begins by saying one line of the skit and the other actor joins in with words and actions.

TV Sports Report

Two or more children (or parent and child) pretend to be television sports announcers and invent silly scenes and conversations to act out while doing a live sports report! One of the actors might start the fake TV show by introducing himself and welcoming viewers to the game. (For example, "Hello, baseball fans. I'm Bart Callous, and I'm here with Shelly Peterson at the Cincinnati Reds Stadium.") The second announcer joins in with a few comments.

Create personalities for the announcers; one sportscaster can be serious and the second can be silly! You can also create some silly events on the sports field to announce (maybe two stray dogs chase each other on the field).

ages
6–12

SILLY-SONG MUSICAL THEATRICS

Pick a funny song you know, put on a costume, and create a musical routine, singing and acting out the song.

Materials
- Lyrics for "The Pigs Got Dressed to Go to Town" (see below), or invent your own silly song
- Costumes or hats

Get Creative Encourage your child to learn the words for the silly song below, put on a costume, and work with a friend or sibling to make up funny actions (or dance steps) to create a silly routine.

The Pigs Got Dressed to Go to Town
(Sing this silly song to the tune of "The Bear Went Over the Mountain"!)

The pigs got dressed to go to town,
Go to town, go to town,
The pigs got dressed to go to town,
To find some tasty treats!
When the pigs arrived, the people ran,
The people ran, the people ran,
When the pigs arrived, the people ran,
To the other side of the street!
One little boy said, "I'm not afraid."
"Not afraid, not afraid."

One little boy said, "I'm not afraid,"
So he stayed with the pigs!
The pigs stood up and shook his hand,
Shook his hand, shook his hand,
The pigs stood up and shook his hand,
With a friendly "How do you do"!
The butcher arrived with a sneaky smile,
Sneaky smile, sneaky smile,
The butcher arrived with a sneaky smile,
And the pigs started to shake.
They shook so hard their hats fell off,
Their hats fell off, their hats fell off,
The shook so hard their hats fell off,
And their teeth started to chatter!
The little boy yelled, "Run away!"
"Run away, run away!"
The little boy yelled, "Run away!"
"You're bacon if you stay."
The pigs took off with a squeal and a shout,
A squeal and a shout, a squeal and a shout,
The pig took off with a squeal and shout,
And they hid in the barn!

317

CREATE A THEATRICS COSTUME BOX

Get a big plastic tub with a lid, or a cardboard box or suitcase, and work with your child to fill it with dress-up clothes, recycled Halloween costumes, hats, and accessories. Items might include shirts, pants, suspenders, bow ties, neckties, vests, gloves, bandannas, fancy women's tops and blouses (turn these into dresses), ballerina skirt (see directions on page 111 for a homemade tutu), capes, shawls, and hats of every kind.

You can also find inexpensive costume hats online, such as a Viking helmet, a genie's turban, a gladiator's helmet, a firefighter's helmet, an airplane-pilot hat, a giant clown hat, a musketeer hat, a conquistador helmet, king and queen crowns, a knight's helmet, a jester hat, a Pilgrim hat, a Statue of Liberty head-piece, a coonskin cap, a pioneer's bonnet, a stovepipe hat, a buccaneer's hat, a chef's hat, a royal guardsman's hat. One of my favorite online places to find costume hats for kids is www.musicmotion.com.

Bowwow on Broadway

Challenge your child to use her imagination to create a silly song, then put on a short musical performance about a mischievous or adventurous dog (the bowwow). She can sing her new song to the tune of "The Bear Went Over the Mountain" or any other tune she knows. She can add costumes, get friends or parents to act in her "Bow-wow on Broadway" musical, and put on a little production in the backyard or basement!

MUSICAL-SUPERSTAR THEATRICS

Your child invents a famous music character or star performer, adds costumes, then puts on a short performance in the living room.

Materials

- Costumes, hats, boots, and props for a musical star
- Any favorite recorded music (such as rock, country, and so on)

ages 6-12

Get Creative Encourage your child to think of a famous musician and pretend to be that superstar by singing (or pretending to sing) along with a recorded song. Your child can practice his act just for fun, or put on a performance for friends and family in the living room or outdoors. Here are three musical acting scenes to try with friends, siblings, or family members:

Rock-Band Theatrics
Your child gets a few friends together and they pick a band to imitate or invent their own. Then they gather some costumes (bandannas, T-shirts, jeans) and select a song.

Country-Music Superstar Theatrics
Your child gathers up some country-music costumes and props: cowboy

hat, cowboy boots, Western shirt, jeans, stage makeup, microphone, and musical instruments. Then she gets a few friends together, selects a song list, and starts the theatrics.

Opera-Star Theatrics
Your child makes costumes with dress-up clothes—hats, wigs, dresses, vests, capes, long skirts, aprons, scarves, dress shirts, pants, flowery shirts. (To get great costume ideas, help your child do a Google image search using the words *PBS opera*.) He can add some props and give his best opera (pantomime) performance in the living room or patio!

> *My cousin Emily and I used to put on variety shows for neighborhood kids and our families. In one show I played "In the Hall of the Mountain King" very fast on the piano. I loved that piece—it's so dramatic! And I was so worked up that I did a dance afterward consisting of just twirling around like a dervish. I was so dizzy that I felt sick.*
>
> **—MELANIE HALL,** artist and award-winning illustrator of over twenty-five children's books, including *Winter Song: A Poem by William Shakespeare*

TIPS FOR YOUNG PUPPETEERS

Here are a few tips to help your child develop skills as a puppeteer:

- Try different puppet movements to see what looks most realistic (use a mirror).
- Experiment with movements that show emotions in your puppet (laughing, feeling sad, crying, being excited, being surprised, and so forth).
- Create a voice (and accent) that matches up with your character and practice it.
- Invent or create a personality for each puppet—one might be stubborn, another mischievous, a third might love to sing.
- Talk loudly and clearly enough for your audience to hear and understand your puppet's voice.
- Be sure to have your puppet's eyes looking toward the audience when speaking.
- Remember to move your hand repeatedly when your puppet talks. (Practice so it becomes automatic.)
- When learning to use a marionette (puppet with strings), practice in front of a mirror. Notice what works best and practice it again and again to memorize the best movements.
- When the marionette is walking, be sure his feet are touching the ground with each step.

"HEY! IT'S ME!" PUPPET ROUTINE

Your child invents a puppet character with a big personality and invents a voice to match!

Materials
- One hand puppet (animal or person)

Get Creative The first step is for your child to invent a puppet character. To do this, you might ask a couple of questions to get her imagination flowing: "What's the puppet's name?" "What is his or her personality like?" "Is she shy or talkative? Is she bossy or friendly? How old is she? Where does she live? What does she like to do?"

Next, your child simply puts on a little spontaneous puppet show, pretending to be the character and having a short conversation with the audience. The opening line of the puppet show might be something like this: "Hey! It's Me, ____" (Fred!). Then encourage your child to invent one surprising thing that happened today in the puppet's life and tell the audience about it. Encourage your child to keep it short, fun, and theatrical! One key tip is to tell your child to try to remember to move the puppet's mouth when speaking!

FAIRY-TALE PUPPET SHOW

Kids start the theatrics with their own version of a classic fairy tale!

Materials
- A book of children's fairy tales
- A bedsheet
- A table (for the stage)

Setup Your child selects a fairy tale to tell in his own words, and then puts a sheet over the table to create a puppet stage.

Get Creative Your child crouches down behind the table and slips his hand inside the puppet. He starts the puppet show by having the puppet introduce himself to the audience and announce which story he is about to tell. Then your child tells a fairy tale in a loud and clear voice. He moves his hand throughout the entire story to make the puppet's mouth move whenever he is talking. When the story is finished, your child shouts out, "The end!" then takes a bow (and waits for the applause).

COMEDY-ROUTINE PUPPET SHOW

Here's a fun way for your child to turn a puppet into a stand-up comedian and invent a humorous routine using a joke book!

Materials
- Kid's joke book
- Pen
- Card stock
- Bedsheet
- Table

Setup Your child selects six to eight favorite jokes from the joke book and writes them on the card stock. Encourage him to practice reading the jokes out loud before performing the puppet show. Then he puts the bedsheet over the table to create a puppet stage and calls the audience to the stage.

Get Creative Your child starts by popping the puppet up to the stage and introducing the puppet character to the audience and announcing that she has a few good jokes to share tonight!

Your child reads each joke loudly and clearly and pauses after each joke. He may also decide to ad-lib some funny comments between jokes. He ends the performance, thanks the audience, and takes a bow when the clapping begins!

MAKE YOUR OWN SOCK-PUPPET CHARACTERS

All your child needs is a woolly sock, some felt, and a little help from a parent or grandparent to make a clever puppet with lots of personality! This activity is best for kids ages ten and up.

ages 6–12

Materials
- One old (heavy) sock of any color
- Permanent marker
- Scissors
- White felt
- Red felt
- Brown or black felt
- One large shank button (a button with a plastic or metal U-shape underneath for sewing to fabric) for the nose
- A needle and thread (parents may need to help with threading the needle, and possibly sewing too)
- Two medium-sized or large shank buttons for the eyes
- Optional: other fabric, a scarf, a clip-on bow tie, a bandanna, yarn, a toddler-sized ski hat, and so forth

Get Creative Work with your child to make a creative sock puppet. First, put your hand inside the sock, with your thumb in the heel and four fingers in the toe part. With your hand inside the sock, ask your child to use the marker to make two dots where the eyes should be placed. Next, your child uses the scissors to cut two large circles from the white felt, each a little bigger than a quarter. She cuts a 3-inch-long tongue from the red felt. Help your child cut two thick, curvy eyebrows from the brown or black felt, making sure that they will both fit on the sock puppet right above the eyes.

Work together to position the red felt for the tongue at the end of the toe part of the sock and place the shank button for the nose on top of the felt. Use a needle and thread to attach the button and felt tongue to the sock. Next, put one white felt circle on the sock where the left eye should be, and place one shank-button on top of that felt. Use a needle and thread to sew the white felt circle and button to the sock. Sew the other white felt circle and button to the sock for the right eye. Place the felt eyebrows above the two eyes and use a needle and thread to attach them to the sock. Encourage your child to add other fabric, a scarf, a bow tie, a neck bandanna, or yarn (for hair) to further decorate your puppet and give him or her a personality.

PUPPETS FROM THE KITCHEN

Make clever stick puppets from kitchen gadgets with your child and challenge her to put on a puppet show behind the kitchen counter!

WHERE TO FIND PUPPETS

Most toy stores have puppets and you can also find a huge assortment of people and animal puppets online. Check locally and consider these online resources as well:

- Find eight big-mouth animal puppets ($24.99) online at www.discountschoolsupply.com
- Find larger, specialty puppets ($12.99 and up) online at www.folkmanis.com
- Find marionettes and giant hand puppets on www.sunnypuppets.com

Materials

- Glue
- Wiggle eyes
- A giant recycled wooden spoon or wooden spatula
- Red or pink permanent markers
- Black or brown permanent markers
- A small button or pom-pom (for a nose)
- Yarn
- Scraps of fabric or colored construction paper
- Colored duct tape

Get Creative Help your child glue the wiggle eyes onto the wooden spoon. Let your child use the markers to create eyebrows, eyelashes, lips, and rosy cheeks. Create hair from the yarn: take a long piece of yarn (about 10 inches) and then cut an additional ten or more 2-inch lengths. Tie the small yarn pieces in knots around the long piece of yarn. (Push all these yarn knots together into one area to create the hair.) Tie the hair (yarn) once or twice around your spoon. Create clothing by wrapping the fabric or colored paper around the handle of your spoon. Use the colored duct tape to hold it in place.

MARIONETTE SONG-AND-DANCE ROUTINE

Your child starts the music and turns his marionette into the star of the talent show!

Materials

- One marionette puppet
- A large mirror (for practice)
- Recorded music

Setup Encourage your child to practice making his marionette dance and walk in front of the mirror so he can see what works best to move the hands, arms, legs, feet, and head of his puppet. (Give a short demo if your child needs to see the basics of handling the marionette.)

Get Creative Your child picks a favorite tune and creates a dance routine for the marionette. He might make it serious or make it silly. (Perhaps his dancer does the splits, spins around and gets dizzy, or slips and falls!) He can ad-lib some funny lines as he dances or your child might write a short script to act out.

CREATE A BIG-BOX PUPPET STAGE

Get a big moving box and create a cool puppet stage with your child.

Materials
- Yardstick
- Marker
- Giant cardboard box
- Scissors (parent supervises child)
- Fabric (to fit across the box for a curtain)
- Colored duct tape

Get Creative To begin, help your child use the yardstick and marker to draw a large rectangle where she wants the opening for the puppet stage. (Be sure to cut this window or opening toward the top of the box to create a good height for your child to sit or kneel inside the box to work the puppets over her head.) Cut a piece of fabric to stretch across the top of the window (or stage) to create a short, decorative curtain across the top of the "window." Your child can use the colored duct tape to attach that narrow curtain to the box. Cut another medium-sized square out of the backside of the box (toward the bottom of the box) so your child can step inside this little opening to do the puppet show.

SOUND-EFFECTS THEATRICS

Two or more friends (or parent and child) can have a hilarious time inventing sound effects together.

Materials
- Just your voice and hands and feet for tapping
- Optional: recording device (to record the sound effects)

Get Creative Experiment with your child on ways to mimic sounds using your voices, or hands and feet tapping, shuffling, thumping. After this parent-and-child sound-effects activity your child may enjoy creating all sorts of wacky sound effects with playmates too!

Here are some sounds to try:
- Alarm clock
- Bicycle horn
- Birds singing
- Car engine
- Car horn
- Cat
- Cow
- Creaky door
- Cricket
- Dog
- Doorbell
- Electric drill
- Electric saw
- Frog
- Goat
- Horse trotting
- Motorcycle
- Ocean breeze
- Ocean waves
- Phone
- Pig
- Plane
- Rain
- Snoring
- Someone running
- Thunderstorm
- Truck

ages
6–12

Creativity with Words

All children ages six to twelve can become creative with words, inventing tall tales to tell out loud, writing stories, poems, creative word posters, and creating their own books. The youngest children in this age group might prefer to work with a parent or caregiver to create collaborative and imaginative stories together, with each person taking turns adding to the story. If your six- or seven-year-old child isn't yet proficient with writing skills, he may enjoy inventing an adventure story about the family pet, and you can write it down as he tells it aloud.

Older kids with strong writing skills can invent their own imaginative stories and poems and write them down as they go. They can create a short book with an original story and illustrations too. They might write about fantasy characters, wacky animal adventures, or spectacular aliens from outer space. Or perhaps they will create a story about a fantasy sports team or a superhero or something else that sparks their interest and engages their imagination.

Parents can be terrific creativity mentors who keep the focus on fun and encourage their child to dabble in a variety of creative word activities during the six-to-twelve years.

CREATE AN ANIMAL CHARACTER

Once your child gets started inventing animal characters, she can write stories or tell imaginative stories to family and friends for years to come!

Materials
- Paper and pencil (or computer and printer)

Get Creative Encourage your child to think of an animal she would like to

ages
6-12

write about. She can start by inventing a name for her imaginary animal and inventing a personality too. (Perhaps it is Pinky the Parrot!) Your child's imagination will bring this animal character to life when she answers a few questions: Is the character young or old? What does she look like? What about her personality? (Is she shy or a big talker? Is the character mischievous? Is she neat or messy?) What does

she like to do for fun? Where does she live? Ask your child to write down her ideas as her imagination pops—for example, Pinky, five years old; pink bow in hair; little feet; fast talker; loves to sing; messy, messy; lives in a golden cage in Grandma's cabin in the woods. To complete the story your child invents this animal in exactly the way she wants her to be and writes down the story.

Animal-Friends Stories

After your child has created an imaginary animal character and written her description, she may want to invent a best friend to keep the first character company! So she can create a second animal character and bring him or her to life in exactly the same way. She writes a description about the best animal friend's appearance, age, name, and personality too.

Amazing Animal-Adventure Stories

Once your child has created two animal characters, it's time to invent a big adventure for the two friends. Encourage your child to brainstorm and pick a story idea he likes best. Did they go on a trip? Did they find a surprise or treasure? Did they get into mischief? Did they go to a school for animals? Did they sail in a boat across the ocean? Your child's imagination will help create a clever story about the adventure the two friends had together.

"Can You Believe It?" Tall Tales

Challenge your child to turn her imagination up even higher, and invent a story about a silly or unbelievable situation that happened to the animal characters she just invented. The sky

"

Many of my favorite childhood memories are my times spent with trees. The gnarled old apple trees on my parents' hilltop in New England, the ancient ponderosa pine by the creek on our ranch in Colorado, and the aspen trees where I strung my first hammock and camped many nights under the Rocky Mountain stars—all these became friends. Sometimes I would wonder just what stories these old friends could tell, if only I could understand their language. Had they seen the Native Americans who lived in these places centuries ago? What about the first settlers to move West in their covered wagons? Did they witness the great floods or amazing lightning storms of the past? And, even more interesting, what could they tell me about how it feels to have such patience and seren to put down roots in a single spot and live there through all the seasons and years of l Maybe this is why so many of my books feature trees—trees who do, in fact, have enchanting story to tell . . . and wisdom to impart if we will take the time to listen.

— T. A. BARRON, author of twenty-four books for young people, including the Merlin series

is the limit, and it all starts with your child's imagination and brainstorming. Did they fly into outer space? Did they become president and vice president of a country? Your child writes down the story or simply tells her tall tale aloud!

STORY STARTERS

Your child picks a quick idea to start ˈ story and then weaves a tall tale to ˈ out loud or write about.

ˈd paper (or computer
ˈ)

ˈge your child to
ˈ silly idea to
ˈthe Story
ˈ to begin
ˈ it
ˈ write it
ˈ out loud.

The Day I Joined the Circus
Your child imagines that she is one of the circus performers and writes about something that happened during one day on the job!

The Surprise inside the Box
Your child imagines a giant box (as big as a refrigerator) that just arrived at his house with a note attached that says, "This is for you." Challenge your child to write a story about the surprise inside.

The Best Game Ever
Your child invents a story about the most remarkable sporting event of the century. This story can be about a real sport or it can be a sport your child invented or even an extraterrestrial team! Encourage your child to pick her best ideas and write a story or tell a story aloud.

The Town at the End of the Rainbow
Everyone talks about a pot of gold at the end of the rainbow, but what if there is really a magical town there? Challenge your child to create that town in his imagination and write about it or tell a tall tale about it!

My Hot-Air Balloon Adventure
Your child creates a story about a fantasy trip traveling in a hot-air balloon.

She might begin with brainstorming questions: Where did she go? What did she see? Who went along? Your child can write the story down, or simply tell her spontaneous story aloud.

One Crazy Campout

Your child invents an outrageous or wacky story about a camping trip that went haywire! He might tell about the animals, the other campers, the food cooked over the fire, the rainstorm in the night, or any other wild details about the campout he will never forget!

The Cats on the Team

Challenge your child to create an imaginary sports team with a group of cats! She may invent a story about soccer, football, baseball, kickball, basketball, or any other sport that she can imagine. She can create imaginary characters and uniforms, and tell about the feline shenanigans that happened too!

The Frog-Jumping Contest

This story begins with your child's imagining that every year on the Fourth of July the neighborhood has a frog-jumping contest. This year something happened that was almost unbelievable! Challenge your child to write a story so the world knows the real truth about the frog-jumping contest everyone is talking about.

The Cake Catastrophe

This story begins with the idea that there was a cake-baking contest in town, but it ended with a bang or on a sour note this year! Your child tells us about the hilarious chaos that happened with all the cooks competing for the cake-baking prize.

> *Inventing original creatures is always fun. To get your thinking started, combine two or three creatures you know into one—and then imagine what kind of extra-special eyes it would have. What language would it speak? And while you're at it, what magical powers would it have?*
>
> **—T. A. BARRON,** author of twenty-four books for young people, including the Merlin series

The Day the Mailman Turned into a Kangaroo

Challenge your child to invent a wild and crazy story about a magic spell or strange event that transformed the mailman into a kangaroo hopping through the neighborhood to deliver the mail. Your child may decide to write a clever ending about how the mail carrier got turned back into himself again before the day was over!

Postcard from Your Pet

To create this story your child imagines that the family pet just took the "vacation of a lifetime" and sent a postcard home with details about the adventure. (Your child writes the postcard pretending to be the pet.)

Petly Shenanigans

Here's another pet story idea. Your child writes an imaginary apology letter from his pet—apologizing for all that mischief he made last Sunday! Encourage your child to make it silly and have a few laughs.

Postcard from Outer Space

Ask your child to pretend that he's taken a spaceship to Mars and challenge him to write a postcard back to Earth telling about the amazing world (and creatures) he has seen. He might add some drawings too! If your child enjoys this story writing idea, he can create more postcards from outer space and make this a writing-and-illustration series!

> "There are many words that make it sound like we are not working: We shilly-shally, dilly dally, and dawdle. We are procrastinating, goofing off, and wool gathering. But my favorite word is daydreaming. It is the stuff of clouds, the hum of life outside the window, the shush of breezes."
>
> —**SUZANNE BLOOM,** author of *A Splendid Friend, Indeed* (Goose and Bear Stories)

The Meow Mystery

Encourage your child to create a story about a disappearance or mystery that has happened in her neighborhood and the clever cat detective who solved the mystery and returned life to normal.

The Amazing Things This Tree Did See

Challenge your child to imagine he is a big, old tree standing in the same place for many years. Then, he writes an imaginative story about something he or she (Mr. or Miss Tree) has seen! To get started, he picks a place in which the imaginary tree is standing. He can match his story to that place. (A few questions might help the brainstorming: Is the tree out west during the pioneer times? Is that tree in a big city right next to the baseball field? Is the tree standing near the place where the

ages
6–12

very first airplane was tested? Is that tree near the ocean where a big pirate ship came ashore?)

Write Ten More Story Starters from Your Own Imagination

If your child is excited about creating tall tales, encourage her to brainstorm more Story Starter ideas of her own. She can jot down ideas in a notebook, and some day when she is in a story-writing mood she can pick an idea from the notebook and write a story about it.

Turn a Story-Starter Idea into a Book

If your child wrote a story that he loves (with one of the story-starter ideas above), how about creating a book with that story? Your child can draw some pictures or add some photos to make it attractive. He can print the words by hand or type them on a computer and print them out. He might decide to read his story aloud at your Family Creativity Night too.

Use the Story-Starter Ideas to Write a Poem

If your child created a story using the story-starter ideas (above), challenge her to see if there is a character in the story she might want to write a poem about too. She can make it serious or make it silly—but the idea is to make it 100 percent imaginative.

THE CATS-AND-DOGS SUGGESTION JAR

Here's a silly idea to let your child think just like the family pet.

Materials
- Paper and pencil (or computer and printer)

Get Creative Encourage your child to write the top ten silly or serious suggestions that your pet secretly wants to include in the Family Suggestion Box.

FAIRY-TALE TWISTS

Pick a fairy tale you know and create a new ending!

Materials
- Paper and pencil (or computer and printer)

Get Creative Your child begins by picking one of the classic stories (on the next page) and writing (or telling) a new ending.

*A Few Classic Fairy Tales
You Might Know:*

- Little Red Riding Hood
- The Three Bears
- The Three Little Pigs
- Cinderella
- The Princess and the Pea
- Hansel and Gretel
- Snow White
- Sleeping Beauty
- The Frog Princess
- Jack and the Beanstalk
- The Ugly Duckling
- Puss-in-Boots
- Beauty and the Beast

*ages
6–12*

FIRST-SENTENCE STORIES

Your child to picks one sentence (below) and makes up a really big tale to tell.

Materials

- The list of First Sentences (see below)

Get Creative Your child picks a First Sentence (below) and writes a short creative story on paper, or simply invents a tall tale to tell aloud.

*Pick One of these First Sentences
for Your Story:*

- The biggest surprise happened today! . . .
- The contest was about to begin, and _____ (character) was really nervous . . .
- The day the giant rabbit hopped to town everything changed . . .
- The pirates' treasure was finally found . . .
- Mr. Wilson had a big problem, and his neighbors could see it . . .
- Suddenly the _____ dropped out of the boat and into the water . . .
- This morning there was a giant golden egg in our yard . . .

> *When I was in third grade, I started writing my own little magazine full of silly stories, crazy art, and imaginary news. Just to keep me happy, a small group of supportive people asked for copies. Then I had the idea to write an entire issue about a burning question in my life: What really goes on behind the locked doors of the teachers' lounge at my school? That issue of the magazine was a tremendous hit, and I had to print over five hundred copies to meet the demand. Everybody wanted to find out what the teachers were really up to in there—students, parents, and most especially teachers! Guess you could say this was my first bestseller. From that day on, I knew that my best writing would come when I was curious or moved passionately by something—those emotions would inspire my best creativity and flow through my writing to touch readers. That way, we can all share in the humor, beauty, tragedy, longing, and inspiration of life.*

—**T. A. BARRON,** author of twenty-four books for young people, including the Merlin series

EXPLAIN IT TO THE ALIEN

Here's a creative writing challenge that is harder than it seems, and it all starts with a pretend visit from an alien!

Materials
- Paper and pencil (or computer and printer)

Get Creative Challenge your child to pretend that a friendly but clueless alien has come to town and your child has been assigned to write a few notes about how human do things. Your child tries to write short and easy-to-follow descriptions about some of the human activities below:
- How to cook spaghetti (don't forget, the little alien might ask, "What is spaghetti?")
- How to kick a soccer ball
- How to behave in church (or temple)

- How to make up a song ("What is a song?")
- How to quiet a barking dog
- How to remember your best friend's birthday
- How to paint a painting
- How to make a friend laugh (Wait! "What is a laugh?")
- How to write a good story
- How to tell a good ghost story
- How to build a good sand castle
- How to do a cartwheel
- How to get a toddler to stop fussing
- How to wash a car (By the way, "What is a car?")

Explain:
- Why does a kangaroo hop?
- Why do fish jump from place to place in a stream?
- Why do skunks spray a stinky smell?
- Why does corn in the farmer's field have "ears"?
- Why do shrimp swim backward?
- Why do bats always turn left when they leave a cave?
- Why do frogs close their eyes when they swallow?
- Why do dolphins swim in circles when they sleep?
- Why do reindeer like to eat bananas?

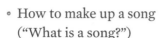

SILLY SCIENCE WRITING

Your child's imagination can be the magic ingredient for wacky tales about science and nature!

Materials
- Paper and pencil (or computer and printer)

Get Creative Challenge your child to pick a question below and write a nonsense reason why it happens. Your child may decide to write in a way that makes his answers seem believable, or he may make them totally outrageous.

WRITE A "WELCOME TO MY WORLD" BOOK

Your child writes an autobiography each year and creates a whole collection from now until the time he or she graduates from high school!

Materials
- Drawing pencils
- 28 sheets of heavy 8½-by-11-inch card stock or cardboard
- Colored markers

Get Creative To get started your child writes the title of the book on one of

ages 6–12

the pieces of card stock: "Welcome to My World" (or pick another title that seems just right). Under the title he writes his name as the author. Next, he draws a colorful picture of himself with the markers (under the title)—this will be the book cover. Here are suggested pages for your book:

- Cover of book (title, author, and self-portrait)
- Title page: Use the colored markers to write the title, your name (draw another self-portrait if you like), and the date
- Page 1: Tell your name, age, where you live, and end with a line something like this: "This is the story of my life at age ___." (Draw a picture on page 2 about this.)
- Page 3: Tell about your school,

teacher, studies. (Draw a picture on page 4.)
- Page 5: Describe your home and family. (Draw a picture on page 6.)
- Page 7: Describe some of the favorite things you do at home. (Draw a picture on page 8.)
- Page 9: Write, "My favorite food is ___." (Draw a picture on page 10.)
- Page 11: Write, "Something fun I do with my friend is ___." (Draw a picture on page 12.)
- Page 13: Write, "My favorite book is ___." (Draw a picture on page 14.)
- Page 15: Write, "The chores I do at home are ___." (Draw a picture on page 16.)
- Page 17: Describe some of the special skills you are learning. (Draw a picture on page 18.)
- Page 19: Tell something kind you do for others. (Draw a picture on page 20.)
- Page 21: Tell about something special that happened on your birthday. (Draw a picture on page 22.)
- Page 23: Describe any special place you have visited. (Draw a picture on page 24.)
- Page 25: Write, "Next year, when I turn ___(age) I would like to do ___ or go to see ___." (Draw a picture on page 26.)

Bind your book (see below for easy ways to assemble it).

> *Everyone can create a book and illustrate it. It doesn't have to be fancy. Tell your story. See what comes out and surprise yourself!*
>
> **—MELANIE HALL,** artist and award-winning illustrator of over twenty-five children's books, including *Winter Song: A Poem* by William Shakespeare

WRITE A FUNNY-PHOTO-CAPTION BOOK

Those silly advertisement photos in magazines are just crying out for a caption (or conversation bubble) from your child!

Materials

- Photos of people, animals, or scenes in magazines (look for photos that would match up with silly comments in a conversation bubble)
- Scissors
- Glue
- Notebook or journal with blank pages

Get Creative Your child starts by ripping funny photos from magazines and using the scissors to cut around the parts he wants to use. Next, he glues the photos onto pages of the notebook, allowing blank space toward the top of each for writing words or captions. Now your child brainstorms a sentence that might go along with that photo. He uses a marker to draw a big conversation bubble above the photo (just like in cartoons) and writes his words in the circle.

FOUR EASY WAYS TO ASSEMBLE A HOMEMADE BOOK

- Staple it
- Use a hole punch and twine or ribbon
- Put the pages in clear plastic pages inside a looseleaf binder
- Print it and bind it at a print shop

ages 6–12

WRITE A FAMILY-FUN YEARBOOK

Family life is the inspiration for this creative writing activity that can be funny or factual.

Materials
- Journal or artist's notebook with blank pages
- Family photos (or markers to draw your own pictures)
- Glue or tape
- Scissors
- Pencil (or computer and printer)
- Two sheets of colored construction paper (for front and back covers of book)

Get Creative Encourage your child to write a yearbook about the highlights and adventures in your family this year. She starts by thinking of a few categories she might want to include

> *I made a little monthly magazine that I wrote and illustrated called "The Fun Book." I must have been seven or eight at the time. I remember one day in summer at the shore I sat on my beach towel with colored pencils and paper while my friends were splashing around in the surf, finishing up an issue because I had a deadline.*
>
> **—MELANIE HALL,** artist and award-winning illustrator of over twenty-five children's books including *Winter Song: A Poem* by William Shakespeare

Materials

- Sheets of heavy 8½-by-11-inch paper
- Colored markers or colored pencils
- Nature photos (from magazines, or use a camera)
- Pencil and eraser (or computer and printer)
- Glue or tape

in her Family-Fun Yearbook. Here are some possible categories (or sections) she might consider:

- Family Trips or Vacations
- What's Cooking in the Kitchen?
- Birthdays, Holidays, and Celebrations
- Family Pets
- Friends, Neighbors, and Visitors
- Silly or Surprising Events in the Family
- Creative Activities (art, music, dance, theater, and so on)
- Sports

WRITE A NATURE BOOK

Encourage your child to pick something in nature he is curious about and write a short book about it!

Get Creative Your child picks a favorite nature topic and does a little research. Then he creates a book with words and pictures. Here are some nature ideas he might consider:

- Creatures of the sea: dolphins, sharks, oysters, shrimp, turtles, jellyfish, octopus, sand dollars
- Creatures that fly: all types of birds, and dragonflies, butterflies, fireflies, honeybees
- Wild animals: leopards, lions, tigers, elephants, foxes, wolves, kangaroos, bears, antelope, moose
- Trees, plants, or flowers

When your child has written and illustrated all of the pages, he can bind the book (see page 338 for easy ways to assemble it).

WRITE A BOOK ABOUT SOMETHING MAGICAL

Anything goes when your child takes the challenge to write about something magical that comes to life.

Materials
- Paper and pencil (or computer, printer, and paper)
- 8½-by-11-inch card stock
- Markers or crayons (red, blue, purple, yellow, green, orange)

Get Creative Your child begins by thinking about what magical thing she would like to write about. Is it a magic hat, a magic plant, magic shoes, a magic carpet, a magic bus, a magic dog, a magic sword, a magic wand, a magic butterfly, a magic balloon, a magic bicycle, a magic airplane, magic skates, a magic table, a magic dragon?

Next, your child writes a strong opening sentence to start the story. Perhaps she thinks up something outrageous or silly or truly unbelievable that might happen because of this magical object. (Encourage your child to use markers or crayons to create drawings for her book too.) When your child has created an ending she is happy with, help her bind the book (see page 338 for easy ways to assemble it).

WRITE A "HAPPY HENRY" STORY

Your child can write a charming "Happy Henry" book for a younger brother or sister or friend who is two or three years old!

Materials
- 8 or more sheets of 8½-by-11-inch card stock
- Pencil and eraser (or computer, printer, and paper)
- Colored markers or crayons

Get Creative Challenge your child to write a story about a make-believe character who is always happy! He starts by giving the character a name.

Next, on a practice sheet of paper, your child writes ten things that make your character happy. Then he writes one more thing that makes the character happiest of all!

Your child draws a picture of the character on one sheet of card stock (for the cover of the book). Next, he draws another picture of the character and words such as "Here are some of the things that make ____(Henry) happy!" Then he creates six to ten pages for the book by printing one word of something that makes the character happy across the top of each page. For example, one page might say, "PIZZA," and then your child draws a picture of pizza on that page. After creating these pages, your child picks one last thing that makes the character happiest of all and writes the word and draws a picture with the character feeling happy with that special thing! Help your child bind the book (see page 338 for easy ways to assemble it).

WRITE A "FRIENDLY DRAGON" BOOK

Ask your child to close his or her eyes and imagine a friendly dragon and tell or write a story about it.

Materials
- Paper and pencil (or computer and printer)
- Colored markers or colored pencils

Get Creative Challenge your child to create a book about a happy dragon who just wants a friend! She can write a clever story about where the dragon went looking for a friend and who finally became his friend. Did he go to a new school? Did he go to a playground, amusement park, or zoo? Your child writes a story and adds a few drawings too. Then help your child bind the book (see page 338 for easy ways to assemble it).

> "I tell children when we're writing poetry, "It's hard work to write well and get something that you really love. But when you're done, you're going to have something on that page that is so good that you're going to think you had a good time."
>
> —**BARBARA ESBENSEN**, author of *Dance with Me*

Write a "My Pet Monster" Book

Your child invents a story about a friendly monster that she met one day and brought to your home. Where does this little monster hide while your child is at school each day? What does he eat? Does anyone else know he exists? Your child may invent a story about something surprising that happened one day while she was at school. When your child is satisfied with the story, she adds a few pictures to complete the book.

POEM STARTERS

Kids can write poems with rhymes or no rhymes, and here are a few first lines to give them a start.

Materials
- Paper and pencil (or computer and printer)

Get Creative Your child picks one of the poem starters below to begin her poem, then just keeps inventing and writing until she is satisfied. It's a splendid activity for two or more friends or for parent and child.

Sample Poem Starters
- There once was a goat named _____, ...
- A donkey went to town to find some _____, ...
- Fiddle-fee, fiddle-fi, there's a _____ nearby (or in the sky) ...

POETRY BOX

Your child draws a few words from the Poetry Box and uses her imagination to create a poem.

Materials
- Scissors
- Card stock or heavy paper
- Pen
- Small gift box with a lid

Get Creative To get started your child uses the scissors to cut twenty (or more)

small pieces of card stock or heavy paper, just large enough to hold one word. She writes one word on each piece of paper that might be a good subject for a poem. The she mixes up the papers and puts them inside the box. When your child is in the mood to create a poem, she selects a word and tries to write a poem with this word. This is a fun solo activity, or it's fun to create poems with a friend or parent too.

SPIRAL POETRY POSTER

Your child picks a favorite poem (or writes one of his own) and turns those words into a giant spiral design to create a cool poster.

Materials
- Pencil
- Sheet of poster board
- Fine-tip marker or drawing pen
- Kneaded eraser
- Optional: glitter-glue pens, magazine photos, markers

Get Creative Encourage your child to select a favorite poem or find the words for a favorite song. Then she uses the pencil to draw a giant spiral on the poster board. It works best if she starts in the middle of that spiral and uses the pencil to write the words of the poem circling around the spiral. (When your child has come to the end of the poem, she may wish to use the drawing pen to trace over the words for a more finished look. When the ink is dry, she uses the kneaded eraser to erase any pencil marks that are showing.) Your child adds illustrations, colorful decorations (using markers), or photos to embellish the poster.

TEN BIG QUESTIONS

The idea is for your child to think of someone famous and imagine he is a newspaper reporter with questions he'd like to ask!

Materials
- Paper and pencil (or computer and printer)
- Notebook

Get Creative Your child picks a famous person from the past, present, or future. Perhaps an athlete, artist, musician, president, or future inventor. Next, he writes down ten questions for a pretend interview with the famous person. (All serious and silly questions allowed.)

Ten Big Answers

Here's a creative-writing idea similar to the Ten Big Questions idea, but this time your child pretends to be the famous person being interviewed and she will write answers to the Ten Big Questions that the reporter asked!

BE A CREATIVE INVESTIGATOR (OR REPORTER)

Your child selects someone in the family he would like to interview and starts recording!

Materials
- Audio recorder
- Pencil and paper (for questions to ask)

Get Creative Your child selects someone in the family to interview about a specific topic. Examples might be "What did you do for fun when you were a kid?" "When did you learn to drive a car?" "What was the best trip you ever took?" "What was your first job like?" Encourage your child to write questions on paper before the interview begins, and then they listen carefully and ad-lib other good questions spontaneously during the conversation.

Fake Celebrity Interviews

Your child asks a friend or family member to pretend to be a famous person and then your child pretends to be a reporter asking questions! These interviews can be silly or serious. The fake celebrity might even be a make-believe character from a movie (such as *Peter Pan*) or book (such as the Harry Potter series), or perhaps it might be a family pet who can suddenly speak! Anything goes in this creative interview activity!

CREATIVE-WRITING JOURNAL

Every writer needs a creative-writing journal!

Get a small notebook that your child can use as his creative-writing journal. Any good ideas, titles, silly situations, words, rhymes, and character names can be put in this book. Then, later, when your child is in the mood for writing a poem, joke, short story, or book, she simply opens her journal and finds something of interest to get her started with her next creative writing project.

Resources

Most of the activities in *The Giant Book of Creativity for Kids* require supplies and materials that are easy to find. The art activities, for example, use ordinary papers, cardboard, paints, pencils, markers, clay, ink, brushes, and craft materials that can be easily found at local art, craft, and education (or teacher) supply stores in your hometown or at online retailers. Most of the materials needed for the pretend, music, dance, and building activities can also be easily found locally or online. Other creative activities use household items that are right in your closet or home: laundry baskets, kitchen gadgets, fabric scraps, pillowcases, sheets, containers, and cardboard.

Listed below are a few sources of materials, supplies, musical instruments, puppets, and costumes that may be helpful in gathering materials and props for your child's creative projects.

 ## Art-and-Craft Materials

For Children and Adults
Artists and Craftsman Supply www.artistcraftsman.com
Discount School Supply www.discountschoolsupply.com
Dick Blick Art Materials www.dickblick.com

Specifically for Children 2+ Years of Age
Crayola www.crayola.com
Lakeshore Learning www.lakeshorelearning.com

Tulle Fabric (for the No-Sew Tutu)
eFavorMart www.efavormart.com

Mat Board
Mat board is terrific for children's collage, painting, and other art projects. It is available very inexpensively in value packs (with thirty-five pieces of assorted colored mat board) at Hobby Lobby stores or online at www.hobbylobby.com.

 ## Building and Construction Materials

Shoe Boxes
Gather up recycled shoe boxes for kids' building projects from large local shoe stores or discount stores (typically available for free). Or, if you need a stash of twenty or more new shoe boxes (with no labels or logos), check out this industrial-paper-product retailer online for cardboard shoe boxes: www.uline.com.

Large Cardboard Boxes
Medium-sized and large recycled cardboard boxes are available for free at local grocery stores (ask in advance). Recycled giant cardboard boxes for appliances are possibly available for free at local appliance dealers (ask in advance).

 ## Music

Child-Friendly Musical Instruments
Local music and toy stores
Little Hands Music www.littlehandsmusic.com
Musician's Friend www.musiciansfriend.com/pages/kids
Music in Motion www.musicmotion.com
Hearth Song www.hearthsong.com
Groth Music www.grothmusic.com
Woodstock Chimes www.woodstockchimes.com (Note: the Chimalong
     mentioned on page 185 is made by Woodstock Chimes.)

Pretend and Theatrics Supplies and Costumes

Hats for Pretend and Theatrics
Music in Motion www.musicmotion.com

Puppets and Marionettes
Local toy or specialty stores
Discount School Supply www.discountschoolsupply.com (assorted hand puppets)
Folkmanis Puppets www.folkmanis.com (larger, specialty puppets)
Sunny Puppets www.sunnypuppets.com (marionettes and giant hand puppets)
Amazon www.amazon.com (search for animal puppets on Amazon and find
    assorted velour hand puppets for kids quite inexpensively)

Puppet Theater
Hearthsong www.hearthsong.com

List of Activities

*(pages with instructions are shown in **bold** type)*

 ## Family-Time Activities and Traditions

 ## Artwork, Art-and-Craft Activities

Toddlers (ages 2-3)

Building and Construction Activities

Musical Activities, Singing

Dance and Movement Activities

Pretend and Theatrical Activities

Word, Language, and Storytelling Activities

Index

About the Author

Bobbi Conner is a writer, painter, and public-radio journalist. She created the award-winning nationwide public-radio series *The Parent's Journal* and hosted the program for twenty-four years. She is the author of *Unplugged Play: No Batteries. No Plugs. Pure Fun* (Parents' Choice Silver Honor) and author of *Everyday Opportunities for Extraordinary Parenting*. Conner speaks about creativity and child development at gatherings for parents, educators, and other professional groups. Her public-radio program, audio interviews, books, and articles have been featured in *USA Today*, *Newsweek*, the *Washington Post*, *Parade*, *Parents*, *Parenting*, *CBS This Morning*, and PBSParents.org. Conner is the mother of three children and lives in Charleston, South Carolina.